Prophet Gentle

ISBN-978-0-578-50355-4

The Gospel Book of God's Laws #1

This Is A Book of Study and Practices God's Laws

www.dgpublisgingpress.com

Acknowledgement

I, Prophet give honor to God who is the head of my life who is the head of my spiritual being I serve in spirits in truth on one accord as the Holiest Highest Priest Prophet ever walk the foundations of the earth in the time of now times. I, Prophet say to you, God supreme existence works through many people in the heavens on earth. Everything that exists in the heavens on earth has its own nature and reason for existence whether good or bad, but without God working spiritually in the inner man of a person, no human would have sense enough to produce anything in the heavens on earth. It is with prime reason God is the first cause for every publishing company in the heavens on earth and everything that exist. God brought nature about before human existence by calling a thing as though it was, and it appeared in the heavens on earth and God saw that it was all good.

Then God call humankind into being to replenish what the spirits of God started in the heavens on earth. God then put God spiritual image in humankind to replenish the earth and have babies. This then brought the world into existence. Supreme reality is the idea of possessing all structural perfection in existence. I, Prophet am an ultimate witness to the ultimate relationship between God and humankind spiritual structural reasons for existence. I, Prophet say to you, God is saying out with the old traditions of humankind and in with the renewed things of God caught up in spirits in truth crossing-over into eternal living eternal life. I Prophet Give honor to the Church of God in Christ Inc. for my up-bring in the Church of God in

Christ Inc. Holy Temples where I was taught to recognize the Holy spirits of God working in my life.

I, Prophet am strong and wise in spirits in truth in God because of COGIC Inc. in my life all through my childhood life unto my adult life. I, Prophet Give honor to my decease father and mother for my up-bring in COGIC Inc. The times are now times of putting away social customs of different religious beliefs knowing only Holiness shall eternally stand forever in the heavens which are on earth. The COGIC Inc. Holy Temples are the elect chosen Holy people (Holy Priesthood) of God called to judge the people in the heavens which are on earth. I, Prophet give honor to the COGIC Inc. Holy Priesthood spiritual being and lifestyle for Holiness in all things pertaining to God. I, Prophet say to you, continue to shepherd God's people before the spirits of God as you wear the crown of eternal life with all authority to judge the people for eternal life in the heavens which are on earth.

The times are now times the chosen Holy Priesthood of Prophets, Bishops, Apostles, Elders, and Evangelists within the COGIC are sitting in the judgment seats of God in the presence of God judging the people with forgiven sins receive eternal life and baptism. The times are now times the people receiving eternal life baptized in the eternal Holy spirits with Holy hands the eternal spirits in the chosen Holy Temple began to get higher and higher in eternal spirits as the multitude of people show up to be judged forgiven sins for the chance of eternal life. The times are now times to remember all things written and spoken unto you are ordered by the eternal Holy spirits of our eternal God leading the people to eternal life in all things said and done daily. The times are always now times all thing be done in a decent and respectful order with eternal living eternal life always in mind.

The times are now times the chosen Holy Priesthood of COGIC has no respecter of person in judging the people remembering the chosen Holy Priesthood are always in the presence of God. The times are now times the chosen Holy Priesthood COGIC allow other Holy Temples to become a part of the chosen Holy Priesthood until there is one big Holy land hath gathered themselves on one accord in all things said and done with same beliefs and same thoughts in eternal spirits in eternal truth. The times are now times no one lay hand on the people in the chosen Holy Temples except the chosen Holy Priesthood of Prophet, Bishops, Apostles, Elders, and Evangelists. The times are now times to remember the chosen Holy Priesthood of COGIC has a great weight of heavy work sitting before them in the presence of God. The times are now times to remember the service of God in the chosen Holy Temples are prolonged if needed in the presence of God to cross the people over into eternal life during judging the people.

The times are now times to remember the justice of God prevail in all things said and done among the people. The people must remember daily they are in the latter days of God's judgments and justice upon the people daily until the paradise heavens on earth appears and there are no more sins, sickness, and death among the eternal spirits of the people. The times are now times to know the presence of God is dwelling in every part of the earth is all things said and done the just judgment and justice of God prevail with the chosen people of God without fail daily. The times are now times to acknowledge the presence of God in all things said and done daily in every part of the earth for the chance of eternal life for eternal purposes without fail.

The times are now times to acknowledge all things said and done are to be said and done in the earth for eternal purposes of eternal living eternal life without fail are eternal spirits now upon the people. The times are times to remember the promises of God are forming among the people daily without notice to the people in all things said and done daily in every part of the earth. The times are now times to keep an eternal focus on all things said and done in the earth remembering the temporary times are ceasing as the permanent promises of God are forming the promise lands of the paradise heavens on earth daily   It is I the Lord your spiritual God say to the people in the heavens which are on earth; without fail all people, places, and things are judged daily until all things called unto you are finished within sins, sickness, and death has cease from the heavens which are on earth. The times are now times to live forever and not die.

Foreword

By Prophet Gentle

Eternal life now presents the foundational and diverse perspectives on key issues engaged in eternal life in heaven which is on earth. It is more rational to believe God gave us the value for gravity that we have right now in our universe when one reads from the Bible book of Genesis. We got the value that we have when God created heaven on earth. In the beginning God created the heavens on earth. The earth was without form and void, and it was dark on the face of heaven, which is the earth. The spirits of God began to move upon the heavenly earth. It was then God said let the waters under the heavens be gathered together into one place. The dry land then appeared. My justification of eternal life is, I believe in the spiritual realm of eternal of life given me by the spirits of God within me. God is the gravity of strong spiritual forces in the heavens on earth.

The stars and the planet God uphold independently that makes our lives possible. It is my spiritual belief that God's spiritual forces dose play a-part in the change of environment that has seasons of complexity of weather in physical, chemical, and biotic forces of factors. These forces mention happen along with social and cultural conditions that influence the life of an individual, or community, and the control of the pollution over all the heavens which is the earth. One must give respect entirely with reference to God in order to explain natural causes of weather, earthquakes, water, and fire which dominate the earth in the call of Gods judgment upon the heavens which is on earth.

The existence of the universe can-not be explained without reference to the spiritual forces of God working within the human being spirits, and human nature that are in the heavens on earth. God is the spiritual naturalism in the heavens on earth working accomplishments of judgment in the physical, and mental of the believer. God's spirits within each person of eternal life is the beginning and the end of all things that exist in the heavens on earth. Genesis book of the Bible explains the natural causes that refer to God the creator and maker of the universe and the people within it. Humankind does not have a way to prove that the spiritual forces of God did not make the heavens on earth. God is spirit saying are ye holy, for I God am holy in spirits and in truth is the spiritual truth.

The systematic world is made by mankind having the spiritual image of God within their heart, mind, body, and soul. God is persistent through the intervention of his divine power independent of humankind in what- ever God does in the heavens on earth to get humankind's attention. There are many people refuse to admit the spiritual power of God cause many things to happen in the earth to exist and to disappear in the heaven on earth. God is the supreme ultimate reality and perfect in spiritual power, spiritual wisdom, and spiritual goodness. God is worshipped as creator and ruler of the universe overall eternal spirits of the infinite mind of all human being in supreme power as a supreme ruler knowing that his/her power come from the almighty powerful spirits of the inside of the mind, controlling the mind.

God is the independent cause for the independent existence of each personal spirits within every person. The cause of God is spiritual independent cause for the existence of all people, places, and things in the heavens on earth. The people, places, and things that exist depend on God to continue to exist. God can bring a storm and tear down every-thing the spiritual mind thought of to build. The God of independent cause gave the spiritual mind to everyone to replenish the heavens on earth and do well. Humankind depends on their spiritual mind to comprehend and do things that are within the spiritual mind. It is factual if humankind did not have a spiritual mind; everyone would be lost not knowing how to organize themselves to walk, talk, write, read, drive, labor, and do many other things done in the heavens on earth. There are some people with good spirits, and there are some people with evil spirits. God allow people to make choices, just like Adam and Eve was allied to make the choice to obey the spirits of God call to their spiritual mind, but they refuse to obey what God told them not to do. God allow individuals to choose good or evil. Now God is bringing all evil to an end into judgment of eternal death beneath the heavens on earth. All humankind depends on God for all things done in their lives. Now you know without the spiritual being of God within your spirits, you can-not exist. We all that are still living among the land of the living in the heavens on earth are depending on God to bring us through this evil bearing money stricken sinful land to eternal life.

God is independent spirits and does not need anyone to exist in the heavens on earth, but we need God to exist in the heavens on earth. All people, places, and things in the earth have a real existence in the heavens on earth. All individual spirits are spiritual beings that God's spirits have given us to comprehend existence whether material or spiritual of humankind we see and hear with our physical being. Everything in the heavens on earth has a reason for being in existence in a specific place even if it has limitations or conditions attached to it.

God continues to manifest every mode of being that is now present in the earth. No-one will ever know the secret ways of God. God covers time and space divinely in the heavens on earth operating the spiritual will of God's power through powerful humankind that God has given power to call a thing as though it were in the heavens on earth and it then come into existence. These things prophesied are the spiritual being of God daily in the heavens on earth as the righteous people depends on the powerful spirits of their mind that God's spirits introduce to them through spiritual utterance forces and spiritual guidance forces from spiritual forces within them from God. It is revealing to the people the insight of God's signs outwardly showed up are the gospel truth of God's laws within judgments and justice. In the earth are now the punishments of God's latter days have arrived upon the people of the chosen generations.

These are the days of the promises of God fulfillment of the holy priests Prophets with words from God that now stand and show up quickly. The present transactions of God are continued by the direct call of the spirits of God. The call of God is not in the calculation of humankind of 7000 years of God's judgments and justice called upon the people in every part of the earth from coast to coast. The penetration of Gods words and spirits are in the Holy services of the Holy Temples of God are uncompromising promises guaranteed protection and assurance of God. The latter-day transformation stairways to the new paradise earth are daily in the works of God east, west, north, and south in all the earth. The visions of righteousness are being performed through righteous spirits of the people of God seeking eternal life. In place are known conditions that reflects God 's promises to cripple the system of unrighteousness with forces of judgments and justice in the earth. Now in its new stages of life are the things of God's judgments and justice operation in every part of the earth catch up with the other new stages of life renewing the earth into a paradise earth.

In the new changes and different stages of life, God control human destiny showing genuine change in one's personal life now in the present times of one's life. The change of many cities and counties where people are isolated by groups are identified by economic inheritance are destroyed bringing hardship to many that lost their estates to the call of natural disasters due to weather and/or fire. This call of God takes focus on the distant future promises of blessings to the people to live on a paradise earth. The blessings of a lifetime are in the making already.

Contents

Introduction

It takes courage to hold visions that are not in the mainstream, but it is exactly that courage to take a stand for one's vision. This book is my visions that distinguish people with high levels of personal mastery in personal spirits of ministry seeing and hearing from God. God is one supreme-being (a person) having supernatural powers that has been given to that person by God. God is the internal spiritual being of individuals working external spiritual powers in the earth universally. God is a perfect being in power within the mind of the person and/or people having spirits of supreme ultimate reality and wisdom spiritually". The spiritual powers and goodness of the person and/or people are worshipped as the creator and ruler of the universe. The spiritual reality over-all are eternal spirits of the infinite mind of a human-being having incorporeal divine principles to rule supernatural spirits that attributes to powerful spirits within the infinite mind, but the ownership of the "supernatural spirits is God.

There are a person and/or people controlling an aspect of reality, or part of reality that has been given to him or her from the supernatural spirits of God. This person or people then are of supreme value and a powerful ruler. God is a spiritual supreme being dwelling on the inside of one who believe and lives by faith with works toward living eternal life. This then gives the person or people free course within because of the supernatural spirits internal and external operating action those things seen and heard in the mind. A person, place, or thing can be of supreme value at any given time. Anyone is free to discuss a subject matter, but belief in God is being free to believe in your own spirits. The spirits of your mind tell you what to do and what not to do; these are spirits of God operating internal inside your mind. The discussion of philosophy does not make one free; anyone is free to believe in their own free-will spirits. There are many people in denial there is a God, which is their own free-will spirits dwelling on the inside of their own mind. The people must understand they guard their own spiritual minds because God allows them to be in control and make good or bad choice as Adam and Eve were given the same "opportunity. Many philosophers aim re-establishing the reality of God and defining the divine nature of laws of God and Society while making theory and contradiction in many subject matters. God is the independent cause of everything that exists or has existed. The spirits of God that are your spirits give rise to cause and effect of all people, places, and things in the heavens on earth. These things mention is enough reason that gives cause to the spiritual minds of the people existing in the heavens on earth are all the spirits of God operating for the good people.

The outward signs of God have showed up in every part of the earth now being revealed to the people. God's judgment calls like never has formed its justice all over the land. The work of God's spirits is nationally showing the effects of wrath within water, fire, accidents, sinkholes, and death roaming the land in the justice judgments of God's spirits. It is now without fail things happen in an instant are the signs and wonders of God overpowering the human judgments bringing the earth to a paradise earth after everyone left living is free from sin. It is now all sins are being dealt with and destroyed in every part of the earth. There will not be any sin left in the earth when God gets finish calling just judgments and justice in all the earth. The people know and feel the effects of God's direct actions in all the earth. These are now the latter times and seasons of God dwelling in every part of the earth making known the signs and wonders of eternal life forming in all parts of the earth as the times are now times to live forever and not die in every part of the earth.

As a Prophet of God, I see past, present and future structures of God and humankind to free the world from sin that resides in the heavens on earth. I see the existence of things God has given me to call a thing as though it were, and it is that I call it to be in the now and the future. Everyone is free to think or call a thing as though it was, but the point is God must honor the call for it to be or exist. Being free to think gives me as well as others the freedom to exercise the ultimate ground of belief in God and to experience expression of spiritual hearing ears as well as spiritual thought and work of God in my life led by the Holy Spirits of God in the heavens on earth.

At this present day we as a people experience arguments reference grammar problems of disagreement and freedom of speech representing speeches written by those who write the government laws of society. One must see ultimate unity with God, and each other in society is the key to a freedom future of success. God is infinite; you are infinite by the image God made you to be in the heavens on earth. You are perfect, God made you in God's spiritual perfect image in mind, body, heart and soul. God is infinite in human nature and God is infinite in human spirits because all spirits belongs to God. God us in control of all spirits but will allow you to be in control with good spirits or a reprobated mind. God is infinite in humankind and human nature operating in human internal spirits only in those who spiritually believe in the spiritual power of God.

Remember you are the God of your spirits over your spirits because God gives you freedom of choice to make good choices or bad choices, which one would you, choose to reach eternal life and never die? There is no one in the heavens on earth that can conceive the powerful knowledgeable existence of God's spiritual awareness of all people, places, and things in the heavens which is on earth; unless God gives it to you spiritually. God is all your good spirits deep within guiding you to all things of righteousness. Remember all good spirits are the gift of God (your good spirits within your heart guiding you) to all good people, places, and things prosperous and not a wrong spirit (a free reprobated mind) guiding you to all the wrong people, places, and things. The gift of good spirits is eternal life for the special appointed people of God with good spirits you can feel about that person.

God have appointed people in the earth with spiritual powers that are a special people God call them arch angels in the heavens which is on earth. If you have not been appointed by God, then you do not have special spiritual powers. Spiritual powers will not work on your behalf if God has not appointed to you that gift. One must practice using and trusting your good spirits within your heart, for it is God spiritual presence guiding you into all right directions of your life in all things. You must trust your good internal spirits to receive eternal life and never die but live forever in the heavens which is on earth after all sins have been destroyed from the heavens on earth.

God spirits are operating daily in the heavens which are on earth in facts and motional actions. To every emotional fact that exists in the heavens on earth, the cause is God spiritual presence being called by spiritual powerful people operating in the heavens on earth, for they are rich, for they are poor operating spiritually calling a thing as though it was and it exist. For these people are the people of God with the mind of God, in the heavens on earth in the image of God; call by the spirits of God. The spiritual call of God's people is making the judgment calls in the earth to make this a better world to live in and a paradise earth. The people of God do not have to be in a church setting to make a judgment call of God.

God allows many things to happen in the heavens on earth that are not good to get the people attention on the things they have no control over, but only the spiritual minds of the anointed appointed people powerfully spiritual minded can control what-ever God's desires are (God's will). God continues to allow sickness and death until the world has been cleansing of sickness, sin, and death, then the rise of eternal life meaning never die from a paradise heaven on earth. God's daily judgment is for seven thousand years in all the heavens on earth. God is operating spiritually ending all sin and sinners in question.

For there be some sinners that are not in question but need to stop sinning while you are ahead. There be some sinners with forgiven sins among them, and there be some sinners with un-forgiven sins among them. The forgiven sinners will inherit the heavens paradise earth after all sickness and sins have cease. The call of the spiritual mind people of God are rich people and poor people form through an infinite divine call of God natural formulation in nature of the powerful spiritual minds in all the heavens on earth.

God is the logical transitional facts of existence working through chosen people in every aspect of life. The people of God are equipped with certain gifts from the spirits of God. God spirits over the world traveling earthly regulate and operate the cosmic systems of this world. God spiritual presence put things in order in the universe in contrast to the earthly need for a paradise earth. God has entered a personal relationship with the appointed anointed ones in all the heavens on earth. God's transcendence spirits are in the world working wonders powerfully. God's appointed work is not to be questioned among the people or those of philosophical thinking in discussion. God is the independent cause of one's thinking spirits that comes to mind knowing all humans are made in the image of God.

God is the independent cause of all individual thinking ability knowing all things thought of is spirits, and all spirits independently belongs to God. Some people have wise strength certain favors with God more than others for certain reasons and certain causes. God's cause brings about effect for enough reason in principles of movement of effective spiritual forces by the spiritual command of God upon the people of God. The authority of God's effect is independent and not control by anyone, but at the same time work through the spiritual anointing of others with independent cause and effect. God is independent unto all; it is the freedom to believe in God. It is one's freedom to believe in God powerful spiritual being in God's appointed people in the earth.

One must desire to communicate with God through spiritual instructional intelligence. God reveals things by clear signs communicating to the open spirits of a common system of awareness through common faith and discipline of the attitude. One must control your spirit of God internal working external through one's being of sound mind and good judgment. To fellowship with God infinitely is freedom to eternal life God gives to all those who believe in their own spiritual being and have forgiven sins among you. Communication with God which is your own spiritual being internal; is to be free from fear knowing God is within you. Look no further, God is within you and has never left you. Listen to your own spiritual being that tells you to be careful and take care of yourself. Those words are the spiritual small voice of God speaking with you and making you aware of your surroundings. God is with you at your side each and every-day if you only believe your good spirits is the spirits of God within your heart.

To believe in God is not a moral duty, but it is a free will of choice to receive eternal life and never die but live on a paradise earth. You do not have to get anyone's approval to know God because it is not an ethical duty to know God. To know God is a free will choice from one's decision to be a follower of God and not a follower of the wrong spirits that may come upon you at any given time. The social interaction with God relates to feeling free deep within one's self. God is spiritual ultimate supreme spiritual reality in a perfect being in power over the entire universe. God is over all people spirits in the entire world that dwell in the eternal heavens on earth. God spirits cause human-being to interact with their internal spirits that operate externally. I, Prophet have given God's spiritual guidance to the subject matter of cross ng-over into eternal living eternal life to study and put into practice that leads to eternal life on a paradise earth. Take heed that ye open your mind to your spiritual being believe in yourself is to believe in God.

It is now within you the things that are your spiritual guide you hear within your mind speak to you the things of God. Read all these words and ponder them within your heart and spirits. Travel with those who are on your same path to eternal life. It is time to seek-out travel companions as soon as possible to go hear the words of God in the Holy Temples. Now living eternal life is living face-to-face in spirits in truth with God. It is time to listen to Gods' direction for your life each day where-ever you go and what-ever you do. It is time to realize it is Gods' spiritual guidance working within your mind guiding you each day. The time has arrived that eyes and ears have not seen nor heard the things God is doing and getting ready to do in your life. The mind of the people can-not perceive the things entering eternal life; nor understand the things that are in the mind of the people of God.

Now is time and talents that no-one can-not climb any-other way, but by the way of eternal life call by the will of God for your life and style. The real life of eternal life unfolds daily awake the people to the spiritual and Holy things of God. The words of this book, I the Lord your God have spoken them to re-build your heart, mind, body, and soul into eternal lifestyle.

Dedication

This book is dedicated to the cherished memories of my loving parents, the late Rev. Roy Sparks and the late Missionary Bobbie Jean Turner Sparks, for giving me the breath of life through the proclamation of their seed foreordained by God. In th s God has given me eternal spirits and said, "Thus you are a blessing to the people in the heavens which is on earth. I God say to you, ye were called to be the Greatest Holiest High Priest Prophet ever walked the heavens on earth in your time at the proclamation of the seed in your mother. I, God called into existence the seed for prophetic ministry predestinated a female foreordained eternal destiny. I, God say to the people in the heavens on earth, there will never be another High Priest Prophet of this nature again. I, God say to the people in the heavens which are on earth, this is the last judgment call upon all the people in the heavens on earth.

I, Prophet further dedicate this book to my husband Colonel, my children and their spouse, son Gentry & Nikki and daughter Katrina & Roderick, with further dedication to my grand-children Destiny and Gentry. This book is further dedicated to my brothers and sisters and their spouse and children; my brother Charles, my sister Joyce & William her husband, my sister Debra, and my brother Curtis. This book is further dedicated to the cherished memories of my late sister, Royce Jean Sparks. I, Prophet further dedicate this book to all my relatives and friends. I, Prophet further dedicate this book to the chosen Holy Temple Churches of

God in Christ in Ministries that have raised me to Prophetic ministry of God true Holy spirits. This book is further dedicated to the Springdale Church of God in Christ Austin, Texas where I was raised, inspired by the Holy spirits of God and baptized by the late Rev. C. L. Crawford. This book is further dedicated to Sister Brantley & the late Rev. Brantley and Greater Love Church of God in Christ Tallahassee, Florida where I attended many years of services.

I, Prophet further dedicate this book to Watson Temple Church of God in Christ Tallahassee, Florida where I presently attend. This book is further dedicated to all Holy Temples Churches and all of God's people in the heavens which are on earth. I, Prophet further dedicate this book to DG Publishing Company & Book Store of Dwayne Gavin, Ingram's Press Printing Company, and Water for The Journey Inc. Photography Editors, Barnes & Nobles Book Store, and Amazon.com. And the spirits of God spoke to the Holiest Highest Priest Prophet ever walk the earth in your time and said write these things in a book I, God speak to you in spirits in truth. I, God say to you write a book and thus go and speak into the hearing ears of the people that thirst for the truth. I, God say to you this is for the gathering of my people with forgiven sins among them a Holy chosen people dwelling in the heavens on earth. I, God say to the people in the heavens on earth all people have sinned and come short of knowing the power of God in the heavens on earth.

1

God's Millennium Years now in Effect

The millennium years of God are now in effect for 7000 years as the sands of the sea without count. The entire world of people is being judged and sinners with un-forgiven sins loose eternal life in every part of the heavens which is on earth. The sinners with forgiven sins among them receive eternal living eternal life. The protection of God's people has many undercover angels watching over them in the heaven which is on earth. There are many evil wicked undermined people with all amounts of evil in their hearts. I, God say to the people in the heavens on earth; the ways of God are covered and concealed for such times as these operating in the heavens which are on earth. There are many secret service angels watching the steps of God's people. , God say to you the ways of God destroy people, places, and things un-expectantly in every part of the heavens on earth without fail. There are many wraths of God upon the people without fail with vengeance roaming the earth.

I, God say to the people in the heavens which are on earth celebrating traditional liars; your celebrating liars are over. The spiritual Prophet Messiah God was born in October. It has been prophesied in past times that God was born in October. I God say to you ye believe not the Prophets then as ye do not believe them today. I, God say to you the times and seasons has arrived and your time is up for foolishness in the heavens on earth. I, God say to the people in the heavens on earth I call these things to your attention that ye take heed quickly without fail. I, God say to you ye have a need to take heed to the false ways of the liars in the heavens on earth. I, God say to you ye have a need to be caught up in spirits in truth. I, God say to you whom are caught up in spirits in truth remain caught up in spirits in truth eternally. I, God say to you celebrate what you know to be true and not a lie. I God say to you all traditional lies are cast beneath the earth from the heavens which is on earth.

I, God say to the people in the heavens on earth; to be save is to have eternal life. I, God say to the people in the heavens on earth I speak my words and I, God change not at no time. I, God say to you all words spoken in this Gospel Book of Laws are faithful and true. I, God say to the people in the heavens on earth I know all things said and done in the heavens on earth. I, God am in control of all good spirits in the heavens on earth upon the people. I, God have turned the evil wicked people over to their reprobated minds that catches up with them in judgments and justice served upon them in many ways that do not appear to the eyes and hearts of the people. I, God say to the people in the heavens on earth woe unto all people in this world. I am God in spirits in truth are one and the same within the spirits of the righteous saying all things said and done in the heavens which is on earth are at the hands within judgments in the earth. I, God say to you the Holy chose n people of God are judging all things said and done in the earth daily.

I, God say to the people in the heavens on earth these are the millennium years of judgments and justice prevail over the entire heavens on earth. I, God say to this people in the heavens my prophecies are now easily understood in this Gospel Book of God's Laws written by the Holiest Highest Priest Prophet ever walk the earth in your times of now times. I, God say to you these words are plain and simple to read with much understanding. I, God say to the people in the heavens on earth, there are no duplicates of these prophecies written in this Gospel Book of God's Laws. I, God say to the people in the heavens on earth in the same hour that anyone adds or take from these prophecies written unto you the judgments and justice of God instantly are upon you without warning. I God say to you ye have now been warned so that ye take heed that ye stray not from these prophecies of mine.

I, God say to the people in the heavens on earth the chosen Holiest High Priest are all the Holy Priest in the Holy Temples Churches of God in Christ Incorporated. I, God say all Holy High Priest will be careful nothing; in that is the speech that cometh out of your mouth in conversation to each other with respect to the Holiest H ghest Priest Prophet ever walk the earth in your times of now times. I, God say to the chosen Holy High Priest judge all things said and done in the earth whether good are bad. I, God say to the chosen Holy High Priest forget not the charge ye must keep in

3

judgments. I, God say to the chosen Holy High Priests have instant respect for each other as one and the same loosing not your crown in Holiness Priesthood in eternal living eternal life.

I, God say to the chosen Holy High Priesthood in the Holy Temples Churches of God in Christ Incorporated ye are a chosen people of God. I, God say to all chosen Holy Priesthood, fast with water, 2% milk, juices, and vegetable juices for two weeks every other month. I, God say to the chosen Holy Priesthood, when fasting there is no eating at any time during the two weeks fast period. I, God say to the chosen Holy Priesthood this is required of you for 7000 years without count as the sands of the sea to correctly judge the people. I, God say to the chosen Holy High Priesthood ye have a need for pureness so that ye hear more correctly in spirits in truth in all things said and done. I, God say to you, see to it that ye take heed to the Holy spirits call unto you.

I, God say to the chosen Holy High Priesthood; preach and teach the un-forgiven sinners in the heavens on earth are struck with the sword of your words call unto them which is the word of God's wrath written and spoken in the judgments of God called unto all un-forgiven sinners in the heavens on earth. I, God say to the chosen Holy Priesthood, preach and teach all children having children cease in the justice judgments of God upon males and females alike committing such acts. I God say to the chosen Holy Priesthood, preach and teach if anyone draw-back after being saved unto eternal life ye loose eternal life. It is all things said and done in the world are judged daily by God and God's chosen anointed Holy High Priesthood in the chosen Holy Temple Churches of God in Christ.

4

I, God say to the people in the heavens on earth forget not ye are in the millennium years of justice and judgments upon the people in the heavens which is on earth. The times and seasons are now days for praying time more than ever before. I, God say to the chosen Holy High Priest, watch over the ways of the congregation during prayer time. When prayers are being said the congregation must bow down their heads and close their eyes as the prayers are being said. There must be a prayer said or read at the beginning and ending of each service in the chosen Holy Temple Churches of God in Christ. I, God say to the chosen Holy High Priesthood see to it that these orders and commards are carried out without fail. I say to you all chosen Holy High Priest watch congregation making sure their heads are kneeling during prayer time showing respect to God and the person praying for their well-being.

I, God say to you if there be anyone with their head not kneel with eyes closed; it be announced prayer be stopped until all heads are kneeling with eyes close so that prayers be not hindered. The chosen Holy Priesthood is to be the only ones looking around watching over the souls of the people. I, God say to you if there be anyone refused to bow down their heads, they have a need to leave because they do not take part in prayer. I, God say to the chosen Holy High Priest the times are at hand for the chosen people to take a stand here in the heavens which are on earth. I, God say to you take it by force the respect due to God and God's chosen Holy people. I, God say to you all things said and done in the chosen Holy Temple Churches of God in Christ are charged to the chosen Holy High Priesthood without fail. I, God say to the chosen Holy High Priesthood ye have a need to give an account of judgments upon the people without respect of person.

I, God say to the chosen Holy High Priesthood it is time to watch over the Holy gates of God and God's people. I, God say to the chosen Holy High Priesthood anyone do not make prayer service do not have a need to come through the doors after prayer is over. I, God say to the chosen Holy High Priest make sure ye start service on time each time as well as the people has a need to be on time for prayer services before the gates are close for prayer services. I, God say to you late drifters cannot come in when prayers services are over. I, God say to you the prayers have a need to not be disrupted destroying meaningful spirits needed. I, God say to the chosen elect Holy High Priesthood; if there be anyone set among you evil remove them from the service at any given time and continue service. I, God say to the people in the heavens on earth ye have a need to cross-over into the Holy land without evil sinners.

I, God say to the chosen Holy Temples Churches of God in Christ; the people stood as the Holiest Highest Priest Prophet entered the pulpit. Then after the Holiest High Priest Prophet Sit down the congregation sit down the service continues. I, God say to you this is the eternal Holiest Highest Priest Prophet ever walk the heavens on earth in your time of now times. I, God say to the people in the heavens on earth there will never be another chosen Holy Highest Priest Prophet to come at no time fulfilling the seven spirits of God in the heavens which are on earth. I, God say to the people in the heavens on earth; test not my spirits that are before you so that ye not lose the way to eternal living eternal life in the heavens on earth. I, God say to the people in the heavens on earth; touch not my spirits in the heavens on earth are my chosen people. I, God say to the people in the heavens on earth the chosen people dwell in the chosen Temple Churches of God in Christ as ye have a reed to dwell among them in spirits in truth.

I, God say to the chosen Holy people of God in the Holy Temples; pray for all things said and done according to purpose. I say to you the order of many people, places, and things change to the good of the people in the heavens on earth. I say to you the voice of God's spirits is roaming the heavens on earth calling a certain of order of people, places, and things to come and people, places, and things to perish without fail. I, God say to the people in the heavens on earth; the paradise earth appears at the end of all sins, sickness, and death cease in the heavens on earth at the end of all judgments and justice.

I, God say to you it is now praying times like never as people, places, and things change according to the spirts of God and God's chosen people call a thing as though it were, and it appears in the heavens on earth. I, God say to you the times are like times of never in the history of humankind. I, God say to you the people in the heavens on earth have a need to pray as changes take place in an instant in a blink of an eye. I, God say to the people in the heavens on earth ye must make a request in prayers in a humble manner that ye may then have a slight chance for an answer from God. I, God say to you, for there be some prayers gone un-answered. I, God say to you there are many un-praise-worthy people praying prayer with no value. I, God say to you I now set an order of prayers for you for directions for worship. I, God say to the people forget not the millennium years of judgments and justice in your prayers determines your

Prayer

successful prayers. I, God say to the people in the heavens on earth, successful prayers bring powerful affect according to the will of God's predestinate affect. I, God say to you open your heart to the spirits of God and pray in the will of God. God we just want to thank you for the angel of God has conceived the Holy spirits of God according to the will of God. The prayers of the righteous are now being heard in the Holy spirits of God, Lord we just want to thank you for your promises now are being poured forth in the heavens which is on earth. Lord we thank you for the resurrection of your Holy spirits being discern and spoken into the heavens on earth as they appear to the good of the people. Lord we know that the paradise heavens on earth will appear in its time and season according to your will. Lord we ask you to please have mercy on us this day and hear our prayers. Lord we thank you for the Holiest Highest Priest that has ever walked the earth in our time and space.

Lord we thank you for the redeemer the Holy one you have so mercifully sent the redeemer of the world. God, we know that your Holy spirits are pure and divine. God it is your grace of love with good counsel along with powerful judgments and justice crossing us over to eternal life. Lord we ask you to crown us with wisdom and knowledge to discern the ways that qualifies us to cross-over into eternal living eternal life in the heavens which is on earth. God it is now we see your mysteries of the visions we have had being reveal unfold comforting our hearts. God we as chosen Holy disciples in the chosen Holy Temple Churches ask you to make us as one and the same in the chosen Holy Temple Churches of God in Christ.

Prayer

God we in the Holy Temples receive your Holy spirits within our hearts. Lord you have so graciously answered our petitions before you. God we just want to thank you for blessing us and making us worthy of your promises poured forth in the heavens on earth. God, we thank you for your divine ways standing before us. Lord we thank you for bringing us out of the depths of un- righteousness. God, we hear your voice and spirits attentive to our supplications. God, we ask for your forgiveness for whatever is not right in our hearts that you help us to make it right. God we as Holy saints have waited for you with patience and relied on your Holy spirits within us to guide and teach us what your will is for us. God we a Holy people ask you to redeem us from all iniquities making us in your image eternally. God, we ask that you continue to allow your light to shine in our lives as a chosen Holy people. Lord we daily show forth your blessings upon us in the heavens on earth.

God, we ask that you keep us free from sins with much mercy upon us than ever before witness. God help us to keep the faith knowing we are the chosen Holy ones inherit the heavens on earth of eternal living eternal life. Lord we thank you for choosing us as the Holy and righteous ones to be your chosen Holy people in the heavens which is on earth. God, we ask that you defend and govern us according to your will bringing us to eternal everlasting life of happiness. Lord we ask that you save us from eternal death showing us the way to remain faithful until the end of all sins, sickness, and death has ceased in the heavens which is on earth. Lord we know that it is you that can save us from eternal death. God, we pray for peace through your righteous Holy spirits that dwells within us. God, we

Prayer

receive your presence standing before us in spirits in truth. God, we thank you for eternal living eternal life you have awarded us for our faithfulness

Lord we want to thank you for labeling us as forgiven sinners in the heavens on earth. God, we give thanks to you an almighty God who lives in our lives in spirits in truth guiding us the right way to eternal living eternal life in the heavens on earth. Lord we know that the reward of eternal life is for all forgiven Holy righteous people in the heavens on earth. God, we know without Holiness no-one can be caught up to the Holy spirits of God that dwells within them. God, we ask that you guide and strengthen our hearts so that we can stand in these last and evil days before us. God, we know your judgments and justice are righteous and true prevailing in the heavens on earth. God strengthen us as we remain caught up in spirits in truth dwelling with you within us daily. Thank God Thank God Thank God Thank God

Prayer

2

Prayer of the Righteous

God it is us your chosen ano nted people standing before your presence humbly kneel in prayer dwelling in your Holy spirits. Lord we thank you for your promises now appearing the heavens on earth, as we continue in faith, hope, and love with true purposes. God, we call to mind and spirits your promises concerning the paradise heavens on earth now forming. God, we thank you for the cleansing of sin, sickness, and death that shall perish at the end of judgments and justice prevailing in all the heavens on earth. God, we realize all have sinned and come short of knowing your powerful spirits in the heavens on earth operating daily to the good of your chosen people.

Prayer

God it is with open minds we a chosen people stand in your presence seeing the heavens appeared on earth entered our hearts, spiritual souls, body, and minds we comprehend the move of God working to the good of your chosen people. God, we believe with reference to your Holy spirits for certain we are your anointed chosen people. God, we give thee thanks for you have so kindly chosen us to be your people. God we cannot thank you enough for giving us favor in your spiritual eyesight. God thank you for favor bestowed upon your chosen Holy people creating thy image in our spirits and outward appearance making us pure in all things said and done in the heavens on earth. God, we thank you for granting us wherein we are perfect in the image of thee. God, we realize it is your granting us favor in the accomplishments of all things we say and do according to your will for our eternal living eternal life. Lord it is with confidence we rise according to your will in our lives.

Lord we resign from murmuring, cursing, swearing, contempt, hatred, judgments of jealousy, revenge, quarrels, injury, bad reputations, excessive drinking of alcohol, and disrespect for others. God, we ask that you change us from lies, fear, wrong desires of the flesh, greed, anger, impatience, stealing, and all other things that would keep us from entering eternal living eternal life in the heavens which is on earth. God, we confess to you in words in deeds in thoughts that you keep us from grievous faults. God, we thank you for pardoning us as forgiven sinners and continue to give us open hearts to your Holy and righteous spirits. God, we promise to avoid faults for the future and be Holy unto eternal living eternal life in all things said and done in the heavens which is on earth. God we will continue

Prayer

to dwell in your chosen Holy Temple Churches of God in Christ. God we again thank you for being appointed an angel to enlighten us in heaven on earth before your throne of grace and mercy.

God, we ask that you guide us in all our actions daily in the heavens on earth. God, we know that we are in the heavens on earth because of thy grace and mercy bestowed upon us. God, we know that thy grace is enough according to your will for all our needs. God thank you because you are so grateful to us for mending our lives unto a new start in things now and things to come in the heavens on earth. God thank you because you granted us peace to be still while you are working to the good of our eternal lives in the heavens on earth

3

The Call of God's Leadership upon the People

I, God say to all people in leadership in the heavens which is on earth; see to it that ye treat the people equal in all things said and done daily for ye have need to remember these are latter days of God and God's people judgments in the heavens on earth. I, God say to leaders in leadership ye have a need to be not caught up in unjust treatment of the people in the heavens on earth. I, God say to every leader in leadership the times are now times of giving an account of unrighteousness imposed upon the people by intent of unrighteous leaders in leadership. I, God say to all leaders in leadership remember that warning comes before destruction in every part of the heavens on earth. I, God say to all leaders in leadership take heed without fail to the call of righteousness leading the way to eternal living eternal life in the heavens which is on earth. I, God say to leaders in leadership gather all things said and done in ways of equal righteousness to all people dwelling in the heavens which are on earth.

I, God say to all leaders in leadership it is my will that all leaders in leadership cross-over into eternal living eternal life judged of good and righteous leadership. I, God say to the leaders in leadership ye have a need to be faithful in all things said and done in the heavens which is on earth. I, God say to you these are the end times of all things done and said in secret imposed upon the people in the heavens on earth. I, God say to you all hidden secrets come to the light of the people who have a need to know in the heavens on earth. I, God say to you the results of destructions happening in the heavens which are on earth have already surface because of the unrighteous ways of the sinful people doing thing in secrets imposed on the people. I, God say to you remember the days of judgments and justice of God is roaming the heavens which are on earth. I, God say to you all things hid surface to the top the people have a need to see and know in the heavens on earth.

I, God say to the people in the heavens which are on earth, the chosen Holy Temple Churches are the Churches of God in Christ are an elect chosen people of God. I, God say to the chosen Holy Priesthood, ye are standing in the presence of God Holy spirits judging all unrighteousness without respect of person. I, God say to the chosen Holy Priesthood, the meek inherit the earth are the chosen anointed called, inspired, and ordained by the Holy spirits of God. I say to the chosen Holy Priesthood, ye are charged to judge the people in all things said and done in the heavens

16

on earth according to what you hear in your spirits. I, God say to the chosen Holy Priesthood, ye are aware and feel the spirits of God within understanding the need for many changes prevailing in the heavens on earth by the call of God and God's chosen anointed people. I, God say to the chosen Holy Priesthood, ye shall judge the people in the heavens on earth for 7000 years without count as the sands of the sea until all sins, sickness, and death has cease in the heaven on earth. I, God say to the chosen Holy Priesthood, stand firm without fail in all things said and done.

I say to you the people must be baptize with forgiven sins among them washed in Holy water by Holy hands to be saved crossing-over into eternal living eternal life. I, God say to you the Holy water is the spiritual blood of God that washes the people hearts clean and pure. I say to you to be saved is to have eternal life and never die but live forever on a paradise heaven on earth at the end of all sins, sickness, and death cease in the heavens on earth. I, God say to you those having forgiven sins among them recover from all sickness, sins, and death, but must endure until the end of all sins, sickness, and death cease in the heavens on earth.

I, God say to all chosen Holy Priesthood, let your yes be yes and your no be no without respect of person. I, God say to you walk according at your level and ability that God has given you. I, God say to you do not stray from the charge entrusted in you to judge the people, for you have a charge to keep. I, God say to you keep the charge without fail in that no destruction follows you. I, God say to you, make it known to the Holy congregation ye have a charge to keep before the presence of God. I, God say to you now is the Holy resurrection of the dead minds to spiritual minds caught up with God in spirits in truth. , God say to you the rise of spiritual

17

judgments of God and God's anointed chosen people are already operating in the heavens on earth. I, God say to you the Holy spirits are within male and female who show actions of powerful works of God in their Holy spirits in faith in truth. I, God say to you there be many Holy Priesthood in spirits in truth rising to call of God to help the people cross-over into eternal living eternal life.

I, God say to you the times are now times of the rising of the chosen Holy High Priesthood in the chosen Churches of God of in Christ Incorporated in every part of the heavens on earth. I say to you this is the last judgment call in the heavens on earth. I, God say to you all things rise to the eyes and ears of God's spirits of the chosen people called to judge the people. I, God say to you there be nothing hid said and done in the heavens on earth from the judgment and justice call of God and God's chosen anointed people. I, God say to the chosen Holy Priesthood, fear not for I, God am with you in every step you take and every breath you take as you speak your mind (what-ever is in your spirits speak it knowing your limits keeping peace) in all things said and done. I, God now form more honor and glory in the chosen Holy Priesthood called to save the people in the cross-over to eternal living eternal life.

I, God say to the people in the heavens on earth now the consequences of forgetting God the value of the soul. I, God say to the people in the heavens, ye have a need to behold the sprits of God and God's chosen people. I, God say to the people in the heavens, I kept back nothing that is profitable to you; ye have a need to know in the heavens which is on earth. I, God say to you by grace ye are saved through your faith. I say to you without faith it is impossible to enter eternal living eternal life in the heavens on earth. I, God say to the people in the heavens on earth, behold all things ye have need of appear in the paradise heavens on earth. I, God say to the people in the heavens on earth doors opened in large important places that has been shut on you. I, God say to you, I, am the truth and the light of eternal life bringing you good tiding of eternal living eternal life. I, God say to you streams of promises bless the people in the heavens willing to give up sins and cross-over to eternal living eternal life.

I, God say to the people in the heavens on earth; hear what the spirits said unto the chosen Holy Temple Churches of God in Christ in the heavens on earth. I say to you, one must read spiritual words of God by inspiration out of this "Gospel Book of God's Laws" written unto you for guidance of crossing-over into eternal living eternal life on a paradise earth at the end of all sins, sickness, and death cease in the heavens on earth. I say to you, ye must be inspired by God to receive these words written in spirits in truth by the Highest Priest Prophet ever walk the earth in your time of now times. I, God say to you read these words written in the order it has been written unto you for guidance in spirits in truth to obtain hearing ears for spirits of God. I say to you, ye then read under the anointing of God as the anointing of God falls upon your spirits within causing you to know who you are and your reasons for being in life. I, God say to you accomplish the anointing spirits of God in your life.

I, God say to you, ye have a need to hear from God in spirits in truth to obtain eternal living eternal life in the heavens on earth. I, God say to you it is good to clearly hear from God in all things said and done in the heavens which are on earth. I, God say to the people in the heavens which is on earth; the millennial of January 1, 2000 started at that appointed time for 7000 years without count as the sands of the sea, the rapture of being caught up in spirits in truth with God crosses the people over into eternal living eternal life in the heavens which is on earth. I, God say to you, this is the first and the last rapture judgment call upon all people, places, and things in the heavens which is on earth. I, God supply the things eternally need through the rapture of smart anointed people with degrees to accomplish things in the heavens on earth that works to the good of the people eternally. I, God say to the people in the heavens on earth; for 7000 years the people in the heavens on earth are resurrected by being caught up in the rapture of their spiritual minds living eternal life in the heavens which is on earth. I, God say to you, forget not ye must endure until the end of all sins, sickness, and death has ceased in the judgments and justice calls of God and God's people.

I, God say to the people in the heavens on earth; ye go through the tribulation periods of life until all sins, sickness, and death has cease in judgments and justice of God and God's chosen appointed people have finish the calls of unrighteousness in the heavens on earth. I, God say to you, there be no unrighteousness escape the call of God and God's chosen people judgments and justice call. I say to you there is no unrighteousness hid in the heavens on earth; for all things said and done in the dark comes to the light of the people in the world having a need to know. I, God say to the people in the heavens on earth; all unrighteousness is buried with sinners of unforgiving sins beneath the earth never to return. I, God say to you, unforgiving sinners' death is eternal beneath the heavens on earth turn to dust. I, God say to you, there is no one returns from eternal death beneath the earth to the heavens on earth. I, God say to you, there have been many people misled that they will see their love ones and friends in the days of the rapture are not true but are false Preachers/Elders and teachers. I, God say to the people in the heavens on earth; be not misled taking heed to these words of mind with intentions of eternal life for yourself.

I, God say to the people in the heavens which are on earth; there be no more dead bodies put in walls of a building in the heavens on earth; all dead bodies are buried in the grounds of the earth. I, God say to the people in the heavens which are on earth; all dead bodies in buildings in walls must come out of the wall and be buried under ground. I, God say to you, there is no need for dead bodies in the cross-over into eternal living eternal life. I, God say to you the dead is dead for eternal as all deaths are eternal death. I, God say to the people in the heavens which are on earth; these things ought not to be done. I, God say to you, forget not the times are now times of judgments and justice upon you daily in all things said and done. I, God say to you, warning comes before destruction in many things ye have had time to take heed without fail. I, God say to you, ye have been warned.

I, God say to you, the wrath of God comes in an instant without warning without fail in every part of the heavens on earth clearing the way to eternal living eternal life. I, God say to you pull every dead body out of the walls in every building where dead bodies dwell in the heavens on earth. I God say to the people in the heavens on earth; only pureness enters eternal living eternal life. I say to you, ye have no need for dead ashes and dead bodies in walls in the heavens which is on earth, for these things are not pure neither healthy for eternal living eternal life.

I, God say to the people in the heavens on earth; I have chosen not to destroy the whole heavens of people, places, and things in the heavens on earth. I, God say to the people in the heavens on earth as ye honor my commanded laws written unto you in this Gospel Book of Laws the good promises of God shall flow quicker leading to eternal living eternal life. I, God speak to you the things that defile the heavens on earth work not to the good of eternal living eternal life. I, God say to you, the death of sinners removes sins from the heavens which are on earth clearing the way to eternal living eternal life. I, God say to the people in the heavens which is on earth; forget not the rapture of God is upon you as you have a need to be caught up in spirits of God in truth enduring the trials and tribulations of the times and seasons upon all individuals in the heavens on earth. I, God say to you the wrath of judgments and justice has been poured out into the heavens which are on earth. I, God say to you there is no stones left un-turn in the heavens which are on earth. I, God say to you all things done in the heavens which is on earth are standing in the middle of judgments and justice daily.

I, God say to the people in the heaves on earth; these things call unto judgments and justice have a need to be fixed by leaders in leadership in the heavens which is on earth. I, God say to the people in the heavens on earth; there be more than ever before in history of humankind, desolation, death, fire, water, accidents, and rain in the wrath of judgments and justice in the over the entire world of people in the heavens which is on earth. I, God say to the people in the heavens which are on earth; it is victorious to attend and fellowship with the chosen Holy Churches of God in Christ merging as one big Holy land called by the spirits of God and God's chosen anointed people. I, God say to you, it is time to heal all nations from sins, sickness, and death clearing the way to eternal living eternal life.

I, God say to leaders in leadership ye have a need to not mislead the people in your leadership duties; forget not these are the times and seasons of judgments and justice prevailing daily in every part of the heavens which is on earth. I, God say to the leaders in leadership, the people have also been misled in every denomination of religious leadership with false teaching. I, God say to you, see to it that these things are not done. I say to you, the people have a need to know the truth and nothing, but the truths reference all things said and done in the heavens which are on earth. I, God say to the leaders in leadership hearken unto my words written in this Gospel Book of Laws written unto you. I, God say to the people in the heavens on earth, see and hear things being called as though they were appearing to the good of eternal living eternal life in the heavens on earth. I, God say to the people in the heavens, the traditions of your forefathers are over never to return in the heavens on earth. I, God say to the people in the heavens which are on earth awake from the dead minds to be caught up in the spiritual minds that work to the good of eternal living eternal life.

I, Prophet say to the people in the heavens on earth; behold I tell you a mystery, ye with forgiven sins among you living according to this Gospel Book of Laws are not sleep in mind, but are caught up in spirits in truth; are now caught up in the rapture of true spirits in the whole armor

23

of God change you in a moment in a twinkling of an eye. I, God say to the people in the heavens which are on earth; the trumpets are sounding upon all unforgiving sinners in the heavens roaming the earth seeking whom they may devour.

I, God say to the people in the heavens which is on earth; at the end of the rapture in 7000 years without count without number as the sands of the sea, the end of all sins, sickness, and death cease in the heavens which is on earth. I, God say to the people in the heavens on earth, at the end of judgments and justice of rapture for 7000 years of millennium without count as the sands of the sea all things said and done in the world are judged until sins, sickness, and death cease and the wrath of God is finish as trials and tribulations ends it course in the lives of all people crossed-over into eternal living eternal life in a paradise world.

I, Prophet say to the chosen Holy Priesthood in the heavens on earth; I, Prophet have already poured out the seven seals upon the seven Holiness Churches in Tallahassee, Florida within were seven letters given to seven Preachers/Elders of the seven Churches. I, Prophet Say to you, the people in the world have a need to be judged daily of incorruptible sins of forgiving sinners being caught up with God and God's chosen people in the rapture of Holy spirits in truth in God with the chosen people of God in the heavens which is on earth. I God say to the people in the heavens on earth; all people with forgiven sins worship with faith enduring until the end of the rapture of God and God's chosen Holy people is finish receiving the forgiven sinners in the cross-over of eternal living eternal life; ye must worship in the chosen Holiness Temple Churches of God in Christ Incorporated in the heavens which is on earth. I, God say to you, the

24

corruptible unforgiving sinners are judged daily until the end of all sins, sickness and death cease in the heavens which is on earth. I, God say to you, at the end of all sins, sickness, and death of the people who have endured enter the paradise heavens on earth with equal treatment of equal living conditions to all people in the cross-over into eternal living eternal life in the heavens which is on earth.

I, God say to the people in the heavens which are on the earth in times like these there is a price to pay for unforgiving sins. I, God say to you hear what the spirits of God said to the chosen Holy Temple Churches of God in Christ, the signs are clear the anointing of God is operating in the light of the world with the chosen anointed people of God. I say to you the Holy Priesthood speak the anointing of God in that ye hear from God clearly telling the people thus what God said. I God say to the chosen Holy Priesthood thus I am showing you are the chosen pattern of people, places, and things according to the will of God for the chosen Holy Priesthood in the order given. I God say to the chosen Holy Priesthood, hear my voice speak unto you that thou commanded to speak unto the people head toward the cross-over to eternal living eternal life in the heavens which is on earth.

I, God say to you everything written in this Gospel Book of God's Laws is done in all the chosen Holy Temple Churches of God in Christ Incorporated. I, God say to the chosen Holy Priesthood stray not from these sayings of mind written unto you in this Gospel Book of God's Laws. I, God say to the chosen Holy Priesthood take heed, in the same hour ye stray from these sayings of mind eternal loss of eternal living eternal life is instantly before you. I, God say to the chosen Holy Priesthood again, take

25

heed to the calling I have entrusted in you a chosen Holy Priesthood a chosen elect anointed special people. I, God say to the chosen Holy Priesthood, see to it that ye not lose your crown of eternal life; see to it ye endure until the end of all sins, sickness, and death cease in the heavens which is on earth at the end of all judgments and justice called upon the unrighteous unforgiving sinners.

I, God say to the chosen Holy Priesthood, have faith in all things said and done with much understanding of this Gospel Laws of God written unto you forgetting not your leadership role. I, God say to all chosen Holy Priesthood, study this Gospel Book of God's Laws to show your-selves approve unto God to speak with confidence to the people in the cross-over to eternal living eternal life. I, God say to the chosen Holy Priesthood, teach no other doctrine than this Gospel Book of Laws written unto you for the cross-over of eternal living eternal life in the heavens which is on earth.

I, God say to the chosen elect Holy Priesthood, in the same hour ye teach or preach other than this Gospel Book of Laws written unto you, ye have eternally lost your way to eternal life, ye then have become confounded in all things said and done. I, God say to the chosen Holy Priesthood, see to it that ye are called by your name with reference to Bishop, Prophet, Elder, Pastor, Evangelist attached to your name. I, God say to you I, God is one and the same God in spirits in truth in the heavens on earth calling justice judgments upon the unrighteous. I, God say to you to be saved; is to have eternal life according to this Gospel Book of God's Laws and none other than this book written unto you for guidance in the cross-over into eternal living eternal life.

I, God say to you, the millennium of judgments and justice sound the trumpets on all unrighteous people in this un-equally yoked world opening the eyes, ears, minds, and hearts of the people. I, God say to you, the creation of people, places and things have special meaning and effect on the chosen elect people of God in the heavens which is on earth. The Holy and righteous saints are operating in the image of physical being of God in the heavens on earth. I, God have sent you a Prophet led in the Holy spirits of God to direct your path in the path of all righteousness without fail in all things said and done leading the way to eternal living eternal life. I, God say to you the kingdom s of the heavens abides on earth. I, God call for the people in this world to repent, the words of God in this gospel truth of Gospel Book of God's Laws must never be forgotten in all things said and done daily in the heavens on earth.

I, Prophet say to you, the appearing of God's Holy spirits in the heavens on earth are earthly felt over the entire world with much affect in the lives of the people. The effect of God calling all people, places, and things to the present laws of God come forward unto the judgments and justice of God. The rising of the Messiah God is in the heavens which are on earth in flesh in blood in body in soul in spirits in truth in Holiness in justice in judgments in God in people chosen by God. I, Prophet say to you, the people in the heavens abiding on earth have a need to be nourished in God in spirits in honesty in truth in Holiness elect chosen Temples Churches of God in Christ Incorporated.

I, God say to you, the fame of the Holiest Highest Priest Prophet ever walk the heavens on earth in your time has been called over 60 years ago in your time has went un-aware to the eyes and ears of the people in

27

the heavens which are on earth. I, God say to you, all people who hunger and thirst after righteousness and truth in the cross-over to eternal living eternal life find it in the gospel writing books of the Holiest Highest Priest Prophet ever walk the earth in your time of now times. I, God say to you, ye must be a wise believer with wise Holy spirits nourished in the spirits of God. I, God say to you, the people of this world can be exempt from sins, sickness, and death who repent being Holy and righteous with equal treatment to the people living conditions in all things said and done in the heavens which is on earth. I God say to you, justice and judgments in the wrath of God takes away the sins of the unrighteousness dishonesty roaming the heavens which is on earth.

I, God say to you, world changing events continue happening until all justice and judgments are finish it course and all sins, sickness, and death have ceased its course in the heavens which is on earth. I, God say to you, all things the people have a need to know are being written and manifested to you for the cross-over into eternal living eternal life in this Gospel Book of God's Laws. I say to you, the spirits of God are eternally in the heavens which are on earth working to the good of the people in the heavens which are on earth. I, God say to you, all leaders in leadership have a need to know ye face the judgments and justice of God daily in all things said and done daily in the heavens which is on earth.

I, God say to you, all unrighteous leaders in leadership face loosing eternal life during your continuing process of unrighteous leadership imposed upon the people; I, God hear the cries and prayers of the people treated unfair. I, God say to you all prophecies; visions and dreams of righteousness are in the mainstream of all things said and done in the

28

heavens which is on earth in the resurrection of God's Holy spirits opening the minds and hearts of the people.

I, God say to you, the resurrection of God's Holy spirits rising to those who hunger, and thirst are in the chosen Holy Temple Churches of God in Christ Incorporated in the heavens which is on earth. I, say to you, eternal life is ascending in all the heavens which are on earth. There is no-one greater than the spirits of God, for God is spirits God is truth. It is the mighty acts of God's spirituality with power upon the people in the heavens which is on earth. I, say to you, ye are now in the days of Pentecost ye see and hear things in your spirits within of God in close relationships with the spirits of God. The purpose of God has eternal value in eternal living eternal life with eternal structure in the heavens which is on earth. The signs and wonders of God are eternal in the eternal heavens on earth. I, God say to you, there will be times arise in the heavens which is on earth ye will not be able to carry Bibles in public; for the end there of will have risen the call of judgment and justice upon the things that were added and taken from the Holy scriptures that were not call by God, but call by humankind writers of Bibles. I God say to you, there not be any Bibles needed in the eternal heavens which are on earth, but the Gospel Laws of God remain eternally in the heavens which are on earth.

I, God say to the people in the heavens which are on earth there is not anything added neither anything taken from this Gospel Book of God's Laws in the heavens which is on earth. I, God say to the people in the heavens on earth, in the same hour ye add or take from this Gospel Book of God's Laws ye have lost your way to eternal living eternal life. I, God say to the people in the heavens which is on earth, there be no more Bibles made in the heavens which is on earth, for ye have confused the people enough with adding and taking from the Holy Bible which already had words added and taken from it in the beginning of Bible days appearing on earth. I, God say to the people in the heavens which is on earth, there are some written lies added to the Holy Bible that the people have not lived neither had any respect for many scriptures in the Holy Bibles.

I, God say to the leaders in leadership in the heavens on earth, take heed, for I am God with all power in my hands to shut the heavens which is on earth since the beginning of times. I say to you I; God change not from these words written unto you in this Holy Gospel Book of God's Laws. I, God say to the people in the heavens on earth, the predictions in this Gospel Book of God's Laws shows up continuously in every part of the world. I, God say to you, the call of justice and judgments stands during the heavens which are on earth destroying all denominations except Holiness denominations. I, God say to the people in the heavens on earth, the lands rise to one big Holy land. I, God say to the people in leadership in the heavens on earth, all these words written unto you became flesh is in the flesh already operating in the spirits of God and God's chosen anointed people. I, God say to you, live in the will God, knowing the will of God for your life. I, God say to you, Holy worship is required of you entering eternal living eternal life. The people of God are singing and praising God in spirits in truth for the promise of eternal living eternal life appearing in the heavens which are on earth.

I, God say to the chosen Holy priesthood, the kingdom of God is at hand operating under the anointing of God by the chosen elect people of God Holy Priesthood in authority. I, God say to you, the inspired light of

Holiness is the covenant of the Holy Pr esthood with spirits of God is God in the Holy chosen Temple Churches of God in Christ in the heavens which is on earth. I, God say to you, all people entering the cross-over are made whole by the baptizing spirits of God and God's chosen elect people. I say to you the anointing of God dwell among the people of God in the chosen Holy Temples renewing their minds daily in all things said and done in the heavens which is on earth.

I, God say to the chosen Holy Priesthood in the heavens on earth, all Holy servants and Holy followers of God are obedient discipleship unto the Holy spirits of God within them in all things said and done with honesty and truth.

I, God say to the chosen Holy Priesthood in the heavens on earth, ye that have entered the cross-over to eternal living eternal life ye are constantly in spirits of God in truth of God's eternal spirits with self-control. I, God say to all chosen Holy e ect Priesthood in the Holy Temple Churches of God in Christ, ye have no need for communion among yourselves for I, God has risen with all power in my hands among you in spirits in truth in the heavens which is on earth. I say to you, the chosen elect Holy people in the congregation must continue in communion for strength in faith in spirits in truth. I, God say to you all chosen elect Holy Priesthood work by internal spirits of God within them with pure hearts.

I, God say to the chosen elect Holy Priesthood in the Holy Temple Churches of God in Christ Incorporated, the Holy Bishops are over the congregation of people in each Temple with 6 Apostles 6 Elders 6 Evangelist and 6 Prophets equals 24 Priest to help the Bishop at each Holy

Temple. I, God say to you, all Holy Priest have abilities according to your faith in God's internal spirits within working according to your faith. I, God say to you, the Holy Priesthood minds are totally different from the congregation of people; for this is latter days of God's justice and judgments call by the Holy Priesthood in the Holy Temple Churches of God in Christ Incorporated. I, God say to you, all Holy Priesthood trust their internal spirits within.

I say to you, the unrighteous people give a daily full account of unrighteousness and un-equableness imposed upon the people. I, God say to you, the elect chosen Holy Priesthood know all things said and done in the heavens which is on earth calling judgments and justice according, I, God say to you, it is time for all people in the heavens on earth to reconcile unto the Holy spirits of God. I say to you, the spirits of God are scattered upon all the face of the heavens which is on earth laying the foundations paving ways to eternal living eternal life working through the minds of the people. I, God say to you, all people, places, and things are renewed paving the way to eternal living eternal life in the heavens on earth.

I, God say to you, pray in the name of the Lord your God and pray not in Jesus name, for there is no return of Jesus to the people. I, God say to you, the people have been misled by false doctrine of false teaching added and taken from the Holy Bible during the beginning of the Bible days appearing on earth. I, God say to you, go back to God, for the people have lost the way to God. I God say to you, put all these things behind you for the chance of crossing-over into eternal living eternal life. I, God say to you, all things are written unto you that ye have clear understanding without fail. I, God say to you this Gospel Laws of God leads and guide you to the cross-over of eternal living eternal life in the heavens which is on earth the promise lands. I say to you, the signs of the times are in the heavens on earth daily until all things are finish I, God have called unto you leading to the paradise heavens on earth. I, God remind you again I have chosen not to shut down the heavens on earth, but restoring the minds of the people spirits as all people, places and things are judged daily according

It is good to remember the spirits of God is traveling in every place in the heavens which is on earth. I say to you, there are those who are hypocrites in the Holy synagogues seeking eternal life. They are the unforgiving sinners with sins among them that are unforgiving sins. I, God say to you, all people in the heavens on earth have sin have come short of knowing the power of God realness operating among them without fail. I, God call this to your attention; the Holiest Highest Priest Prophet that has ever walk the earth in your times of now times has been operating among the people for over 60 years without notice in the Holy Tabernacle Churches of God in Christ. I, God call this to your shame while you are looking for the return of Jesus; there is no return of Jesus to come at no time. I, God say to you, ye have been misled, it is such times as these ye have a need to renew your minds in the realness of God in spirits in truth.

I, God say to you, the return of Jesus was false documentation when people added their own spiritual words and took spiritual words out of the Holy Bible at the beginning of times in the days of writing the Bible. I, God say to you I have come to receive my people in spirits in truth in a better understanding for such times as these of judgments and justice upon the people in the heavens which is on earth. I, God say to you, ye have a need to come to yourselves in spirits in truth in realness of God in awareness, for ye have entertained angels of God among you as you are unaware and refuse to hear from the Prophets I God sent to you. I, God say woe unto you in spirits in truth in all things said and done in the heavens which is on earth. I, God say to you, for generations and generations the people entertain themselves and others with lies to reach self-gain in false ministries as so many do this every day.

I, God say to you, put on the whole armor of God in that ye hear clearly in spirits in truth wanting in nothing. I, God say to you, the people wrote the Holy Bible in the days of writing the Bible many of them were in reprobated minds because of adding and taking spirits from the Holy Bible. I God say to you, it is for you to use common sense in putting things together in all things said and done that ye be not deceive by paper nor spirits. I, God say to you, ye have fail the test of trying spirits in the Bible by spirits of common sense and what you see going on around you. I, God say to you again, many things in the Bible have not been lived by neither abided by for generations and generations up to this very second.

I, God say to you, if I call judgments and justice upon the people for not truly abiding by the Holy Bible, the world would be wiped out without people. I, God say to you renew your minds with this Gospel Book of God's laws without fail in the cross-over to eternal living eternal life. I, God say to you, the line is drawn with this generation of people and the people to come. I, God say to you, this is the reason why sin without end is in the world until God steps in calling judgments and justice like never upon the people refuse to stop sinning. I, God say to you, sex and money have ruined the minds of the people with grieve and lust, with many people the more they have the more they want.

I, God say to you, the secret works of God are in the heavens which are on earth operating in combinations of people, places, and things. I, God say to you, there are new identities new lifestyles upon the people of God shown forth. I, God say to you all power is in my hands is exceedingly great over the universe of this world. I, God say to you, the world cannot continue in the ways of the people for self-gain of money and sex in the left hand, many with the Holy Bible in the other hand. I, God say to you, this Gospel Book of God's Laws are fulfilling upon the people in the heavens which is on earth.

There be no-one in the heavens on earth take the glory of God. I, God say to you, the seed of the Prophet was called over 60 years ago with the spiritual mind of God given gifts from God is God within her. I, God say to you, the seed was called and blessed in the mother's womb to conceive the Holy One before the intercourse of the father and mother took place 65 years ago. I, God say to you, up to this very day, I have raised the Holiest Highest Priest Prophet with the mind of God in flesh in body in soul in heart in spirits in Holiness in chosen Holy Temple Churches of God in Christ ever walk the heavens on earth in your times of now times. I, God say to you, the Holiest Highest Priest Prophet have gone unnoticed by the people surrounds her.

I, God say to you, there is no Holy Priesthood over the Holiest Highest Priest Prophet; she is not a member of one church, but is a member of the chosen Holy Temple Churches of God in Christ as a whole she is over the kingdom of chosen Holy Temple Churches of God in Christ. I, God say to the chosen Holy Priesthood, see to it that ye abide within the Gospel Laws of God written unto you in this book without fail I God can

35

shut the heavens on earth for the Holiest Highest Priest Prophet ever walk the heavens on earth in your times of now times. I, God say to you, all people, places, and things in the heavens which are on earth belong to God. I, God say to you, provoke me not at no-time with much more anger. I say to you, the anger of God is in the heavens on earth paving the way to eternal living eternal life.

I, God say to you, all people who cross-over to eternal living eternal life behold the realness of the spiritual face of God in the heavens on earth. I, God say to you, remember the lives of the people crossing-over into eternal living eternal life is at stake at any given time until all judgments and justice is finish and sins, sickness, and death cease in the heavens on earth. I God say to you, the transfiguration of your body takes place in a twinkling of an eye the moment ye believe in this Gospel Book of God's Laws written unto you. I, God say to you, the people of God inherit the paradise heavens on earth at the finish end of judgments and justice. I, God say to you take all things said and done by force are serious for the sake of crossing-over to eternal living eternal life. I, God say to you, these words in the Gospel Book of God's Laws are sealed Holy spirits faithful and true.

I, God say to you there are generations of people to come and go until the people seal their hearts with eternal living eternal life in truth in faith in equableness treatment of others in peace in the will of God and God's people judging the people for eternal living. I, God say to you, all sins, sickness, and death shall pass from the face of the heavens on earth. I, God say to you the heavens on the earth for people judged with forgiving sins among them. I, God say to you, blessed is unto all people who are not offended by this Gospel Book of Laws written and spoken unto you. I, God say to you, the seven seals have been poured out in the heavens which are on earth. I, God say to you the promises of God have taken affect already upon you in many ways without notice.

I, God say woe unto you instantly who by mouth by hand try to reverse the words of this Gospel Book of God's Laws written unto you in Holy inspirations in spirits in truth. I, God say to you, the reverse of these words from you, ye instantly loose the way to eternal life on your behalf. I, God say to you, repent of your false thoughts and live eternal life. I, God say to you, all people laboring in the chosen Holy Temple Churches of God in Christ are rewarded greatly learning all things ye have a need to know reference the cross-over into eternal living eternal life. I, God say to you, these are the real now times to fear God and live eternal life. I, God say to you again, all things are at hand judged until the finish of the people stop sinning. I, God say to you, ye that find eternal life have a need to hold fast to it by way of enduring without fail.

And I heard the voice of God saying unto all the chosen elect Temple Holiness Churches of God in Christ; hear what the spirits of God said unto the most Holiest Highest Priest Prophet ever walk the face of the heavens which are on earth in spirits in truth in flesh in body in blood in prophecy descending spirits over the entire heavens on earth. And the spirits said write these things down I, God speak to you in spirits in truth in that you thus go tell the people what thus I, God speak unto you. Thus, speak into the hearing ears of the chosen elect people of God; gather all the forgiving sinners in the heavens which are on earth.

Thus, the chosen people of forgiving sins are a special people of God abiding in the heavens on earth inherit the paradise heavens on earth. The chosen elect people enter the Holy Gates of the elect chosen Temple Holy Churches of God in Christ. I Prophet Give honor to the chosen elect Holy High Priesthood in authority over the sheep of God's Holy disciples, the Holy Priesthood shepherd the Holy flock of God. I, Prophet give honor to the Holiness saints the Holy followers of God in all the chosen Temple Holy Churches of God in Christ in the heavens which are on earth abiding by the Holy spirits of God within their spirits inherit the paradise heavens.

4

The Chosen Elect Holy Temples COGIC Appointed the Call of Judgments

I Prophet Give honor to the elect chosen Temples COGIC appointed the call of judging the people to receive eternal life. I, Prophet say to the people in the heavens which are on earth, it is Holiness or hell within the loss of eternal living eternal life on paradise heavens on earth. I, God say to the people in the heavens on earth; be ye Holy in all things said and done in the heavens on earth perceiving judgment call of God is daily in all things said and done in the heavens on earth. I, God say to you, from the beginning of times the people were called unto Holiness, but there were those who sought their own religion their own way as of this very day. I, say to you, now is the last just judgment call upon all people, places, and things of traditions of the forefathers in the heavens which is on earth. I, God say to you, this is the chosen generation of the elect chosen people to judge the people of unrighteousness in the heavens which is on earth.

I, God say to the people in the heavens which is on earth, take heed unto all these prophecies written and spoken unto you; for you have a need to receive all these prophecies in spirits in truth. I, God say to you, ye have a need to abide by these prophecies in spirits in truth instantly quickly without fail. I, God say to the people dwelling in the heavens which are on earth, your life is at stake for eternal living eternal life or the loss of eternal living eternal life. I, God say to you, judgment call begins at the chosen elect Holy Temple of Churches of God in Christ Incorporated in the heavens on earth.

I, God say to you, judgment call ends at the elect Holy Temple COGIC Incorporated. It is the times are now high times in all the heavens which are on earth to gather the sheep from the goats. I, God say to you, see these things in spirits in truth in Holiness and take heed instantly that ye be not removed from Holiness. The chosen elect people of God have entered in the heavens on earth changing and calling all things according to the spirits of God in spirits in truth unto the people in the heavens which are on earth. I, God say to you, these prophecies now called unto you, a Holy elect chosen people of God.

I, God say to the elect chosen Holiness COGIC Inc. ye have a need to start all Church services on time. There are many people coming down from the Holy heavens on earth God hath appointed unto Holiness COGIC

Inc. in every part of the heavens on earth. At no time the 11:00 a.m. worship services are not to be schedule for service at other Temples, but at your own Temple. At no time the 11:30 a.m. services are not to start late but start on time every time every service, no service starts late, but on time. The 11:30 a.m. Holy COGIC worship services are the main ingredients to the chosen Holiness people of God. , say to you, Holiness is right for all people dwelling in the heavens which are on earth.

There be no second coming after the judgments and justice calls of God and God's people are finished and say well done, it is done. The troubles of this world will be done when the end of all sins, sickness, and death has cease in the heavens on earth and the paradise earth will have appeared complete. I, God say to the people in the heavens which is on earth, there be no second coming after the 7000 years of judgments and justice without count as the sands of the sea. I, God say to you, all ungodly unholy people, places, and things in the earth are swallowed up in judgments and justice in the victory of eternal justice and judgments destroyed from the face of the heavens on earth.

I, Prophet say to the elect chosen people of COGIC Inc. my name is blessed from on high in the heavens or earth for I see God spirits to spirits face to face. I, say to you, I am that I am, for I am sent unto you that you inherit eternal living eternal life a chosen Holy people of God. I, Prophet say to you, eternity in the heavens which are on earth is my home. I, Prophet say to you, this is a memorial to all generations of people in the heavens which is on earth, heavens are your home on earth. I, Prophet say to you, God said to me, go gather my people unto me that are scattered in the heaven which is on earth; for my people are the elect chosen Prophets,

41

Bishops, Apostles, Elders, Evangelists, and all Holy saints entering the COGIC Inc. Holy Temples remaining in the cross-over to eternal living eternal life. I, God say to the Holiest Highest Priest Prophet ever walk the earth in the now times; I, God have surely visited you in spirits in truth, for I seen and judge the people, places, and things wrong done unto you. It is I; God brought you up out of the lands of the living unto the spiritual lands of the living.

I, God say to the elect Holy Priesthood, shepherd my sheep separating the sheep from the goats driving the goats away from the sheep the Holy chosen people of God in all the Holy chosen Temples as the Holy Prophet stood up and help guide the sheep to eternal living eternal life. The Holy Priesthood watered their sheep in baptizing them for eternal living eternal life in the heavens on earth. And the Holy Priest watered their flock coming down from the heavens as the Prophets drew enough water (speaking the prophecies of God) for 7000 years without count as the sands of the sea of the judgments and justice calls of God.

I, God say to you, the most "Holiest One" (the Holy One) is before you, in the heavens which are on earth. I, God say to you, there be no-one escape the latter day's judgments and justice of God daily in the heavens which is on earth. And the angel of the Lord appeared out of the midst of the people with a tongue as a flaming fire and consumed them in the midst of her; saying now you see me for I have come to pass in the heavens on earth and save the Holy elect chosen people of God unto eternal living eternal life in the heavens on earth. I, Prophet say to you, this is for them that believe and not for unbelievers as ye are un-evenly yoked from the chosen elect people of God in the heavens on earth. I, Prophet say to you, prophecy is written and spoken unto them that believe and hearken unto the Holy spirits written by my hands. This prophecy written in this book is for the people living and dwelling in the Holy spirits of God as they all live and dwell on one accord in the Holy chosen Temples of God.

I, God say to you, the first sign given you is the Holiest Highest Priest Prophet the Holy One before you in the heavens which is on earth as the chosen Holy Priesthood speak the latter days judgments and justice of God. And during all things said and done in the elect Holy Temples the Prophets only show up at the appointed times and seasons appointed unto them by the spirits of God in the heavens which is on earth. There is no Prophets at the Holy Temples continuously at every church service unless God hath called into your spirits to be at an appointed church service. The spirits of the Prophets interrupt many services not appointed unto them to be there. Apostles must be over the congregation of people as Bishops and Prophets are over seers to the congregations.

It is I; the Lord your God has not appointed Prophets to be at every elect chosen Holy service. This gives the Apostles over the chosen elect congregation to organize the Temple and the congregation of people according to all things called by the spirits of God without the judgments of the Prophets on every occasion. If God speaks unto the Prophet or Prophets to be at all the elect chosen Holy Temple services for this is your season, then the Prophet or Prophets will be at every service judging all things said and done according to the spirits of God hath called upon them in spirits in truth. I, God say to you, all Prophets must write down all things called unto your spirits at all times at any time of morning, noon, night as the chosen elect Holy Priesthood must write things down God spoke to

43

your spirits that ye have need to speak to the elect chosen saints of God. I, God say to you, the elect chosen Holy Priesthood must study this Gospel Book of Law to show yourselves approval unto the spirits of God.

I, God say to you, ye the chosen elect Holy Priesthood must study this Gospel Book of Law that ye feed the chosen followers of God correctly in spirits in truth. The Holy Apostles continue to bring the congregation unto their subjections of God's Holy spirits according that hath been called unto you in spirits in truth. I, God say to you, there be no female Preachers among you, for man is always the head of the household chosen elect Holy Temples of God. I, God say unto you, the spirits present at the appointed times and seasons are subject to the Prophet or Prophets.

The Prophet may stand at any given time during service and speak, for there are no certain times. I, God say to you, that Prophet must move by the spirits of God within speaking at any given time God speaks to the Prophet to speak without fail without confusions. I, God say to you, it is good to write things down spoken to you by the spirits of God that there is not any adding neither taking from the spirits God called unto you. I, God say to you, the Priest and everyone in the Temple is subject to the spirits spoken by the Prophet or Prophets without fail at any given time. When the Prophet stand to speak all people in the Temple is quite and listen to the voice of God speak through the Prophet. For all things done and said in the chosen elect Holy Temples will always be done and said according to the Holy spirits of God. At no time the Church services are cut off according to clock time, but according to the spirits of God moving in the Holy elect Temples.

For all things are called to order according to the spirits of God in the chosen Holy elect Temples of God. The spirits of God are called into strict order according to the Holy Temples over-seer with the help of the Prophets according to the spirits of God. I, God say to you, this Gospel Book of God's law will be strictly followed abiding by the calls of God upon the chosen elect Holy Temples; in that is the call of judgments for 7000 years crossing the people over into eternal living eternal life. I, God say to you, all things in this Gospel Book of God's Laws are written and spoken and easy to read that the blind spirits can comprehend with understanding. It is time to recognize the voice and spirits of God without fail trusting with much faith in God. It is the spirits of God at work in the lives of the people of God crossing the people over into eternal living eternal life. I, God say to you, it is eternal life or the loss of eternal life one must choose. The time is now times of latter days judgments and justice daily of God in the heavens which are on earth working to the good of the people. I, God say to you, who-so-ever speak abide not by the Gospel Book of God's Laws have lost the way to eternal living eternal life.

I, God say to you, it is time for the body of Holiness to wake up and live eternal life according to the Holy spirits of God. And I, God say to you, who-so-ever seek not the words of this Gospel Book of Laws have lost the way to eternal living eternal life. I, God say to you, whether rich or poor whether young or old whether male or female ye must make a choice to live eternal life or loose eternal life. I, God say to the people in the heavens which are on earth, ye must choose ye this day to behold the spirits of God face to face or face the loss of eternal living eternal life.

And all the people in the chosen elect Holy Temples COGIC Inc. with spiritual hearing ears beheld an angel, the Holiest Highest Priest Prophet in the midst of them, the author of the Gospel Book of God's Laws; the Holiest Highest Priest Prophet ever walk the heavens on earth in your time of times now. And the High Priest Prophet said with a loud voice unto the people, woe is unto sins, sickness, and death at the end of justice judgments of God and God's Holy elect people. And we all will walk around heaven all day in equableness in peace in love in spirits in truth in God in the heavens which is on earth. I, Prophet say to you, it has been a long time coming, the change has come to cross us over into eternal living eternal life in the heavens on earth at the call of God's spirits dwelling in the entire world governing judgments and justice on all unrighteousness. For the paradise heavens on earth is appearing daily as changes are brought about in the heavens on earth; the judgment calls of God and God's elect Holy people are progressing daily is hear working to the good of the people.

I, God say to you, all leaders in every area of leadership in the heavens which is on earth with unforgiving sins among you have lost the way to eternal living eternal life. I, God say to all people in the heavens which are on earth, ye that have unforgiving sins among you have lost the way to eternal living eternal life. I, God say to you who have forgiving sins among you, ye are awarded eternal living eternal life in the heavens which is on earth. I, God say to you, ye are face with the sprits of the Holyest Highest Priest Prophet in the spirits of the almighty God's spirits in truth in the heavens which are on earth. I, God say to you, the people walking around in the heavens on earth are over-powered by the spirits of God and the Holeyest Highest Priest Prophet ever walk the heavens on earth in your time of now times. The times are now high times of judgments and justice in all the heavens on earth for 7000 years without count as the sands of the sea.

The first time the Holeyest Highest Priest Prophet sounded giving official order in Holiness Temples; 7 churches in Tallahassee, Florida were given letters of God's last judgments and justice calls has surface upon the face of the heavens which are on earth. The spiritual being of God is in the heavens which is on earth are the spiritual being of the Holy spirits of God in the most Holy High Priest Prophet ever walk the heavens on earth in your time of now times. I say to you God is a supreme spiritual being requiring worship in the universe as ye have a need to dwell in these spiritual messages written unto you for the cross-over into eternal living eternal life. There are many people in the heavens which is on earth do not have spiritual hearing ears to hear the voice of God speak unto them; now have a chance to cross-over into the Holy spirits of God and fellowship with the chosen elect Holy Temples of God to learn faith and the voice of God already within you. I, say to you, be not bitter in all your getting knowledge of God has brought about a new change in the heavens which is on earth working to the good of the people; working to the good of a paradise heavens on earth appearing.

I, God say to you, all denominations have been judged false except Holiness denominations; as it is written of me, be ye Holy for I am Holy in spirits in truth. I, God say to you the Holiest Highest Priest Prophet have called the 7 judgments in the heavens on earth already as she calls a thing in the heavens on earth and it appear that she calls it to be. I, God say unto you, there is no other High Priest with power like unto the Prophet at any

47

time in any denomination as I, God say to you question not the authority I give: for there will never be another. The Holiest Highest Priest Prophet is the one and only one Prophet of all times in your times. I, God say to you, the Holiest Highest Priest Prophet have prophesied, written, and spoken unto all kindred's and nations of the entire world.

I, the Lord your God say to you, the book of eternal life has been opened by the most Holiest Highest Priest Prophet ever walk the heavens on earth in your time of now times seeing and hearing all things said and done in spirits in truth. And I, Prophet heard a voice saying eternal judgments and justice are in the heavens which is on earth paving the way to eternal living eternal life on a paradise earth. And the Prophet measured all things said and done in the Holy Temples of God in the heavens which is on earth. For all other denominations hath been judged false religions. There be one religion left standing in the midst is Holiness appearing one big Holy land in all the heavens which is on earth. I, say to you, all things said and done in the heaven ungodly perish in judgments and justice of God.

I, the Lord your spiritual God say to you, the Prophets now come to you have power from the spirits of God from on high. I, say to you, the Highest Priest Prophet has power to ask God to shut the heavens on earth ending all people, places, and things in the earth; smite the whole earth with all plaques or unforgiving sinners. And I, Prophet heard the spiritual voice of God saying out with the old traditions of humankind and in with the new things of God. And the spiritual voice of God said to me there are many changes made in the entire heavens on earth.

I, the Lord your spiritual God say to you, there are no female Preachers, Bishops, Apostles, Elders in the chosen elect Holy Temple Churches of God in Christ; females are Evangelists and Prophets are not called to Preach in the elect chosen Priesthood, females are called to speak to the Holy congregation. I, the Lord your spiritual God say to you, males are called to Preach as Bishops, Prophets, Apostles, and Elders in the elect Holiness COGIC Inc. I, the Lord your spiritual God say to you, males are not Evangelists in the elect Holiness COGIC Inc. I the Lord, your spiritual God say to you; the Prophets Prophesy at any given time in the elect Holiness COGIC Inc. services because of the spirits of God speak to the Prophets at any given time. I, the Lord your spiritual God say to you, see to it that ye an elect chosen Holy people of God abide by these Gospel Book of Laws written unto you for the cross-over into eternal living eternal life in that there be no confusion among men and women seeking eternal living eternal life in Holiness Priesthood. I, the Lord your spiritual God say to you, the chosen elect Holy Priesthood consist of Bishops, Prophets, Apostles, Elders, and Evangelists in the COGIC Inc.

I, the Lord your spiritual God say to you, make room for all Holy Priest in the COGIC Inc. pulpit in that there is no Holy Priest sitting in the congregation disturbing the Holy spirits operating before you. I, the Lord your spiritual God say to you, male and female Holy Priest always sit in the pulpit during service. I, God say to the elect chosen Priesthood, ye must always keep a clear understanding of what ye see and hear in the spirits of the congregation, in that all things seen and heard in the spiritual realm be addressed correctly in spirits in truth. I, the Lord your spiritual God say to you, out with the old traditions and in with the new things of God eternal

49

spirits within the cross-over into eternal living eternal life. I, the Lord your spiritual God say to you, no female cannot own a Holy Temple in the COGIC Inc. at no time. I say to you the days of God and God's Holy people reign in the heavens which are on earth. And the renewed Holy spirits fell upon the chosen elect Holy Priesthood people of God as they spoke the judgments and justice of God in the COGIC Inc. Temples a great fear fell upon the people before them. And the elect chosen COGIC Inc. Holy Priesthood ascended into the renewed Holy spirits of God has risen in the heavens which are on earth.

And I, Prophet saw Apostasy had risen in all the heavens on earth and all religious denomination were abandon except COGIC Inc. Holiness Temples as the Apostolic spiritual authority in COGIC had risen. I Prophet Say to you the divine Apocalypse appeared in the heavens which are on earth pertaining to the book of God's Revelation renewed the heavens on earth in judgments and justice for 7000 years without count as the sands of the sea. And I, Prophet saw the Holiness Temples COGIC Inc. reign in every part of the entire heavens on earth calling a thing as though it were, and it appeared in the heavens which is on earth over the entire world. I, Prophet say to you, God's ultimate divine purpose is in affect by spiritual powers of the elect Holy chosen people of God dwelling in the heavens which is on earth. And all COGIC Inc. Priesthood reign over the entire world of people in spirits in truth in faithfulness in God in all things said and done in the heavens which are on earth. And I, Prophet saw the spiritual prayers of the elect working spiritual power forces upon all unrighteousness dwelling in the heavens which is on earth.

I, Prophet say to you, I have poured out the 7 seals in the heavens which are on earth with reference published in the Gospel Book of God's Laws #2. I, Prophet say to you, the time is up for spiritual dead minds of the people whom have been misled and found guilty of believing the return of Jesus is coming. I, Prophet say to you, ye have already been judge guilty as ye have a chance to go back to God in spirits in truth and cross-over into eternal living eternal life. I, Prophet say to you, it is the powerful spirits of God over the entire world in the heavens which are on earth not Jesus. I, Prophet say to you, ye have sin and come short of knowing God putting Jesus before God in spirits in truth.

I, Prophet say to you, Jesus was a Prophet given authority to rule the people in the heavens which were on earth. And I, Prophet heard God saying Jesus was not a spirit; Jesus was a person with spiritual powers of authority. And I, Prophet heard the spirits of God saying, I, am God all by myself in spirits in truth in people whom receive me within to guide them. And I, Prophet heard the spirits of God saying there is no Jesus to come; for the people have been misled by the adding and taking of the Holy Bible, by the people in the beginning of times of writing and the people writing Bibles is the reason why they are the people of the past with no return to the heavens on earth. And I, Prophet heard God saying the people of the past use the name God for self-gain as many in Christian leadership do this very day have been judged lost the way to eternal life.

I, Prophet heard God saying, I, God am not the God of confusion as are now in Bibles in the heavens on earth. I, God say to you, many people have come short of knowing God and put Jesus in the fore-front of God. I God say to you, the chosen elect people of God are a spiritual mind people

51

hearing true words from God in the time of now times. I, God say to you, the people unholy fear the Holy people hearing in the spirits of God in the heavens which are on earth.

I, God say to you, the elect chosen Holy Temples are opened in all the heavens in earth; there is seen and heard the call of God's judgments and justice for life eternal or the loss of eternal life. I, God say to you, the voice of the elect Holy chosen Priesthood is as lightening and thundering roaring as an earthquake followed by great hail across the entire world of heavens which are on earth. I, the Lord your spiritual God say to you, the elect chosen Holy Priesthood judge without respect of person; in that ye not be caught up in the wrath of judgments of God upon you.

I, the Lord your spiritual God say to you, the voice of the chosen elect Holy Priesthood is like unto consuming fire burning all spirits of evil wickedness before them with verbal and spiritual speech. I, the Lord your spiritual God say to you, the Holy kingdom of God is at hand before the eyes and ears of all people dwelling in the entire world of heavens which are on earth. I, God say to you, there be no exception of family neither friends in the call of true judgments and justice of the Holy chosen elect Priesthood judging the people.

And I, Prophet seen the chosen elect Holy Priesthood sat before God in spirits in truth in the chosen elect Holy Temples COGIC Inc. giving thanks for a Holy Priesthood called on in these last and evil days to judge the people. And I, Prophet seen the chosen elect Holy Priesthood praying thank you Lord for we are glad to be in that number counted as the sands

52

of sea without number as your righteous and Holy people in the heavens which is on earth. And I, Prophet seen them continue praying saying; Lord we realize the Holiest Highest Priest Prophet come from you with spirits in truth in the heavens which is on earth as we thank you for power and strength to judge the people. And I, Prophet seen the chosen elect Priesthood praying; Lord we except our mission you have called us to do as you guide us in these 7000 years of judgment call placed upon us to call in the heaven which are on earth.

I, Prophet say to the people in the heavens which are on earth; the Biblical judgments of Revelations of God are before all people, places, and things standing before God's spiritual judgments and justice daily. And I, Prophet heard God saying the Holy spirits and Prophecy is one and the same. I say to you, I am God of spirits and truth and I change not. I, God say to you, all people, places, and things stand before the Holeyest Highest Priest Prophet in spirits in truth dwelling in the heavens which is on earth. I, God say to you, there be nothing left undone for all things have need to be done be done. I, God say to you, to be save is to have eternal life. I, God say to you, there is no other way to be saved other than having eternal life crossing-over into eternal living eternal life in the heavens which is on earth.

I, God say to you, "Thank God Thank God" is to be said at the end of all prayers replacing the words "A-man and A-man" at the end of all prayers. I, God say to you, see to it that ye take heed to these gospel laws written unto you in that ye loose not life eternal. Now speaking unto all Holiness followers in the heavens on earth are the Holy spirits of God that dwell in the heavens on earth. I, God say to you, the elect chosen

Priesthood Ministers are always identified in the Holy Temple wearing tabs and collars around the neck in the presents of the congregation. I, God say to you, when preaching to the congregation the Priest will always have on a robe with a stole around the neck hanging down on robe. I, God say to you, take heed to this prophecy in that ye loose not the way to eternal living eternal life. I, God say to you, all elect chosen Holy Priesthood have a need to be respected and identified as Holy Priest in leadership in the chosen elect Holy Temples.

I, God say to you all things are decent and in order at the chosen elect Holy Temples. I, say to you, there be many chosen elect anointed ones among you unannounced before you. There are many among you in the elect chosen Holy Temples rise speaking the anointing testimonies of God. I, God say to you, ye must endure all these prophecies written and spoken unto you in this gospel book of laws as an elect Holy chosen people of God changing all things where change is needed. I, God say to you, ye must always abide by the Holy spirits of God as elect chosen Holy Priesthood. I, God say to you, all things said and done in the elect chosen Holy Temples are judged for 7000 years as the sands of the sea without count until all things are finished in judgments and justice of God and God's chosen Holy elect people.

I, God say to you, in the elect chosen Holy Temples, watch all money handlers closely, changing up as often as needed. I, God say to you, there be many people in the Temples steal the church funds often. I, say to you, ye have need to watch the church funds calling judgments where needed making changes where needed. I, God say to you, ye have a need to monitor all things said and done in the Temples. I, God say unto you,

54

abide by these prophecies written and spoken unto you. I, say to you, in that, I God continue to abide in you a chosen Holy people of God having spiritual hearing ears in the Holy gospel of God in the Holy gates of God the elect chosen Holy Temples of God. I, say to you, there be always ushers at the Holy gates (at the Holy doors) of God; the Holy keepers of the Holy gates.

I, God say to you, all elect chosen Holy Temples will congregate with one another in scheduled services. I, God say to you, there be no congregations of elect chosen Holy Temples congregate with other denominations other than the chosen e ect Holiness denominations. I, God say to you, take heed to these prophecies in that ye loose not the way to eternal life. I, God say unto you, a faith¯ul Holy chosen nation of people of God that ye continue in eternal life on a paradise heavens on earth at the end of all things I, God hath called unto the spirits of the chosen elect Holy people in the heavens which are on ear¯h. And the spirits of God nourished the Holiness followers a chosen people of God time after times for all eternity in the heavens which is on earth. And the chosen elect Holy Priesthood seen in the spirit the word "God" written on the forehead of the elect chosen people of God with forgiving sins among them. And the chosen elect Holy Priesthood seen in the spirit the word "unforgiving sins" written on the forehead of the unforgiving sinners.

I, God say to you, all people, places, and things are in judgments and justice of God is seen and heard in spirits in truth. There be no one in the heavens on earth see and hear what the chosen elect Holy Priesthood hear and see at no time. I, God say to you, take heed to these prophecies making room in my Holy house for my people in that my house is full. I,

God say to you, pass these prophecies unto all the Holy elect chosen people of God separating the sheep from the goat. I, God say to you, the sheep set separated from goats and visitors in the elect chosen Holy Temples. I, God say to you, take heed to these prophecies making room in my house for the people come before you.

And the chosen elect Holy Priesthood seen judgment call upon adults, babies, and children, young and old people alike. And all people, places, and things in the heavens on earth were judged according for 7000 years in the entire world over all heavens which are on earth. –I, say to you, there be nothing left undone as there be no exception because of age. I, say to you, all people with eternal life must endure until all judgments and justice is finished in the heavens which are on earth. And all the chosen elect Holy Temples congregate on one accord in all things said and done, in that there is no confusion to the people. I, God say to you, these are not just days of having church, but have judgment call when the sprits move in that area at any given time during service at any service which have been place upon the chosen elect Holy people of God.

I, God say to you, let the spirits move in services by the Holy spirits; not according to clock time. There are many chosen people of God entering the chosen elect Holy Temples to be saved unto eternal life at any given time at any service as needed. I, God say to you, take heed to these prophecies that the Holy gates do not be shut from my people having a need to receive eternal life. I, God say to you, all chosen people of God saved unto eternal life is baptized in the Holy Temples by Holy hands. I, say to you, all elect chosen people of God must be baptized, in that the anointing of God come upon them.

I, say to you, all things are heard and seen in the spirits of the elect chosen Holy Priesthood according to God's judgments and justice. I, God say to you, there be many Bishops, Prophets, Apostles, Elders, Evangelists and many people joining the Holy elect Temples. I, say to you, the gates of God are open to the need of many more Priesthood and servants as the Temples grow with many people seeking eternal life. I, God say to you, take heed unto these prophecies, in that the mission of God is complete and wanting (lacking) in nothing. I, God say to you, see these things called unto you.

I, the Lord your spiritual God say to you, all things done and said in the chosen elect Holy Temples are heard and seen in the spirits of the most Holiest Highest Priest Prophet ever walk the heavens which is on earth in your time of now times; who continues writing and speaking the Holy words of God unto a chosen elect Holy people of God. I, God say to the chosen elect Holy Priesthood, see to it that ye speak and preach the judgments and justice of God leading to eternal living eternal life; fulfilling all prophecies I, God have called unto you without fail in spirits in truth.

I, the Lord your spiritual God say to a chosen elect Holy Priesthood, speak not healing unto no one. This is not seasoning of healing, but seasons of judgments and justice for 7000 years as the sands of the sea without number without count. I, God say to you, I will speak healing unto those I will heal in due season in due times. I, God say to you, there are many unforgiving sinners among you receive not healing but have lost the way to eternal life. I say to you, forget not these are the latter days of eternal judgments and justice dwelling upon all people, places, and things in the heavens which is on earth.

57

I, the Lord your spiritual God say to all elect chosen Holy Priesthoods will take heed to all prophecies call unto you without fail, in that ye are not cast from eternal life from among the elect chosen people of God. I, say to you, there be those who hear in spirits in truth act instantly and quickly according to the words of God; call to take the place of Holy Priests who do not act on the spiritual prophecies of God because they cannot hear in spirits in truth in the spiritual realm of God; because they were never call to be Holy Priests of God.

I, the Lord your spiritual God say to you, all things are at hand being judged in the spiritual realm of the Holeyest Highest Priest Prophet ever walk the heavens on earth in your time of now times. I, God say to you again and again, there be nothing left undone that has a need to be done that has been call to be done through the mouth and writings of the most High Priest Prophet ever walk the heavens on earth in your time of now times in the heavens which are on earth. I, God say to you, all false religious leaders in leadership that were not call are in judgments and justice daily until there way is lost from eternal life. I, God say to you, all false religion and false religious leaders stands before judgment and justice daily. I, the Lord your spiritual God say to you, all death is eternal since the beginning of times.

I, God say to you, all prophecies written and spoken in this gospel book of laws are operating in the entire heavens which are on earth. I, the Lord your spiritual God have given you directions and instructions in that ye loose not the way to eternal living eternal life in the heavens which are on earth.

I, the Lord your spiritual God say to you, ye now are caught up in the rapture of true spirits in truth in the heavens on earth in the chosen elect Holy Temples. And I, Prophet heard the eternal spirits of God saying, let the elect chosen people of God hear what the spirits said in the elect chosen Holy Temples of God in the heavens which are on earth. I, God say to you, all things are written ye have a need to know in judgments and justice in the heavens processing the paradise heavens on earth. The times are now times to live and not die knowing the times and seasons are at hand forming the promises of God to the people. The times are now times to trust your eternal spirits within and take actions according to your faith on what you hear God speaking to you knowing God brings you through all things said and done daily.

The times are now times to know what God has for you is for you to receive knowing many things happening try your faith as you acknowledge God's eternal presence before you. The times are now times to show forth your trust in your eterna spirits within you daily. The times are now times to pick up the broken pieces of your heart knowing these are the eternal changing times God's eternal spirits are forming the paradise heavens on earth through all things said and done in the earth daily. The times are now times to forsake not the presence of God before you as you entertain angels of God unknowingly. The times are now times to know this is not the end of life even though things are happening all around you, know that God is present in spirits in truth making ways out of what seems to be no way.

5

God's Purpose and Spiritual Affect Felt upon the People

The millennium of God's judgments is felt as God and God's person sounds the trumpets of judgments and justice now standing during the heavens which are on earth; opening the eyes, ears, and minds of the people. It is the time of now times and seasons the elect chosen people of God are identified by God's words "be ye Holy" in all things said and done in spirits in truth "for I am Holy" in spirits in truth. I, God say to you, the effect of justice in all things pertaining to the people have special meaning of judgments and affect upon the people daily. I, God say to you, the image of God is within the chosen elect Holy people of God. I, God say to you, who deny the Holy spirits of God in heavens which is on earth have lost the way to eternal living eternal life. I, God call for all people to repent in spirits in truth knowing the Kingdom of God have been identified here before you in the heavens on earth. I, say to you, ye have a need to go back to God in eternal spirits in eternal truth.

I, say to you, forget not the year of January 2000 began the last call for judgments and justice for 7000 years as the sands of the sea without number without count until all unforgiving sinners have perished from the face of the heavens which are on earth. I, say to you, forget not the Holiest Highest Priest Prophet call eternal judgments and justice into effect over the entire world of heavens which are on earth. I, God say to you, cause and affect are here because of sins the effect of judgments and justices are spread over the entire world with much affect upon the people. I, God say to you, it is important for the world to understand the coming of God is here as there is no Jesus to come at no time. I, God have call judgments and justice throughout the world through the mouth of the Holy elect chosen people of God. I, God say to you, be careful who you entertain angels of God unaware. I, God say to you, the chosen elect Holy angels of God are judging the people daily in the heavens which are on earth.

I, God say to you, I am real in spirits in truth of the chosen elect people of God. I, say to you, ye must be open to the Holy spirits of God allowing God to speak to your spiritual mind. I, God say to you, the victorious earth is appearing daily until all things are finish. I, say to you, the chosen elect people of God are living in the image of God is God in the heaven which are on earth daily. I, God say to you, the Prophets of old hath spoken there would come a woman High Priest Prophet in the image of God call all seven spirits of God in the heavens which are on earth. I, God

62

say to you, the people have been misled have strayed away from the spirits of God; leaning toward their own misled spirits of self. I, say to you, the times are now times of giving an account of foolish ways and thoughts. I, say to you, the lust of the flesh has caused much sin to spread over the entire world in the heavens which are or earth.

The trumpets of God and God's people sound over the entire world written and spoken by the Holiest Highest Priest Prophet ever walk the heavens which are on earth in your time of now time. I say to you this is the voice of the Holy One preparing the way in spirits in truth in God in judgments in justice; making straight the path for the elect chosen people of God with forgiving sin among them. I, God say to you, the Holy spirits of the Holiest Highest Priest Prophet has gone out into the enter heavens which is on earth calling for justice and judgments. The elect chosen Holy Ministries of God speaks out among the people in the chosen elect Holy Temples of God.

The people are being drawn more and more like never to the chosen elect COGIC Inc. Holy Temples of God. I, say to you, the flock of God attends the chosen elect Holy Temples of God in the heavens which are on earth. The chosen elect anointed saints attending the elect chosen Holy Temples of God are acquainted with the Holy spirits of God operating within them the voice of God. The chosen elect anointed people of God have a special relationship with God. I, God say to you, all other religious denominations have been judged false except the elect chosen Holy Temples of God chosen as the righteous ones to judge the heavens which are on earth. All other denominations abandon their denominations crossing-over to the chosen elect denomination of Holy COGIC Inc. to receive eternal living eternal life. I, the Lord say to you, be ye Holy in all things said and done for I God am Holy in spirits in truth.

I, the Lord your spiritual God say to you, my chosen elect Holy people are identified by the words "be ye Holy for I God am Holy" in spirits in truth. I, God say to you, the spirits of Holiness strengthen faith, honesty, and truth in spirits within people. I, say to you, all chosen elect people see the salvation of God working to the good of the people of God forming eternal living eternal life in the entire world. I, God say to you, ye must be equal in treatment to each other ye must be honest to each other ye must be true to each other ye must be faithful to each other ye must live in the spiritual mind of God called to your spirits within you trusting what you hear within working to the good of you.

I, the Lord your spiritual God say to you, the Holiest Highest Priest Prophet write and speak to you from the roots of the Holy spirits dwelling within her. Thus I, God have to comfort my people speaking and writing in books thus I tell you to speak to my people; in that ye lead them to eternal living eternal life on a paradise earth forming out of eternal judgments and justice daily in the entire world. I, God say to you, the Holiest Highest Priest Prophet have called for judgments and justice in the heavens on earth to destroy all sins roaming the entire world heavens which are on earth. I, the Lord your spiritual God say to you, many things have lifted in the heavens on earth only the Holiest Highest Priest Prophet can see and hear. There be many things lifted in the plain in the heavens on earth, the people see what they have a need to see and hear. I, God say to you, there be many things lifted up in the heavens which are on earth only given to the chosen elect Holy people of God to see and hear within their judgments call to judge the people whom have a need to cross-over into eternal living eternal life.

I, God say to you, the chosen elect people of God inherit the paradise heavens which appears on earth at the end of judgments and justice all sins, sickness, and death cease in the entire world. The glory of God is revealed unto the entire world without fail recognize the glory of God in the heavens which are on earth. I, God say to you, this is the end forming of all unforgiving sinners in the entire world heavens which are on earth. I, say to you, the highway to eternal heavens on earth now stands before you in this gospel book of laws written and spoken unto you. I, the Lord your spiritual God say to you, take heed that ye loose not the way to eternal living eternal life forming in the heavens which are on earth.

I, Prophet say to you, forming in the entire world are all things pertaining to God having special meaning and effect on the elect chosen people of God. This is the chosen generation of people warned reference the wrath of God's judgments and justice over the entire world. The wrath of God is destroying sins, unforgiving sinners, sickness, decease, and death by fire, water, earthquakes, sinkholes, and accidents allowed by increasing more and more than ever before over the entire world. The wrath of God has increase more and more upon the people whom have not repented continue to sin in the world heavens which are on earth. I, Prophet say to you, out with the old traditions of humankind and in with the renewed people, places, and things of God in spirits in truth.

I, Prophet say to you, the world is changing in all areas of life, literally creating a massive resistance of reactions of the people roaming the entire world not seeing it is the work of God's wrath in judgments and justice paving the way to eternal living eternal life. I, Prophet Say to you, the time of now times are serious judgments and justice on all things said and done in spirits of unrighteousness in the entire world. The times are now times of all false religious congregation that are unholy "shall not stand" in the entire world. I, Prophet say to you, no-other religious denominations will not stand in the heavens except the chosen elect Holy Temples of COGIC Inc., called by the spirits of God; the chosen elect righteous people to judge the people in heavens on which are on earth.

I, God say to the religious leaders whom resist true leadership refusing to cross-over to Holiness leadership, ye have lost the way to eternal living eternal life. I, say to you, these are the critical times of judgment calls upon the people. The subject of the matter is teaching and preaching "crossing-over into eternal living eternal life judgment call", true doctrine under the inspirational spirits of God's Holy spirits. I, say to you, without the Holy spirits of God dwelling within you, ye cannot live in the heavens which are on earth. I say to you, now is the time to understand the true meaning of living Holy by the Holy spirits of God.

I, God am calling for all nations of this world to live Holy in all things said and done without sins, sickness, and death at the end of all judgment calls and justice. I, say to you, ye must worship in chosen elect Holy Temples. I, say to you, everyone left after the calls of justice judgments has ended shall abide under the spiritual structure of God's gospel laws wherein everyone is able to go directly to God for their own self in spirits in truth. I, say to you, the eyes and ears of the lost sheep are now opened to the spiritual ways of God in spirits in truth. The times are now times to withdraw from sins and old traditions of this world cleansing your life and be drawn to the renewal of your mind. It is time to have spiritual relationships with God remembering the call of judgments are daily upon all people, things said and done, and places in the heavens on earth.

I, say to you, in order to please God ye must be baptize in Holy water with a renewed mind in the new things of God putting away the lust of the heart. It is time to determine your status with God's Holy spirits living on the inside of you, and then God's directions enter your heart; ye then fully obey the voice of God heard within you keeping trust and faith in the spirits of God ye hear within you. You then walk in the spirits of God as God direct you in all things said and done. The kingdom of God is within the Holy and righteous saints made in the image of God receiving inner directions from God for eternal living eternal life. The symbolize zeal of God's image is in the heavens the ascension of the Holiest Highest Priest Prophet is on earth saying now is the time of the Pentecost spreading into all the heavens on earth. I say to you, the times are now times of judgment for all denominations one accord in Holiness in spirits in truth in God in the heavens on earth.

The benches filled with the Holy saints of God dwelling in the Holy spirits of God in all the chosen elect Holy Temples. The chosen elect Holy saints are kneeling at the chosen elect Holy Temples alter praying and crying out to God thanking God for eternal life as a chosen elect people. I, say to you, the heavens are right here on earth. Life is eternal only to those who have forgiving sins among them. Life is not eternal to those who have unforgiving sins among them. I, say to you, death is eternal, there is no other side of heaven in the grave. All dead bodies in the grave turn to dust

67

beneath the earth. The reserved time has appeared in judgments to end all evil wickedness stubborn contrary practices that do not work to the good of the people.

And God told the Holiest High Priest Prophet ever to walk the heaven on earth in your time of now times to go Prophecy and write all things in a book I have told you, thus and go tell my people. I, say to you, there have been many people to change their glory for things that do not profit them. The people are bitter in all things said and done are, perverse evil, unjust, unholy, unrighteous, and jealous haters of others that have favor with God. I, God now say to you, who are in error in fault, stubborn, contrary to Holiness, difficult to deal with, turn from what is right to do evil, ye are in judgment daily have lost the way to eternal life. I, say to you that deny the Holy spirits of God in the heavens which is on earth, ye have lost the way to eternal living eternal life.

I, the Lord your spiritual God say to you that deny the heavens are on earth have lost the way to eternal life. I, The Lord your spiritual God say to you, all generations of past and now generations have misinterpreted the scriptures by not using inspired spirits with common sense of knowledge; which have brought worse destructions upon the people more than ever before. I say to you Pastors not call to preach speak more after their evil hearts for monetary reasons. I, say to you so-call pastors not call to preach not inspired to preach not dwelling in the Holy spirits have increase more and more over the entire earth for monetary reasons as they have greatly misled and deceived the people with Jesus is coming. I, the Lord your spiritual God say to you, there is no return of Jesus at no time now neither in the future. I, God say to you these preachers that were not called to preach mislead and deceive the people after imaginations of their heart.

There are so many spiritual leaders have caused the people to backslide in confusion unto this very day. I, God say to you so-call religious leaders in leadership, ye have not obeyed the voice of God because ye hear not in the spiritual realm and ye mislead the people for monetary reasons in all things said and done. I, God say to you that refuse to hear in the spiritual guidance of God because you are not ordained in the Holy spirits of God, ye have no understanding and many people fall with you supporting you in unrighteousness.

I, God say to you, the Land is greatly polluted in unrighteousness accompanying the unforgiving sinners of this world. I, God say to you, those that have waited upon the Lord have been renewed in strength and faith in God; are the chosen elect people of God caught up in the rapture of the Holy spirits of God in spirits in truth.

I, God say to you, the chosen elect Holy Temples are name "The Holy Temples of God" in that there is no confusion to the people. I, God say to you, I call judgments and justice against the perverse generation of people in this world doing all amounts of evil wickedness to the people in things said and done in secret. I, God have poured out my fury on all evil doers revealed secrets in the light of the world heavens which are on earth. I, God say to you, my words are swifter than lightening and sharper than any two-edge sword. I, God say to you my words are loosed in the entire world saying now is the focal point of destiny heaven is right here on earth.

I, say to you, the paradise earth appears when all sins, sickness, and death are finished in judgments and justice over the entire world.

I, Prophet say to you the entire world is being over-haul under spiritual renovation with final destruction wherein all unforgiving sinners are before eternal judgments and justice. The names, pictures, and slogans of Jesus fade in perish judgments and justice of unforgiving sinners, places, and things destroyed from the heavens which are on earth. I, say to you, God is a supreme being of human beings that requires worship having authority over the universe with super natural powers and spirits; seeing all scriptures are given by inspiration of God and is profitable for corrections in giving instructions in righteousness from inspired spirits of God. I, say to you, one must see God is the head of the body within spirits of truth and righteousness in all things said and done according to the spirits of God.

I, say to you, God have preeminence over your life in all things said and done; saying God has all power which is in the heavens on earth. I say to you, learn to put wisdom and knowledge before all things said and done in your life today. I say to you, wisdom and knowledge comes from God by whom all people, places, and things exist in spirits that work to the good of human beings. I say to you, these are unseen forces of God given by God unto human beings for the good of human beings in righteousness in truth in faith in God in all things said and done. The true facts at appointed times such as these are Jesus is call Jess-us (Just Us) who are followers of God in Holiness in truth which have been a comfort unto God receiving eternal living eternal life. These are they whom are my fellow workers in the kingdom of God abiding in righteous spirits in truth in faith in God in all

70

things said and done. I say to you, awake to righteousness and equableness in all things said and done in that ye perish not in judgments and justice of the latter-days judgments of God and God's chosen elect people calling judgments and justice. I say to you, it is an individual affair with God as all individuals give an account of deeds done good deeds done not good.

I, the Lord your spiritual God say to you, ye have a revised understanding of being saved crossing-over into eternal living eternal life within the call of judgments and justice. I, God say to you, take heed in that ye have been warned not to fall out of the new creations of the heavens on earth forming the new paradise heavens on earth. I, God say to you, the Holy spirits of judgments and justice over the entire world wins every battle in the heavens on earth. I, say to you, see to it that ye be not deceived by your own disbelief of these things written and spoken unto you being misled by your own unrighteousness.

I, God say to you, my words are not void written and spoken to you by the Holy One in this gospel book of laws. I, God say to you, these Prophecies are upon everyone among the living in the heavens which are on earth. I, God say to you, in a quick instant there are many things happening in the heavens which are on earth. I, say to you, no one is free from eternal judgments in the heavens which are on earth daily. I, say to you, all things are being gathered separating evil from good in judgments and justice are all people, places, and things destroyed by fire, water, accidents, and death. I, God say to you, anyone deny the Holy spirits of God operating in this "Gospel Book of God's Laws" ye have lost the way to eternal living eternal life as ye give an account before the judgment seats of God.

I, God say unto you, all people of this world it is required of the Holy One's hands to bring these prophecies unto you in that ye are saved unto eternal living eternal life in the heavens which are on earth. I, God say to your warnings come before destruction as ye have needed to put away your pride. I say to you, these are days of few unto those who have unforgiving sins among them. I say to you, it is already too late for many people to commit yourselves unto the Holy spirits of God. I say to you, time is not on your side as judgment calls God and God's chosen elect people has already began as ye have a need to put on the whole armor of God in spirits in truth in the heavens which are on earth.

I say to you, the call for the people of this world to repent for the kingdom of God is here at hand in the heavens which are on earth. The chosen elect people of God are identified within the COGIC Inc. Holy Temples. The washing away of old traditional world of things is in force as the renewed cleanse people, places, and things appear forming the paradise heavens on earth. I, the Lord your spiritual God say to the forgiven sinners, ye are to remain sinless in the heavens. I say to you, all unforgiving sinners are sifted out of the heavens by the spirits of God and God's elect chosen people in the heavens. It is the now times of all unforgiving sinners have much destruction among them daily until they are no more dwelling in the heavens on earth. I say to you, the people in the heavens are examine carefully daily within the judgment call of God and God's chosen elect people as no one escapes the final latter days judgments and justice roaming the heavens which are on earth.

I say to you, all of God's people are mark with a sign visible to the chosen elect Holy Priesthood. All people obedience to the words of God show respect to the chosen elect Holy people of God. All people see God's kingdom rules in the heavens on earth are the chosen elect Holy COGIC Inc. Ministries in the heavens. Holiness baptism clearly shows and identifies the people of God with forgiving sins among them; as COGIC clearly mark indications of Christianity observed in Holiness Temples. The mark of Holy discipleship through Holy baptism raise the dead minds of the people to spiritual minds caught up in the rapture with God and God's people in spirits in truth. This shows the glory of God walking in renewed lives of the people in the heavens. These things mention announce the purpose for God's words "be ye Holy as I am Holy" for ye have need to be Holy in all things said and done in the heavens.

I say to you Holiness rule the heavens the newness of God bringing salvation unto the chosen elect people of God with forgiving sins among them. All have sin coming short of wisdom and knowledge of God's spirits operating in the heavens among them. There are many people have no relationship with God no relationship with God's spirits within them no relationship with God's words no relationship with God's chosen elect people among them in the heavens. The heavens on earth have gone out into the entire world straight-way in spirits in truth. The Holy spirits of God and God's chosen elect people are descending like a dove opening the minds of the people in the heavens.

And lo I, Prophet heard a spiritual voice from heaven speaking about the elect chosen people of God saying, these are my beloved chosen followers in the heavens in whom I God am well pleased. I, Prophet heard a loud spiritual voice saying all Holiness people are a chosen people of God, but the elect chosen are people of the COGIC Inc. Holy Temples are forever of this generation and generations to come. The confirming of divine final judgments pronounced unto all people whether good or not good judgments prevail in this world over the entire earth the elect people prevail in the entire heavens on earth. The judgment calls are an earthly messianic awareness proven true unto all the people of the entire world there be nothing left undone for all things be done have need to be done in the heavens. The times of now and the times to come stand before daily judgments of God and God's chosen elect people in the heavens.

I, Prophet Say to you, this world of humankind has pierced themselves through and through with many sorrows ruining their lives and lives of others. It is the now times ye must become aware of the spiritual voice of God uttering guidance to you for the cross-over into eternal living eternal life. I, God say to you, these things are written unto you plain simple in that ye have understanding and true to the good of you receiving eternal life. I, God say to you, ye have a need to know I God is dwelling among you within your spirits in truth to guide you and have never left you. I, God say to you, these prophecies are no duplicates, but are written for your guidance in the cross-over into eternal living eternal life on a paradise earth in the heavens on earth. I, the Lord your spiritual God say to you, in the same hour anyone add or take from these gospel book of laws ye have lost your way to eternal living eternal life. The times are times to know the people of God in the heavens which are on earth prevail in all things said and done. The times are times to be at peace with God in spirits in truth in belief in God. The times are times to know God is God all by God self. The time is time to pray to God and pray to God only because Jesus is not a spirit, but God is eternal spirits and eternal truth. The times are times

74

to know God is not Jesus God is not the father, God is always the Holy spirits dwelling in the earth dwelling within the good spirits of the people. The times are times to know God is blessing the people.

6

Those Who Hunger After Righteousness Find It

It is God's appearing felt over the entire world has risen in spirits in truth as the world is nourished by true righteousness. The call of things as though they were is in the entire world over the heavens which are on earth. The call of the Highest Priest Prophet ever walks the heavens on earth in your time of now times are here. Those who hunger after righteousness find it in the heavens which are on earth. The religious systems of this world take a supernatural change of religious beliefs and attitudes unto Holiness belief crossing-over into eternal living eternal life. The ultimate reality relating to God's words are observed in all religious beliefs in all congregations regardless of their denomination unite with Holiness congregations for the chance of eternal living eternal life.

There are no other denominations to stand without fail accept that of Holiness in true gospel in true religion. The seasons and times now are felt on all religious ministries dwelling in the heavens which are on earth. All unholy organizations fade with time and seasons are not able to stand in the heavens. I, God say to you the original plan and purpose for the people stand in the heavens. I, God say to you, the world is forever changing people, places, and things daily. I, God say to you, all people, places, and things are measured in the world unto Holiness in all things said and done daily. The acts of God are among all people, places, and things that have need for change is felt. The spirits of God and God's elect chosen people are felt over the entire world. I, Prophet Say to you, now are times and seasons for concrete faith in God in all things said and done.

The time is now times of grief and sorrows more than ever before felt upon the people over the entire world. The time is now times the acts of God are felt upon the people as God prepares the way to paradise heavens on earth. I, Prophet say to you, there be many people, places, and things destroyed in the heavens which are on earth are not Holy acceptable to God neither fit to be in the heavens on earth. I, Prophet say to you, take heed to this gospel truth in that ye perish not, but live eternal life in the heavens which are on earth. I, God say to you, those who hunger after righteousness find it in the gospel truth written and spoken unto you in this gospel book of laws ye have need of to cross-over into eternal living eternal life. The divine inspiration of prophecy and predictions of the Holy One are felt over the entire heavens the call of God.

I, God say to you, the Holiest Highest Priest Prophet utters divine inspired revelation foretelling future events knowing the past and future of one's life. The Holy One is prophylactic by inspired spirits of God within her. I, God say to you, ye have a need to eternally live by every word written and spoken unto you from her nspired spirits of God within her. I say to you, the fame of the Holy One has ascended in the heavens over the entire world judging all things said and done in her hearing the call of God. The power and fame of the Holy One is automatically felt in spirits in truth. I, God say to you, the Holiest Highest Priest Prophet is the supreme being of God with supernatural powers of God as ruler over the universe with supreme value.

It is I the Lord your spiritual God accomplish my fury upon the foolishness of unforgiving sinners refuse to stop sinning. I, say to you, the lust of the world started from the beginning of time giving birth to sins brought forth eternal death. I say to you, the appetite of evil self-gain activities stands before judgments and justice in all things said and done. I say to you, the mind of humankind has demonstrated carnal minds for pleasure and desires of the flesh ye are measured in judgments; I God put a stop to carnal minds of imaginations of tempting spirits in the hearts replace with righteous spirits. I say to you, it is good to remember eternal judgments are upon you daily in all things said and done.

I, God say to you, the chosen elect Holy Priesthood are shown all the kingdoms of the world heavens on earth. I say to you, money loose its power and effect on the people in the heavens which are on earth. I, God say to you, with control and power over money ye have inflicted the pain of poverty, not having enough money upon the people. The pain of crime

79

has caused much crime in the heavens which are on earth. I, God say to you the entire continents of this world are conquered by the spirits of God and God's elect chosen people have been over-thrown. I say to you, in the globe of the entire world are the powerful actions of God's great victory over-come the unjust unrighteous wicked ones.

I, God say to the wise believers of this gospel book of laws; I receive your spirits as wise believers in spirits in truth. I say to you, the angels of God are caught up with God in spirits in truth showing powerful Christianity standing firm in chosen elect Holy Temples of God. I say to you, the original plan of God is in force over the entire world despite all difficulty's righteousness prevails in the universe. I say to you all the wicked evil done is done in the heavens which are on earth. The treasured values of the heavens are recognized in judgments and justice of God and God's chosen elect people. I say to the different religious groups who are not inspired by the Holy spirits and words of God; ye have lost the way to eternal living eternal life. I say to you, righteousness over-power all the heavens on earth. I say to you, the fall of unforgiving sinners is the power of God's wrath unfolding in mysteries of the heavens which are uncompromising. It is the condemnation of God's justice judgments upon the people.

I, the Lord your spiritual God say to you, only God's elect chosen people who cross-over into eternal living eternal life are immortally exempt from eternal death. I, God say woe unto you who are unholy in all things said and done in your daily lives. The world changing events brings judgments and justice by force on all ungodly people, places, and things. I, God say to you, ye are communicated to by the mouth of many people surrounding you; take heed to righteousness spoken to you for a just call are just reasons from God working through anointed people surrounding you. The seven spirits of God went out into the entire world for all seasons. I God say to you, all religious leaders and congregations' unholy not teaching and preaching eternal life loose the way to eternal life for lack of knowledge. The vision 'God's resurrection' of God's Holy spirits is in the elect chosen Holy Temples call by the spirits of God and God's chosen elect people.

It is the voice of the Holiest Highest Priest Prophet making straight the way to God's spirits for eternal living eternal life within paradise heavens on earth. I, God say to you, these prophecies in this book lead the people out of the wilderness of their minds making plain the path to eternal living eternal life. The call of all people, places, and things into existence in the heavens has uncovered the mysteries of God religious truths making known the revelations of God in the heavens on earth. The Holy Kingdom of God is here to lead the people into eternal life making plain all things said and done by divine sanctified quality of the COGIC Inc. elect people of God.

The judgments and justice of God are brought on all people, places, and things in the heavens on earth unholy. The Holy plans of the seven seals have been poured out upon the people accomplish judgments and justice in the heavens on earth replacing evil with Holiness paradise heavens on earth. The light of God shines in all dark places in the heavens on earth. I, God have sent the Holiest Highest Priest Prophet to you to bear witness of that light that shines in dark places as all things that are hiding are uncovered. I, God say to you, I have sent the Holiest Highest Priest

Prophet to you in that ye are not lost from eternal living eternal life. The minds of people are open spreading the gospel truth opening the minds of the people that are hindered from the gospel truth. The Holy salvation of eternal life spreads among the chosen people of God free from sin.

The times are time for sinners to repent of their sins and be caught up with God in spirits in truth in the full grace of God. The resurrection of God's Holy spirits dwelling among the people is spread over the entire world bringing an end to evil hearts. The shame of the unrighteous are manifested has went forth in all the heavens on earth. Those who refuse Holiness are now at their last chance before it is too late. These words written and spoken unto you are not void but have accomplished the original purpose of God's plan for the people. It is all things said and done stands in the front door of judgments and justice daily without warning instantly upon you. These words predicted, written, and spoken are fulfilled over the entire world upon the people daily without fail. I, say to you, see to it that ye take heed in righteous spirits in truth without fail. Remember the call of judgments and justices are upon the people for 7000 years as the sands of the sea without count without number in the entire heavens on earth.

The justice of God and God's chosen elect people take away the sins of the world by force daily in the call of just judgments upon the people. The current conditions and situations change in every part of the world heavens on earth. It is destruction upon all people, places, and things of unrighteousness nesting in the heavens on earth. The power of God's devastating judgment calls defeats the unrighteous sinners nesting in the heavens on earth. The presence of divine circumstances is upon the

82

people; God's eternal judgments with awesome contexts of justices. The people with forgiving sins among them has the vision of eternal life within their spirits. The days of God's just ce occur in current events and conditions.

The promises of God have begun, bringing the needs of the nations of people a peaceful heaven on earth at the end of all sins, sickness, and death cease in the heavens which are on earth. It is the commands of God upon the people of the world. The spirits of the people are renewed to spiritual images of righteousness. The heavens on earth are restored in all places have a need to be restored over the entire world. The people are comforted by the massages of eternal life preach to them in the Holy Temples. The great changes in the heavens on earth represent God's presence existing in the heavens on earth in sprits in truth in the Holiest Highest Priest Prophet in the chosen elect COGIC Inc. Temples; have direct great excess to God by spiritual hearing ears during the people. The covenant between God and the chosen elect people of God is sealed. I say to you, blessed is the ones who walk in the counsel of this gospel book of laws for the crossing-over into eternal living eternal life.

The spirits of God and God's chosen elect people break the bonds of all unrighteousness in the heavens on earth as they sit on the Holy Hill judging all things said and done. It is God and God's people angry with the unrighteous people every day. The hearts and minds of the people are tested for righteousness. I say to you, beware the name "Jesus called Ha-sues" is a name people wear among you as ye look for the return of Jesus there is no return of Jesus. There are many tears shed because of love one's decease and perished in the heavens on earth.

Whatsoever God do is eternal judgment calls; there is nothing can be added to it neither taken from it. The chosen elect Holy Priesthood are in the judgment seats of God, it is required at the hands of the Holiest Highest Priest Prophet and the elect chosen COGIC Inc. Holy Priesthood to judge the people. It is for every purpose of every work God gives humankind good insight for eternal living eternal life on all things said and done. It is God gives wisdom, knowledge, and joy to sinners with forgiven sins prevails in the heavens which are on earth standing before God and God's people daily. I say to you, to everything there is a season and a purpose dwelling among the people.

It is I, God communicating to you through the gospel writing of the Holy One the Holiest Highest Priest Prophet saying take heed for a just reason for a just cause of eternal living eternal life. I say to you, awake see and hear the things written and spoken unto you work to the good of your increase in spirits in truth. It is required at the hands of the Holy One to spread the gospel truth. The times are now times salvation spread to all forgiven sinners extends eternal living eternal life in the heaven on earth. The Biblical Prophecies in this book are faithful and truth leading to eternal living eternal life in the heavens on earth. The Holy One has paved the way for the elect chosen Holy people of God to receive eternal living eternal life.

The spirits of the Lord went out into the entire world in all high places breaking down idols of strong wholes. The answers to God's people prayers prevail in the entire heavens on earth. The lift of all the ways of God are in the heavens on earth for all seasons. The break-down of cities and towns in sin are rounded up in great slaughter of God's wrath before them in judgments in justice in truth. The dark ways of the unrighteous brought to judgments and justice daily in the heavens on earth. The presence of God's judgments and justice is looking at the people walking around in the heavens all day.

It is time to put away social customs of religious beliefs knowing it is Holiness or hell beneath the earth. The only religion left standing in the heavens on earth is Holiness unto all eternity forever have already come forth. I God say to you withdraw from your traditional religious gatherings and belief for your soul is at stake for eternal loss of eternal life. I, God say to you, be ye Holy for I am Holy, ye have strayed away from Holiness to all other different denominations of this world. I say to you, ye must be Holy in all things said and done. I, God say to you, ye have been warned to take heed before destruction come upon you. The Holy saints of God dwell in things pertaining to the things of God call by God in the chosen elect Holy Temples of God.

It is time to move away from spiritual elementary and be serious about being caught up in spirits in truth with God and God's Holy chosen elect people. It is time out for playing with God or your soul will be loss in an instant blink of an eye like a thief in the night. It is all souls are at stake for eternal life or eternal death at the loss of eternal life. I say to you, choose this day who ye will serve God or the lust of the flesh. The lust of the flesh cannot enter eternal life. The times are now times of the people must be caught up in spirits unto God in truth. The Holy Temples are anointed in the Holy spirits of God. The chosen elect people are always open unto the Holy spiritual voice of God. I say to you, to be saved, is to have eternal life being filled with the Holy spirits of God baptized in Holy water with Holy hands of Holy Priest.

I say to you, to be saved you must have forgiven sins among you call by God and God's chosen elect Holy Priesthood sitting in the judgment seats of God. The judgments of God and God's people are fulfilled upon the people dwelling in the heavens which are on earth. The last an evil days of sins are before the people. The forgiven sinners are heirs of eternal life in the heavens on earth. The chosen elect Holy Priesthood are men and women of God thoroughly furnished unto all good works as mediators between God and the people. These things written and spoken unto you are a sign of the times now at hand. The chosen elect Holy Priesthood must with joy not with grief give an account of all souls saved crossed-over into eternal living eternal life.

I, God say to you, anyone cause the Holy Priesthood grief, ye have lost the way to eternal living eternal life. The time is out for the people playing with the Holy Priesthood of God in all things said and done in the chosen elect Holy Temples of God. The chosen elect Holy Temples are the ark of God where God choose to allow the Holy spirits of God to dwell. The chosen elect Holy Priesthood are sitting on the throne of God in spirits in truth judging the people. It is I, God has established and chosen the Holy saints to be my people and I am their God in spirits in truth in the heavens which are on earth. I, God say to you, the elect chosen people of God possess the land by force, in all the heavens which are on earth. I, God say to you, I know all hearts, I search all hearts, and I know the imaginations of the thoughts of all living souls in all the heavens on earth.

I, God say to you, I have prepared you for all things in seasons and out of seasons. I, God say unto you, watch as well as pray, for all things ye have a need to know have been revealed unto you. I, God say to you, ye are in the last days of judgments for sins and sinners who continue to sin. I say to you, take heed unto these things revealed unto you. I say to you, all people, places, and things are in the ast latter days of judgments and justice prevails over the entire heavens on earth without fail. I say to you, all things said and done in the heavens are exposed in the bare open discovered by judgments and justice. I say to you, the unrighteous are not prepared neither equipped for the wrath of God's justice daily arranged in seasons and out of seasons.

The people are starting to pay attention and take note of the wrath of God prevailing in the heavens on earth are many things happening in an instant that has been ignored regarding the just judgments of God. The people can no-longer disregard the wrath of earthquake, sinkholes, fire, water, accidents, decease and death are happening now more than ever before in the history of the world. I say to you, the ways of God must be observed without fail pay attention to the ways of God prevailing over the entire world; there are continued people, places, and things perish in an instant from the foundations of the earth, never to be found swallowed up in judgments of God. It is time to listen to the words of God written and spoken unto you knowing God is dominant over the entire world of people places, and things that exist.

7

Powerful Eternal Strong Intense Words of God

I say to you the spirits of God and God's chosen elect people prevail over the people in the heavens which are on earth. The spirits of God and God's chosen elect people hear all things said and done by the ungodly people in the heavens on earth. I say to you, eternal living eternal life has ascended into the heavens which are on earth. Eternal life reign in the heavens has over- come the world in spirits in truth succeeds without fail. There is no-one greater than the Holy spirits of God living, walking, and talking in the spirits of God. The spirits of God are felt through the chosen elect people of God as never before as the presence of God's spirituality is felt in the chosen elect Holy Temples of God. The living spirits of God and

God's chosen elect people forever have power to reign in the heavens on earth. The people in the heavens on earth are in the latter days of Holy Pentecostal of the elect chosen people of God.

The mouth of God's people is a consuming fire with strong intense words of encouragements and judgments. I, God say to you, my visitation of the people come in judgments of justice prevailing in all things said and done. The wages for sowing continuing sins in the heavens is the loss of eternal living eternal life. It is an individual affair; all people must bear their own wages of continued sins causing the heavens to be corrupt. The signs and wonders of God and the chosen elect people of God are in the heavens on earth. The roots of eternal life have come forth out of the branches of life. The people cannot see for looking, the signs and wonders of God and God's chosen elect people are continuously before them in the heavens on earth. There are many people trouble to know the heavens are on earth as there are many people trouble to know there is no return of the people from the graves beneath the earth as there are many people trouble to know there is no return of Jesus from the dead.

It is time for the people to come to themselves with common sense of things written, said and done surrounding you. There is a need for the forgiven sinners to learn by being among the elect chosen people of God. There is no need for the unforgiving sinners to be among the elect people of God; the unforgiving sinners have lost the way to eternal life. The just judgments of God and the elect people of God are far and near governing entire heavens on earth. The anger of God is stretched out against the hypocrites of continued unforgiving sinners. It is time to look at the heavens on earth that surrounds you and live faithfully toward yourselves and others with equal treatment toward each other. The light of God is shining on all people, places, and things in the heavens making change where needed. The prey of judgment call and justice of God is upon all people, places, and things in the heavens which are on earth.

The written voice of the Holiest Highest Priest Prophet has lifted a standard in high stature have come forth leading the people to eternal living eternal life within the call of judgments and justice in the heavens on earth. The people must realize the storms of life are raging before them over the entire world. The light of the heavens on earth are before the people walking around the heavens without notice because of corrupt sins roaming the entire heavens on earth.

The cries of the people within oppression of cruelty, repression, and domination are before the hearing of God and God's elect people calling judgment against all unrighteousness dwelling in the heavens which are on earth. The righteous must endure until the sins of the unrighteous cease in judgments and justice of God. The eyes and ears of the chosen elect people of God continuously see and hear near and far all things said and done from one end of the heavens on earth to the other end of the heavens on earth in spirits in truth bringing all things to judgments and justice of God. Ye that endure until the end of eternal judgments are exalted and lifted daily in all things said and done.

The sign of God and God's elect chosen people operating in the heavens on earth appears daily in judgments and justice in all things happening working to the good of the people. The judgments and justice of God comes in swift speed in an instant upon the people. The people are smitten with their own ways recompensed upon them bringing many sorrows to themselves. The elect chosen people of God sit in the heavens high and mighty lifted in judgments and justice of God. The actions of God and the elect chosen people of God speak louder than words. The hidden lies of unrighteousness are brought forth daily in the entire heavens on earth. The unrighteous are ill with their own doings brought against them in judgments and justice of their stiff neck and stiff faces.

The righteous people fear not neither be faint hearted for ye have over-come the world and have possess the lands already. The fierce anger of God has gone out into all the world is the sign of God working to the good of the people in the heavens on earth. The signs of sins being punished without fail have appeared over the entire world. The high looks and stout hearts of unforgiving sinners have lost the way to eternal living eternal life. The sting of judgments and justice burns until God is satisfied with the results of judgments and justice over the entire world. There are many lands ruined with water and fire as many lands dry up from not enough water. I, God say to you, the spirits of my just judgments are in the earth among the living. I, God say to you, hear my words that are written and spoken unto you, for I God sits upon the mount of the heavens on earth broke forth in spirits in truth.

I, God stretch forth my unforgiving spirits against unforgiving sinners who continue to sin. I say to you, my purpose is accomplished at hand unto this chosen millennium generation of people, places, and things at hand. I say to you, my will be done in every life in the heavens which is on earth. I say to you, the salvation of God works according to the purpose of eternal life shinning a light in the pathway of all the chosen people of

God. The people have played a shame confusion frustration guilt superstition guessing game of telling the people the return of Jesus is near. In question in judgment this is far from true facts and proof that the return of Jesus is near. The people must be sensitive unto the Holy spirits of God, hearing all of Gods plans for eternal living eternal life. The direct will of God are spiritually before the people with listening and hearing ears. The people have a need to be sensitive and cooperative unto the spirits of God. The forces of God's will be upon the people with mature spirits following instructions from God in the will of God.

The commands of God are gone forth in the spirits of the chosen elect Holy priesthood. The restoring and rebuilding of a paradise heaven on earth is in process. There is much respect for the Holy one laboring in the presence of God in spirits in truth. The royal presence of God's spirits in the heavens on earth cause much fear upon the people. It is time to be aware God is bringing down to naught the unforgiving sinners who continue to sin. I, God say to you, I make a full end of all unforgiving sinners who continue to sin. I say to you, bold strokes of violent storms come unto every part of the land destroying people places, and things ungodly in the heavens on earth. The true is spelled out the vision of dramatic effects emphasizing the presence of God and God's people on the mount of the heavens on earth.

The golden halo of wisdom within much understanding and knowledge are over the heads of the people. The truth of eternal life is spelled out with much wisdom to this chosen generation than the generations of the past. The people in the presence of God make change for the good of eternal life. The spirits of repent is spelled out to the people seeking eternal life on a paradise earth. It is according to the will of God women and men must take a stand for God with much study and insight of what the will of God is for the people. The spirits of God must penetrate through the hearth of the people. The women are called to speak by inspiration of God to the people as men are called to preach by inspiration of God to the people. The times are now times to hear what the spirits of God is saying to the people for the cross-over into eternal living eternal life. The women use loud voices to sing in the Holy Temples of God. The heavy voice structure is given to men to be head of the house (Holy Temples) of God. I say to you, know that ye give an account of all things said and done unholy in the house of God (Holy Temples) of God. It is the chosen elect Holy Temples of God who are in-charge of preparing and helping the people cross-over into eternal living eternal life in the call of judgment.

I say to you, ye have a need to meditate on these things written unto you in spirits in truth. The times of woe unto you who scatter the people of God and have not attended to them. I, God now gather my people that have been scattered, for the days have come I, God raise a righteous Holy people; they shall not fear of being lost anymore neither be dismayed because of a lack of knowledge. The days are upon the people of dwelling safely in the kingdoms of a paradise heavens on earth. I say to you, I am the Lord your spiritual God call these things written and spoken unto you. I, God am not Jesus as many of you have confused yourself lacking in wisdom and knowledge.

Behold the days has come said God; I now bring from all the heavens on earth my Prophets whom I am well please have overcome the world by spiritual hearing ears and by these Holy and righteous words written unto them but the lands are full of ungodly deeds are standing before God's judgments and justice. Many of these ungodly deeds are in the religious places which are now in the wilderness dried up and their course is evil forces used on the people under their evil forces. These are they that are unforgiving sinners have lost the way to eternal life. The false Ministers in Ministries have slippery ways in darkness. Ye now drive into your own dark slippery ways falling therein. I, God bring your evil deeds upon you in all the heavens destructions are upon you instantly.

The false religions having a form of religion have caused the people to error in committing adultery and fornication with false religious leaders in leadership. I God therefore feed false religious leaders with gall from the plaques of the land. I, God say to you, hearken unto the words of the false Prophets prophesying peace saying, saying no evil shall come before you. That false Prophet walks after the imagination of his or her own heart and not the prophecy from God. The people walking around in the heavens which are on earth can see evil is spread over the entire world of heavens on earth. I, God say to you, the Prophet's whom have stood in my counsel are in spirits in truth; mark that Prophet's words shall come to pass. The Prophet's in my counsel have gone forth.

Behold a whirlwind speaking my fury is gone forth upon the greedy unrighteous spirits of liars. I, God say unto you, I execute and perform my words written and spoken to you from this gospel book of laws. These are the ladder days of my words perform its purpose. There are many people do not understand and have not been taught the truth. I say to you, consider it, I God make my words show perfect affect over the entire world. I, God say to you, I have not sent false ministries I have not sent false Ministers to preach and speak prophecy to the people. I, the Lord, your spiritual God say to you, if they had stood in my counsel, they would not have caused my people to error. I say to you, it is the false Ministries and false Ministers cause my people to error.

I the Lord your spiritual God give the inspired words to the Holiest Highest Priest Prophet standing in my counsel hearing my words with open spiritual ears. I the Lord your spiritual God say to you, I dwell in spirits in truth in all things said and done in righteousness. I God say to you, there is not any place hid, I see in the secret places in the heavens which is on earth. I God say to you, I am not far off, my spirits dwell near and far in the heavens which is on earth. I the Lord your spiritual God say to you, I give you the inspired words of mine from the Holeyest Priest Prophet ever walk the heavens on earth in your time of now times. I, God say to you, I am God at hand in the heavens on earth dwelling in soaring in spirits in truth. I, God have heard what the false Ministers in false Ministries have said false prophecies of lies saying I God said it. I say to you, ye are false Ministers of deceit of your own hearts, which cause my people to forget I am God in spirits in truth is not Jesus, many people have been misled to call me Jesus. I, God again say to you the false Ministers in false Ministries have not stood in my counsel.

I the Lord your spiritual God say to you, the true chosen elect Holy Ministers in Ministries that have stood in my counsel have dreams of visions speaking prophecies and preaching my words that are faithful and true bread to eternal living eternal life. I, God say to you, my words are just like fire burning the unrighteous to ashes. I say to you, my actions speak louder than words causing explosions of judgments and justice where needed in the heavens on earth. I say to you, my words produce change striking instantly over the entire world heavens which is on earth. I say to you, my just judgments destroy the minds of the unrighteous. I, God say to you, I am against false Ministers in false Ministries that have not stood in my counsel neither has not been ordained nor inspired by the Holy spirits. I say to you, ye have caused my people to error in their thinking. I, God say to you, ye shall not continue to profit.

I the Lord say to you, when you see the unrighteous burden down, it is because I the Lord your spiritual God has forsaken them. The times are now times of punishment for their unrighteous hearts. I say to you, judgments are already upon the unrighteous in every part of the heavens on earth. They speak about their burdens being heavy upon them; their burdens are the words they speak. I say to you, they take did not take heed while they had time before it was too late. I say to you, I am the living God in the heavens on earth in spirits in truth. It is I the Lord your spiritual God stand before you in all things said and done. I say to you, ye now see all kinds of things happening in the heavens on earth. It is I the Lord have utterly forsaken many unrighteous people casting them from eternal living eternal life for their sins. It is the unrighteous sinners who continue to sin have lost the way to eternal life in the heavens on earth. It is I the Lord your spiritual God bring change upon the earth shaming all unrighteous sinners who continue to sin. I say to you, hear my word and forget not that I am not Jesus; for there is no return of Jesus to come at no time now neither times to come in the heavens on earth. The unrighteous is forgotten by the righteous.

97

I, Prophet say to you in all the heavens on earth. God's eternal spirits are loosed in every city every country in every part of the earth. The eternal judgments of God are upon everyone whether good or bad, ye give an account of all things said and done daily. There is nothing hid that will not be uncovered, all things hid are in judgment brought to the light. The times are now times to fear the judgments of God upon your life daily. The latter days of all things said and done brought forth in the earth stands before judgments and justice. The spirits of God's image and eyes are the elect chosen people of God are in every place on earth see and hear all things said and done. The spirits of God's wrath are risen more and more raging in every corner of the earth. I, Prophet Say to you, whosoever doubts these words, are in danger of losing eternal living eternal life thereby.

I the Lord your spiritual God say to the people in the heavens on earth, whosoever speak a word against these sayings of mind; ye then has blasphemed against the Holy spirits of mind, ye are not forgiven as ye have lost the way to eternal living eternal life in the heavens on a paradise earth at the end when all sins, sickness and death cease in the earth. I the Lord your spiritual God say to you, the resurrection of the COGIC Holy Saints in all the earth has raised in the chosen elect Holy Temples on earth. I the Lord your spiritual God say to you, all things are ready according for the call of judgment charged unto the elect chosen Holy Priesthood. The Kingdom of God is within the chosen elect Holy Temples. I, God know the hearts of all who believe these inspired words written of me. I, God say to you, behold all these things written of me are accomplished in the entire earth. I say to you, immediately many things have already appeared as many things continue to appear instantly. The heavens on earth have fulfilled upon this chosen generation of people for the eternal purpose of eternal living eternal life.

I say to you, be aware of things taking heed for things you are unaware of come upon you at unexpected times. There are many adults and children have gone into captivity of their own faults because they continue to sin as they are before the judgments of God and God's chosen elect people. I say to you, life is eternal for those with forgiving sins among them in the heavens which is on earth. I say to you, those who are decease in the graves shall never return to the face of the heavens on earth. The dead in the graves know not anything, for they are without breath and spirits. I say to you, all dead bodies turn to dust without fail. There is no other side of death for the dead to cross-over into. I God have told you; the heavens are on earth and not beneath the earth. I say to you, after the 7000 years as the sands of the sea are periods without count in numbers the judgments and justice continue to be served upon the people. I say to you, after judgments and justice are finished in the heavens which are on earth, the paradise heavens shall appear without fail.

I say to you, one day with God is without number in count without calculation. I the Lord your spiritual God, have commanded all that is written in this gospel book of laws. I say to you, be careful about nothing, ye entertain angels unaware are before you. I God say to you, this is the end of all things said and done in unrighteousness. The people of this world are in great grieving and mourning because of constant death, sins, and sickness in the heavens on earth. I say to you, ye now see and hear in the lands of the living the things ye have need to know. I God say to you, I am the living God in spirits in truth in the heavens on earth in people that are making good choices in life. I God say to you, all false religions with a form of religion are done away with in judgments and justice. The chosen elect Holy Temples shall be the only religion left standing in the heavens on earth. These are the days, nothing but the words of God shall stand in the entire heavens on earth. I the Lord your spiritual God say to you, the resurrection of the heavens on earth have appeared over the entire world on earth.

I say to you, all flesh with forgiven sins among them is made Holy in spirits in truth. I say to you, ye have need of Holy spirits, all things ye have need of are manifested unto you in Holy spirits in truth within your spirits. I say to you, ye must have a Holy heart with clean spirits for God to enter your spirits. The times are the now times to seek the Holy spirits of God until you find it in the chosen elect Holy Temples of God. I say to you, ye have need to the Holy spirits to inherit eternal life. I say to you, to be saved is to have eternal life. I say to you, ye must be caught up with God in spirits in truth to live Holy. The times are now times to depart from all other denominations except that of Holiness. The new world orders exist in the elect chosen Holy Temples of God in the heavens on earth. It is time to comprehend these things written unto you before it is too late.

I say to you, ye that desire to live Holy in spirits in truth must attend the chosen elect Holy Temples of God. I, God speak to you plain enough that you understand enduring my Holy and righteous words written unto you. I say to you, all people living unholy have a need to cross-over into Holiness in the elect chosen Holy Temple to become inspired by Holy sprits and truth. I God say to you, the times are the now times to abandon all

100

religious denominations except the chosen elect Holiness. It is time for the unholy nations to accept the truth and be ye Holy for I God am Holy. I God say to you, my voice is heard in the spirts of the Holy elect chosen people of God. I God say to you, all people hear not the voice of God speak to them, your prayers are unanswered. I say to you, ye have a need for your prayers to be answered but ye cannot hear in the spirits of your mind to receive the answer from God. The people in the world have a need to pray and be answered from God in spirits in truth. The people must be caught up in the Holy spirits of God, hearing from God in spirits in truth baptize in Holy water by Holy hands is being born again caught up in the rapture of God.

I say to you, none but the righteous shall hear from God in spirits in truth. There is no one who has seen the Holy spirits of God, the spirits of God cannot be seen; the spirits of God are felt and heard within the mind which are spirits telling you what to do and what not to do. I say to you, it is a choice to except or reject Holiness. The times are now times to stop making bad choices not seeing the outcome until it is too late. It is God who manifests good choices to you in spirits in truth within your mind. I, God say to you, ye have a need to live in a spiritual world according to God's purpose for your life in all things said and done daily. The times are now times to have a peaceful life in the heavens on a paradise earth when all sins, sickness, death and judgments cease in the heavens which are on earth. The times are now times eternal living eternal life ascends over the entire world unto all forgiving sinners baptized in Holy water in Holy Temples.

The times are the now times severe eternal judgments of God's Holy spirits have entered the entire world. The chosen people of God continue to enter eternal life in the heavens which are on earth. I, God say to you, I am all power in the heavens on earth in spirits of the people in truth of the people. The way to God is through the Holy spirits in the chosen elect Holy Temples of God. The times are now times all people must live in the Holy spirits of God to be justified unto eternal life on a paradise earth. It is then at the end of all judgment's sins cease when all unforgiving sinners have perished from the face of the heavens on earth. I the Lord your spiritual God say to you; so many of you have gone out of the way of eternal living eternal life. I God say to you, ye are walking in ways of self-gain instead of eternal-gain of eternal living eternal life. The temporary things of this world are in the lustful hearts of the people. The war-fairs of the heart war against others. The war-fairs of the heart wander into deep things of eternal death.

I, Prophet say to you, there is no one greater than the Holy spirits of God. The Holy spirits of God bear-witness God is real because of God's existing spirits in people spirits making good choices in life. The will of God is that all people be saved gaining eternal life. The world needs God's spiritual guidance in every area of life in every situation of life. The spiritual forces of God are in every part of the world making straight the way to pure paradise heavens on earth. I, Prophet say to you, there is no one that can hide or escape from the spirits of God in the heavens which is on earth. The times are now times to live, walk, and talk in the Holy spirits of God.

I, Prophet say to you, a wise understanding heart walk in the ways of God that are commanded by God according to the gospel laws of God. I

102

say to you, the statues of God prevail into a crown of life of eternal living in peaceful heavens on earth. I say to you, the foundation of eternal life has been laid for you to live according to these words written unto you in spirits in truth. The lights of Holiness have been written unto you, in that ye loose not eternal life. The chosen elect Holy Temples is the Thrones of God ready to receive God's chosen people with forgiven sins. The set order of spiritual judgments and justice are already operating over the entire world. I, Prophet Say to you, see with your eyes hear with your ears understanding within your spirits the things of God appointed to take place according to the words of God written in the gospel book of laws.

I, Prophet say to you, it is for 7000 years count without numbers as the sands of the sea; this world is being revised to the standards of God in the spirits of the people in the truth of the people. All the peaceful Holy lands continue processing daily over the entire world heavens on earth when sin will have ended, and all judgments and justice will have finished its course in the heavens on earth. The lands of Holiness are processing itself to be without sins, sickness, and death in every land of the living in the heavens on earth. The people shall walk, talk, and live according to the spirits of God directing them daily in the heavens on earth. I, Prophet say to you, the spirits of God reign over the entire world forever and forever.

I, Prophet say to you, the people see and hear the work of God operating in the heavens on earth more than ever before. The words of God are scattered abroad in the heavens behold the people of this world in spirits in truth. The elect chosen Holy saints of God are laboring with plain clear intercessions from God unto the people resolving disputes about religion bringing a better understanding to the people. It is the voice of God communicating with the people of God in a very spiritualistic way that can be interpreted by inspirational hearing and listening ears. I say to you, there is a time for every purpose concerning the manifestations revealed reference the original plan of God for eternal life for the people.

I, Prophet say to you, the presence of God's spirituality is in all the heavens on earth. The spirits of God are over everyone that dwells in the world heavens on earth. The spiritual flow of God is in the air roaming the entire world without distance separating the people from God. The Holy spirits of God freely receives the people of God with forgiving sins among them. I say to you, there are happy spirits there are sad spirits there are laughing spirits there are crying spirits there are lying spirits as all things work by way of spirits within a person. I say to you, all people speak the spirits of their mind when they talk to others. I say to you, all people have spirits within whether good or bad. I say to you, the desire to know the will of God is a spiritual feeling. And I, Prophet heard the spiritual voice of God saying, I the Lord your spiritual God have made all things in spirits in truth plain to understand for the people to comprehend dwelling in the spirits of God.

I, God say to you, ye have not understood the ways of God; the spirits in you now know how to receive the spirits of God within you. I say to you, the spirits of God will not dwell in an unclean heart, mind, body, and soul. The spirits of God are standing at the door of your heart ready to receive you. It is your choice; you can receive or reject the spirits of God. I say to you, many people have lost the way to eternal life because they cannot accept the ways to eternal life. There are many people bound up by their own everyday routines and traditions of their temporary life which leads to eternal loss of eternal life. It is the things of God unseen that are for eternity. The times are now times to live by faith and not by the things seen which are temporary. The people must pass the test of living by faith within receiving eternal life. The spirits of God test the people faith at any given time.

The things of God are permanent in life; I God have call judgment against the temporary things in life such as the traditions of humankind. The greatest mysteries of God are revealed unto the people of this world. The power of God has over-thrown the power of humankind. It is the things of eternal life are drawn from the spirits of God within the people. I say to you God is not a painted picture; God is the spirits in control over the minds of the people by supernatural forces in the waves of the air. The requirements of God are everyone in the heavens on earth live in spirits in truth worshiping in the chosen elect Holy Temples of God.

I say to you, there is no one who can escape the spirits of God in the earth. The traditions of this world have kept the people from discovering and living in the spirits of God. I, God command the people to live by the good choice of spirits in your mind directing you on your everyday journey in life. I say to you, take heed unto these things written and spoken unto you, in that ye cross-over into eternal living eternal life. I say to you, remember these are the days of Pentecostal. The hour has come wherein ye shall worship in spirits in truth in Holiness. The times are now times for everyone in this world to get on one accord with God worshiping God in the chosen elect Holy Temples. The spirits of God will not dwell in an unclean heart; your heart and mind are the dwelling place God wants to dwell in your spirits. The heart and mind must be fit for God's spirits to dwell inside of you. I say to you, without the spirits of God dwelling inside of you ye fade away.

The days and times are latter days and times without number without count accomplish God's purposes. The times are now times all things happening in the earth are unto whom and where God sends it. The hours of God have spread over the entire heavens on earth. I, God say to you, all spirits go to whom they belong to. I, God say to you, seek righteousness in all things said and done. I, God say to you, I am a just God in all things in judgments and justice. I, God am divine with no respect of person in eternal judgments and justice. I, God have sent you divine doctrine written unto you ye have a need of to cross-over into eternal living eternal life. I, God have revealed divine revelations ye have a need to know. All things of God are accomplished upon the people without fail. I, God say to you, continue to comprehend these things written unto you in spirits in truth in that ye are not rejected from eternal life.

I, the Lord your spiritual God have sent you insight ye have a need to know by the Holiest Highest Priest Prophet with foresight inspired knowledge and wisdom of God. I, God say to you, there is no one that can stay the hands of God. I, God say to you, I have all power in the heavens on earth. I the Lord your spiritual God say to the people in the heavens on earth, come out of the wilderness of your mind and open to the spiritual ways of God. I, God say to you, every chosen elect Holy Temple is Holy grounds. I say to you, up on the mountain top, look and see the things I God have in store for you after crossing-over into eternal life. I, God say to a blind world of people, I God have sent you help to lead you out of the wilderness of your minds. I God say you; there is no path way open in your heart to lead you out of the wilderness of your mind if you do not hearken to eternal spirits within your spirits as   the Lord your spirit God speak to your heart in spirits in truth.

I the Lord your spiritual God say to you, I God am a supernatural being with supernatural powers within chosen people with supernatural spirits. The times are now times to know God is fulfilling the promise of eternal life to the chosen people of God. The times are now times to claim the promises of God taking actions on spirits heard within knowing God is speaking to you. The times are now times to live in eternal spirits in eternal truth. The times are now times to know the people have error in things said and done because they have refused the ways of God since the beginning of times as the people do this day. The times are now times judgments of God are upon all things said and done in the earth daily. The times are now times the people give an account quickly of all things said and done daily. The times are now times to know God is forming the paradise heavens on earth through all things happening in every part of the earth.

8

The Heavens on Earth Forces of God

The times are now times of seeing and feeling God's Holy spirits dwelling within you to comprehend the eternal things call by God in the heavens which is on earth. It is important to know the eternal values of God and structures of God's purpose for all people, places, and things forming in the heavens on earth. The signs and wonders of heavens forces are forming before you. The times are now times to remember death of the people is eternal turn to dust in the graves. The crown of life is eternal living eternal life in the heavens on earth. The times are now times the chosen elect Holy Priesthood preaches sermons by inspiration of God in the chosen elect Holy Temples of COGIC. The times are now times to remember, this is God's world and not men world. It was the spirits of God call the world into existence and not men. The predictions of this world were called into the heavens which are on earth through the spirits of God operating in the chosen elect people of God.

The times are now times for the forgiven sinners to hear, see, and feel the things of God within you. The times are now times to follow the things of God you hear in your mind. It is good to follow up without fail on the things of God you hear in your mind. There are things in your mind of good sound judgments you must do to be a follower of the spirits of God. The spiritual mind must use sound judgments before doing things call to you by the spirits of God. There are times you will do things you hear in your mind and there are times you will doubt the things of God you hear in your mind. I say to you, ye must know where to draw the line in all things said and done. These things written and spoken unto you are for the forgiven sinners with forgiving sins among them receiving eternal life.

The times are now times to act on these things of God written and spoken unto you, then God deals with you on a one to one basics. The times are now times to trust your spiritual instincts of God you hear in your mind. The times are now times to know you are the God within you. The times are the now times to know you are the image of God living in the image within you making good choices leading to eternal living eternal life. The times are now times to live by faith more than ever before as ye stand the test of times now upon you. The tests of times are upon you more away from the Holy Temples than within the Holy Temples. I say to you, ye have a need of these things written and spoken unto you in that ye live spiritually hearing from God in all things said and done.

The times are now times to know the chosen elect people of God have already spied out the lands in the heavens which are on earth. The times are now times to remember people are destroyed for lack of knowledge. The people must be spiritual minded in agreement with God in all things said and done in the heavens which are on earth. The gain of eternity for all seasons is before you as a gift from God as you spiritually consecrate your mind. The times are now times to reframe from consecrating your mind in the lust of the flesh. The times are for all people to consecrate their mind in the spiritual mind seeing the light of eternal life. I say to you, the way to God is made clear to you. The times are now times to awake to your faith in the spirits of God. The times of dwell in the spiritual mind of God's image mentally and physically are before you in spirits in truth.

The times are now times to hear the still quite voice of God speak to your mind standing before you in spirits in truth. I say to you that have blind ways to the spirits of God, ye now have been restored in sound mind in spirits in truth. The times are now times the spirits of God dwelling on the inside of you remain for eternity. The will of God comes to you during everything happening in all things said and done in the heavens on earth. I say to you, all people have come short of knowing the powerful spirits of God dwelling within their mind. I say to you the spirits of God behold you anointed with Holy spirits strengthening you in all things said and done daily in the heavens which are on earth. The eternal people, places, and things of God are called by the spirits of God daily. The kingdoms of God are the chosen elect Holy Temple Churches of God in Christ in every part of the heavens on earth. The promise lands of God are processing in all the heavens on earth. The redeeming of the chosen people of God is processing the minds of the people into eternal spirits in faith in truth.

The fullness of God's spirits is operating in the people of God in every part of the heavens on earth. The people of God take the promise lands by force from the unrighteous. The unrighteous are not operating by the spirits of God. The spirits of God are mandatory to operate by the eternal spirits of God. The times are now times to choose eternal life and live in the promise lands before it is too late, and your time has expired to receive eternal living eternal life. The time is out for playing with God for monetary reasons. The times and seasons are times for saving the souls of the people as the chosen elect people of God must give an account for saving souls of the people. The times are now times to choose eternal life or choose eternal death now standing before you in the spirits of God within you.

The future of hope of God is now changing people, places, and things in every part of the heavens on earth for the betterment of paradise heavens on earth. The salvations of God are before the people of God with the promises of God. The times are now times standing in awe of God's majesty in every part of the world destroying mankind traditions. The power of God and God's chosen elect people are operating in the twilights of the heavens on earth overthrowing the unrighteous traditions in every part of the world. The special deliveries of God are before the people daily processing eternal living eternal life. The eternal purpose and values of God are in the structured spiritual minds of the people of God. The purpose and values of God are made known to the people in spirits in truth. The cries of the people have entered the spirits of God and God's people. The minutes, hours, days, months, and years are bringing an eternal end to ungodliness in the heavens on earth. The heavens on earth are made perfect without sins, sickness, and death in the eyesight of the people of God. There is evident of God's spirits operating in the heavens on earth. There is evident all people, places, and things are becoming new as all old traditions of the people fade away from the heavens on earth restoring Christians faith in God.

There is evident the eternal spirits of God are operating in the minds of the people has lifted in every part of the heavens on earth. The people in the heavens on earth bear witness of God's powerful spirits within the people creating the new paradise heavens on earth. The people see the signs and know that the kingdoms of God are here in the heavens on earth accomplishing the purposes of God for the people. The people have a need to grow in wisdom in knowledge in spirits in truth without spots of blemish confound spirits. The times are now times to hold fast unto these things written unto you learning to follow the words of God written unto you. The instructions of God have been written unto you plain, in that ye understand without fail. It is time for the people to repent and receive the new things of God. The word of God's salvation to the people is now being performed daily in the heavens on earth.

The new heavens on earth are being filled with nothing but the righteous people, places, and things of God. The righteous people, places, and things are caught up with God in spirits in truth replenishing the new heavens on earth. The spirits of God have reach humanity establishing the end of all sin, sickness, and death at the end of judgments and justice as the relationships between God and the people bear witness of the heavens forming the paradise earth. The new birth of all people, places, and things are established in the daily lives of the people. God's new creation brings about all things renewed in the heavens on earth. The covenants of God are fulfilled under an oath with the chosen people of God. The new birth of all the heavens on earth brings about the healing of all nations as the plans of God are accomplish.

It is in times like these all the plans of God are force upon the abilities of the people forcing them to endure until the end of all judgments and justice prevailing in the heavens on earth. The unforgiving sinners are destroyed daily until all unforgiving sinners are no-longer residing in the heavens on earth. There are many circumstances of things happening among the people they can comprehend what must be done in all things said and done. The political powers and military powers of the people will not be needed in the paradise heavens on earth. There are no stones left un-turn for all things are possible with God. Things are constantly happening in an instant bringing the people to heart felt tears work to the good of the chosen people of God.

The lights of the heavens are shining in every part of the heavens on earth. The spirits of God are formed in the air of the heavens controlling the spirits of the people in the heavens which is on earth. It is in the waves of the air God control all people, places, and things in the heavens on earth. The eternal ark of God has moved upon the face of the heavens on earth. The ark of the eternal spiritual waves of God in the sky is an open structure reforming the way the people think has over-powered the people to think in the eternal spiritual mind of God. The human mentality has improved mentally and physically by the forces of God's spirits upon all things said and done in the heavens which are on earth. It is in all things said and done in the heavens on earth, the spirits of God exist according working to the good of the people crossing-over into eternal living.

These are the days and times to have faith in God and see the signs and wonders of God bringing about eternal changes to the heavens which are on earth. The times are now times eternal life is brought forth in plain to the eyes and ears of the people in certain situations working to the glory of God. There are many people in a grieving state of mind that will never see the light of eternal life because their state of mind is dim by the decease love lost in dead love ones. The times are now times to come to yourselves and endure all things happening around you in such times as these. The people that cannot endure in times like these loose the way to eternal life crossing-over into eternal death. The pains of life are brought forth everyday as the wages of unforgiving sins is death. There many people in the heavens on earth continue to live in the wilderness of their mind because of their evil hearts. The chosen elect messengers of God continue to speak the words of God to the people of God in the heavens which are on earth leading the people to eternal living eternal life.

I say to you, in the heavens on earth, the decease is eternal dust in the earth. All dead bodies are not dry bones but quickly turn to dust in the earth and beneath the earth in every place in the earth. All preserved dead bodies in the brick walls turn to dust n every part of the earth. Take all dead bodies out of the brick walls and bury them while there is time before accounts are given in judgments of God. It is not good to breathe the air of dead bodies living in the brick walls of the earth. It is not good and very unhealthy to breathe the dust of dead ashes now turn to dust smell rotten;

115

I say to you bury all dead bodies beneath the ground. The dead bodies are not kept any more above the earth but beneath the earth. I say to you, these things being done are deadly air to the living human being in the heavens which is on earth.

The people in the world have gone astray doing things that ought not to be done for monetary reasons that are in judgments and justice of God. I God say to you, all things said and done daily stands before the eternal judgmental spirits of God. I the Lord your spiritual God say to you, all things hid in the earth uncovered in judgment. There be nothing left unjudged in the heavens which is on earth. I, God say to you who are responsible for these things mention is in judgment have a need to come to yourselves doing the right things that leads to eternal living eternal life. I, God say to you, undo quickly that which I have spoken to you as ye are judged daily for these things I God speak to you in spirits in truth. I, God speak plainly to you that ye see and hear these things in order that ye save your life unto eternal life. I, God say to you, ye have been warned of your wrongdoing unrighteousness being judged daily.

There are many people continue to die never to return to the heavens which are on earth, for death is eternal dust beneath the earth. I, God say to you, those sick with eternal sins shall not recover from their sickness but turn to eternal dust beneath the earth after their death. I, God say to you, when you pray, say if it be the will of God. I, God say to you, there be many in the earth who will recover from sickness receiving eternal life. I, God say to the people in the heavens on earth, ye live in the shadow of death daily judged of all things said and done in every part of the heavens on earth. I, God say to you, all people live in the shadow of death in all things said and done until all sins, sickness, and death has ceased at the end of judgments and justice and the paradise earth appears. The clearing of the earth of sins, sickness, and death from the face of the heavens on earth take place daily clearing the pathway to paradise heavens on earth in all things said and done.

The wicked evil spirits of the unrighteous are cast out of the heavens which are on earth. The spirits of betrayal spirits of the unrighteous are cast from the heavens which are on earth. The hatred spirits of the unrighteous are cast from the heavens which are on earth. The jealousy spirits are cast from the heavens which are on earth. The adulterous fornication spirits of the unrighteous are cast from the heavens which are on earth. The lying spirits of the unrighteous are cast from the heavens which are on earth. The theft spirits of the unrighteous are cast from the heavens which are on earth. The back-biting spirits are cast from the heavens which are on earth. The harden hearts of the unrighteous are cast from the heavens which are on earth. The killing spirits of the unrighteous are cast from the heavens which are on earth. The things said and done that ought not to be said and done are cast from the heavens which are on earth. The cause of sins, sickness, and death spirits are cast from the heavens which are on earth. The causes of unhappiness are cast from the heavens which are on earth. The unforgiving sinners are cast from the heavens which are on earth. I, say to you, all cast spirits turn to dust beneath the earth.

The Highest Priest Prophet ever walk the heavens on earth in the now times speaks and writes with divine authority, power, wisdom, and knowledge in the lands of the living making plain and straight the way to

117

eternal living eternal life. These are the days the scriptures are being fulfilled upon the people; the original plans of God are standing before the people in every part of the world. The light of the world is God's spiritual and physical plans in the spirits of the people in the truth of the people. The Highest Priest Prophet walking the heavens which is on earth bringing sight to the blind spirits of the people. The spiritual thoughts of mankind have already been conquered by the spiritual powers of God and God's chosen elect people spiritually operating in the heavens which are on earth.

The chosen elect Holy gospel heals the people with eternal life in the heavens which is on earth, but the unforgiving sinners' days are numbered have lost the way to eternal life. The times are now times all unrighteousness perish from the face of the heavens which are on earth in due times in due seasons. The times are without number without count saying for everything under heavens there is a time and season that be done which God had purpose from the beginning of times in the Bible days of Genesis. There be nothing left undone in all the heavens in every part of the world all things have a need to be done, be done in times and seasons. The times are now times to watch as well as pray in the will of God. The times are now times of all things done and said must be in the will of God working to the good of the people in the heavens which are on earth.

I, God say to you, all thing the people have a need to know are manifested unto you are written unto you in spirits in truth by inspiration of the Holiest Highest Priest Prophet ever walk the heavens which is on earth in your times of now times. The times are now times to see the lights making straight pathways to eternal living on a paradise earth. I, God say

118

to you, all things are now at hand before the face of the people in the heavens which are on earth. The words of God shall not pass away void but accomplish all purposes of God in the spiritual will of God. The times are now times to take heed without fail in all things said and done daily. The times are now times to remember all people stands before the shadow of death until the end of all things is said and done God hath called into the heaven on earth forming the parad se eternal living of eternal life. It is in the favor of the people in the heavens which are on earth to do not stray away from these gospel laws written and spoken unto you. I say to you, in the hour ye stray away from these gospel messages written unto you, ye lose your way to eternal living eternal l fe on a paradise heaven on earth.

The Holiest Highest Priest Prophet bear witness of inspirational spirits of God within the chosen elect people of God brings divine reality of God to the light of the people. The people in the heavens on earth now hear the words of God with a much clear understanding of what God is calling unto the people. The voice of the Holiest Highest Priest Prophet has lifted out the heavens which are on earth. The Highest Priest Prophet ever in your times of now calls a thing as though it were to whom and where it belongs in the heavens which are on earth and it appears. The times are now times all things said and done are standing in the plain for the people to hear and see in the heavens on earth. There is nothing unknown to the Holiest Highest Priest Prophet making straight the pathways to eternal life written and spoken unto you. The things said and done in the eyesight and hearing of the Holiest Highest Priest Prophet are judged quickly without fail. The greatest command is the respect unto the Holiest Highest Priest Prophet that has paved the way to eternal living eternal life written unto you in spirits in truth. The elect chosen Holy Temples are quite whenever the Holiest Highest Priest Prophet stands to speak. I, God say to you, take heed that these things be carried out without fail; forget them not and write them down that ye have a need to know. I, God say to you, there is no need for mistakes in the kingdoms of God. I say to you, ye now see and hear plain the many things ye have a need to know.

The chosen elect Holy Priest always preaches sermons by inspiration of God in the chosen elect Holy Temples. The Preachers that are preaching in the synagogues of Temples that are not inspired neither ordained whom were not called by the Holy spirits of God to preach have a need to step down in that you lose not the way to eternal life. These are they have misled the people for monetary reasons causing many people to be destroyed for lack of knowledge. I the Lord your spiritual God say to you, women have not been called to preach, women have been called to speak as Prophets and Evangelist in Ministry in the chosen elect Holy Temples. There are those who grieve the Holy spirits of God have lost the way to eternal life. There are those who have no faith in God who have lost the way to eternal life. These are they who have denied the Holy spirits of God within them.

I the Lord your spiritual God say to you, I, God proves to them my spirits are in the heavens which are on earth. I say to you, the fear of God is in the heavens which are on earth spread over the entire world. The people that deny the spirits of God operating in the heavens on earth are in all parts of the world have lost the way to eternal life. There are those who it is not their intentions to label their Temples Holy Temples. I the Lord your spiritual God say to you, ye have need to merge with the chosen elect

Holy Temples of the Churches of God in Christ Incorporated before it is too late ye then loose the way to eternal life. The people in the heavens on earth are overthrown by the spirits of God overpowering them in all things done and said change to the will of God. This is known to all people in the world, God's spiritual heavens on earth reign over the entire world. The times are now times more than ever before to be ye Holy for I, God am Holy in spirits in truth. I the Lord your spiritual God say to you, all people stand in awe of eternal judgments in the shadow of death till the end of things of God are said and done over the entire world. I say to you, the wages for sins of sinners who continue to sin ye have lost eternal life.

I, Prophet say to you, this is not a man's world, this is God's world. It is God that has given men women boy and girl free will choices to choose right choices over wrong choices. I, Prophet say to you, nothing but the righteous shall stand in the heavens which are on earth as all unrighteous fails. The times are now times there are nothing hidden as many things are happening in an instant. There are many landmarks moved out of place never to return over the entire world. The people see whole cities, countries, towns, and states destroyed in the judgments of God over the entire world. There be many people, places, and things perish from the face of the heavens on earth without a trace as has been predicted in the days of the Bible being written. There be many people in the heavens on earth groaning and crying mourns for people, places, and things of value perish from the face of the earth gone in an instant. The rising of crime in the earth has dug deep over the entire world cease in the judgments of God in due seasons.

The rising of heat drought, rain, water, fire destroy many people, places, and things cease in the judgments of God in due seasons. These things are happening over the entire world because of the sins of sinners has dug deep into unrighteousness without care for others. The high-minded people with pride brought low in all the heavens on earth. There are many funerals on the rise in every land until the people refuse sin opening their hearts to righteous minds and turn to God in spirits in truth. The times are now times don't let it be said it is too late for you to cross-over into eternal life. There are those who have lost the way to eternal life as their days are numbered in every part of the earth. The times are now times to take a stand and live right as the graveyards increase in record numbers with funerals. The times are now times there are no stones left un-turn in the judgments and justice of God. There are many without count has seen the spirits of God face to face see eternal life. The times are now times to take heed to the things that guide your souls to eternal life.

The times are now times to hear what the spirits said to the people, for these things save your soul. The times are trouble-sometimes standing at the door of the people because of those who refuse to stop sinning. The times are now times out for playing with God; it's time to be real in spirits in truth. The times are now times are up for playing church for monetary reasons. The times are now times to save souls unto eternal life. The times are up for pretending to be a Christian. The times are now times ye give an account for things said and done daily. The times are now times to not take things for granted in the heavens which are on earth knowing God is in control and have the last say so in the lives of all people dwelling in the world. The times are now time to remember these things written unto you, for ye know not what a day may bring. I say to you, let each day speak for itself meaning each day will bring about changes in your life in due seasons and times which were preordained.

9

The Words of God Standing during the Heavens on Earth

The words of God are standing during the heavens on earth destroying all false denominations. I the Lord your spiritual God say to you, all denominations are false except the chosen elect Holy Temples. I the Lord your spiritual God say to you, eternal judgments and justice set during all congregations that are unholy. I, God say to you, cross-over into the chosen elect eternal Holiness COGIC while you have a chance. The words of God written and spoken unto you are now made flesh operating in the call of judgments and justice daily. The times are now times to know the voice of God and operate within the call of God in Ministry in truth of God call by God. The times are now times to be obedience to the voice and words of God; in that ye are in the will of God. The spirits of God are supreme divine spirits with existing superpowers in the chosen elect people of God.

The times are now times to see the existing inspired lights of spiritual truth operating in the chosen elect people of God. The anointing angels of God are operating in the chosen elect Holy Temples call by God in spirits in truth. The times are now times to be made whole in spirits in truth in God in the chosen elect Holy Temples of God. The times are now times to renew your minds in the spirits of God by accomplishing hearing the voice of God operating within you. The fulfillment of all things of that which has been written and spoken unto you is already upon you in waves of the air above you in spirits in truth. The times are now times to face reality of God's words now standing before you before it is too late. The times are now times all nations become as one big Holy land as all grounds become Holy grounds. The plaques of judgments are upon all people, places, and things that refuse to live eternal righteousness.

The people judged eternal life are redeemed by the Holy spirits of God in truth in righteous spirits with understanding of eternal living eternal life. The time is over for excuses of saying; I do not read the Bible because I do not understand it and I do not believe in the Bible. The times are now times to find the words you believe in with evidence and proof of the truth operating in the heavens which is on earth. The commands of God are that everyone lives according to the Holy spirits of God on one accord in one big Holy land without sins, sickness, and death. The gifts of God are given to the people according to their abilities. I, God say to you, to whom much is given, much is required. I say to you, forget not these things ye read, write them down in the contents of your heart in that ye walk in the path of righteousness unto eternal life. I say to you, this world is God's Holy land forever. The things call by God is in the righteous spirits of the people as you hear it and read it. The people ir the heavens on earth sin much through their ignorance; it is good to keep no company with them in that ye not detour from the words of God and take wrong paths to eternal living eternal life.

The time is up for sins to constantly continue in the heavens which are on earth. The people that live by the words of God in their heart, it shows outwardly by their faithful and true actions daily. The people that have strayed away from the words of God, it shows outward in their unrighteous actions. The times are now times to put away the outdated traditions of the people and come into the newness of God by way of renewed spiritual minds. The words of God are written and spoken unto the people of this world. The times are now times the people are expose to nothing but the truth about God and eternal life. The chosen elect preachers preach only in the chosen e ect Holy Temples. I say to you, all other denominations have been spiritually defeated by the Holy spirits of God.

The voice of God is within the mighty chosen elect people of God. The voice of God is always omnipresent reign in all places with all power and authority in all things said and done by the people. All corruption in the earth destroyed with the unforg ving sinners in every part of the heavens. The days of God's voice are upon the people in the heavens are here. The people are call to repentance in every part of the world. I the Lord your spiritual God have sent anointed Prophets to you many times as

127

ye were not able to determine false Prophets from true Prophets because ye do not have hearing spiritual ears. I say to you, all things are judged daily until all sins perish from the face of the heavens on earth. The days of God ruling in judgments and justice are established in the heavens on earth. The powers of God have already defeated the people bringing more and more devastating eternal judgments upon the people. These are the latter days of God that has put fear in the people. The times are now a time the people in the heavens on earth are in horrible situations and disappointments appears in the lives of the people.

The new remnant of God gives new directions changing the world of people making new paths to paradise heavens on earth. The times are now times to grasp without fail the calls of God changing times and seasons that have taken place in every part of the heavens on earth. The lifestyles of the people change to the ways of God in the will of God. The changes of life affect everyone living in this world. The people in the heavens on earth take heed immediately walking in the straight pathways of eternal living eternal life. I God say to you, without fail, comprehend these things written unto you as ye study much to show yourselves approved in wisdom and knowledge of the things of God. I say to you, write these things down that ye forget them not for ye have a need to know these things written unto you in spirits in truth.

The chosen elect Holy Shepherds reaching out unto the lost souls in the heavens on earth. The Holy flocks of God's chosen people recovered in all the heavens on earth. The noise of moaning and crying is driven through all the heavens on earth. The thick clouds of darkness are hanging over the heavens from coast to coast unto all the inhabitants of the earth.

The captivity of the unrighteous is already before them the wrath of God's judgments and justice. The hidden sins of the people are uncovered in every part of the earth. There is no peace unto the unforgiving sinners in every part of the earth. The times are now times to listen to God's voice being obedient to the voice of God and know the will of God for your life. The people with listening hearing ears hears what God is saying unto the Holy people in the Holy Temples. The times are now times to hear the still small voice of God speak unto you that ye have a need to hear from the voice of God. There are great multitudes of Holiness people of God are filled with the spirits of God hear the spirits of God speak unto them. These are they are the chosen people of God, the disciples of God dwelling in the true work of the Holy gospel of God. These are they that are given salvation through the grace of God in the heavens which are on earth. These are they the wise people of the world. These are they that have wash their robes and made them white as snow.

The people of God are Holy people of God; these are they who shall never be moved from the face of the paradise heavens on earth. The Holy people are the chosen people of God because they know and understand the deep things of God believing in God by the promises of God with faith and hope in God. The Holy people of God dwell in clean spirits of God in righteousness in spirits of truth. The thrusting out of God's spiritual people is in every land reaching out to the lost sheep of God that have been misled by false doctrine in every part of the earth. The keys to eternal life are within the Holy people of God dwelling in the Holy Temples of God. The Holy one is dwelling in the heavens which are on earth with the keys to eternal living eternal life written unto you are these words in spirits in truth. I say to you, nothing but the righteous can see and hear from God. I say to you, nothing but the righteous receive eternal living eternal life in the heavens on a paradise earth.

The spiritual words of God stand within the chosen elect Holy Temples. The Holy foundation of the gospel religion was called by the Holy spirits of God unto the people of God. I say to you, ye must be Holy in all things said and done to hear from God in spirits within, I say to you, to be Holy, ye must be caught up in spirits in truth in God. I say to you, to receive eternal life, ye must be caught up in the realness of God's spirits within you. The evil spirits of the people do not prevail in false religious colts; palm reading, witchcraft, and the laying around of pennies are types of evil spirits of the unrighteous. I say to you; the unrighteous sins perish along with its maker in judgments and justice of God. I, God say to you, I see your evil works under the sun are not hidden; I, God pull out all hidden sins in the heavens on earth. I say to you, know that the time is here without warning the wrath of God stands before the unrighteous workers of evil thoughts. The times are now times to dwell in the Holy spirits of God leading to eternal living eternal life.

The times are now times to realize the supreme divine existence of Gods existence of God's spirits over the entire world of human beings. The justice of God's commands prevails over the entire world of people. The justice spirits of God spread abroad over the entire heavens on earth in all things the people say and do. The justices of God pull out all things the people say and do in leadership are in judgments and justice daily. There is no unrighteous left un-turn clearing the path to a better world. The dishonest leaders in leadership are cut off from eternal living eternal life. I say to you that reject righteousness, ye have lost the way to eternal life. I say to you, these words written unto you are plain and clear. I say to you, every word written unto you in this gospel book of laws prevail over the entire world of people, places, and things. I say to you, there are those who are cursed with eternal death unknown to them because of their unforgiving sins among them.

The revelation prophecies of this gospel book of laws are sealed in spirits in truth in the heavens on earth The gifts of God have come forth more and more within the people of God in every part of the heavens on earth. I the Lord your spiritual God say to you; it is a woman made known to you the eternal ways of God leading to eternal living eternal life on a paradise earth. I, God say to you, all that is commanded of this people come forth. There are great things being done and great things to come in the entire heavens on earth. The people in the heavens on earth are convinced the spirits of God and God's people spread over the world is in control. The manifestations of God's power of eternal judgments bring eternal life in a new divine order called by the spirits of God. There is no one can stop the works of God within the chosen elect people of God. The times are now times the whole earth stands in awe of eternal judgments and justice of God daily giving an account of all things said and done face to face with the call of judgments and justice of God. The times are now times to see God's actions speak louder than words in all things said and done. It is I; God call all things to your attention said and done in the heavens on earth.

The spirits of true prophecy stand before the people in the heavens on earth. The spirits of the people stand before the Holiest Highest Priest

131

Prophet ever walk the earth in your times of   now times. The spirits of revelation have come to pass on the unrighteous. The resurrection of real prophecies prevails over the entire world of heavens on earth. I the Lord your spiritual God say to you, there be no other doctrine prevail other than this doctrine leading to eternal living eternal life in the heavens which are on earth. The people surround the Holiest Highest Priest Prophet see the power of God prevail within the life of the Prophet. The spirits of God and God's chosen elect people have taken by force the control over the spirits of the people. The times are now times to remember your spiritual body is the Holy Temple of God in all things said and done. The times are now times to remember to take heed to these things written unto you in that ye loose not eternal life.

I the Lord your spiritual God say to you, the times are now times to preach eternal life; the time is out for preaching traditional Bible stories. The Preachers must preach to the people how to be saved receiving life eternal in the chosen elect Holy Temples. The people in the heavens which are on earth have a need to know how to receive eternal living eternal life. The people in the heavens which are on earth have a need to know, death is eternal beneath the earth turn to dust. I say to you, all things being reveal and manifested have been called beforehand in all the heavens on earth. I say to all the nations, the mouth of the messiah is in the earth speaking through the Holiest Highest Priest Prophet ever walk the heavens on earth in your times of now times. The translations of the Holy spirits which are in the waves of the air is now being spoken and written unto you by the Holiest High Priest Prophet.

I say to you, the times are now times confusion is destroyed as the people bear witness to the words written and spoken from inspired spirits of the Holiest Highest Priest Prophet. The written commands of God operating in the heavens on earth bear witness of the presence of God before the people in all things said and done. The inspired true spirits of God are standing before the people with judgments and justice. The brilliant wisdom and knowledge of God are truly written unto you for guidance and understanding leading to eternal living eternal life. This is the chosen generations of people God now draws the line upon for righteousness in eternal living eternal life. The times are now times unrighteousness comes to an end with this generation of people and the generations to come. The Holy gospel of God has been updated for guidance to eternal life.

The inspired spiritual light of God's spiritual truth is daily standing before the people spirits in truth. The spiritual truth is beyond all things said and done in the earth. The Holiest Highest messenger from God stands before the people with written and spoken inspired spirits of the true Holy gospel of God spread in every part of the earth. The things of God called upon the people are being accomplished upon the people daily until all things called by God are accomplished and finished in judgments and justice upon the people. The speaking of visions and dreams are being accomplished in leadership upon the people. The world of people has a need for change. I say to you, all things said and done are already in judgments and justice. The times are now times, immediately all the chosen elect Holiness leaders in leadership see the light of God shinning in spirits in truth. There is much more leadership needed in guidance of eternal living eternal life. The chosen elect Holy Priesthood are called to take the lands of God by force in spirits in truth.

The deep things of God are seen and heard in the presence of the people as they are overwhelmed in astonishment by the consequences and circumstances of judgments and justice of God over-powering the people in every part of the earth. The paradise heavens of God are building through the wrath of God's eternal justice that has been poured out upon the people in every part of the heavens which are on earth. The times are now times for the people to be truthful with much faith in God to fix all things in the people minds that have leadership over the people in every area of life. The understanding of God's times in judgments and justice are brought forth to the understanding of the people in that there are no confusions. The proper understanding brings the people out of the confusions of their minds. The people now know, all things said and done daily in the earth stands before the judgments of God and God's chosen elect people calling judgments on all things said and done in unrighteousness.

The things said and done in the heavens on earth have entered the minds of the chosen elect people of God in spirits in truth. The people in the heavens on earth are learning to live by faith in spirits in truth in God in the people of God. The Holy chosen elect people of God must "fast" constantly that ye hear and perceive the spirits of God before you in all things said and done. It is good for the chosen elect people of God to not eat too much meat in that ye hear and perceive the spirits of God standing before you at all times in spirits in truth. The chosen elect Holy disciples must "pray and fast" together opening the pathway to one accord hearing from the spirits of God in spirits in truth in a stable mind set in the Holy gospel. The need for all people in this world to humble themselves under the mighty spirits of God on one accord in all things said and done is for the crossing over into eternal living eternal life. It is then God can enter the depths of the minds of the people in which the spirits of God can flow clearly hearing from God in spirits in truth. It is then the natural mind becomes spiritual mind as ye fast and pray ye becomes stronger in clearly hearing the voice of God's eternal purpose for a paradise heaven on earth. It is then God lifts your spirits in all leaderships in all things said and done. It is then ye hear things in your mind are the spirits of God calling all things in decent order for eternal living eternal life in all areas of leadership.

The people of God, the natural mind becomes the spiritual mind in all things said and done. The people of God in all areas of leadership follow the spiritual order of God's voice without fail. The change for eternal life is in all things happening in the wrath of God working to the good of the people receiving eternal living eternal life. The times are now times the things with eternal purpose are accomplished in the will of God through the people. The things that have no need in eternal life fades of the earth without fail. The times are now times, the ringleaders of sins fade from the earth. The times are now times all sins will have finish its course in the heavens which is on earth. There is no room for daily mistakes in judgments and justice as all people in the world have need to take heed to daily judgments and justice of God dwelling in the heavens on earth. The times are now times to take heed, the sins of adults affect the lives of their children having a need for their parents to raise them without sin in the lives of the children.

The prejudice of this world is not forgiven is call up front in eternal judgments and justice of God is dealt with in any form in any fashion. The times are now times to know what is right between you and God on a one on one spiritual basic. The spirits of God will minister to your needs for eternal living eternal life. There is plenty good room at the cross-over into eternal living eternal life. The call of all things said and done in the earth have been call up front inspected by the spirits of God and God's Holy elect chosen people. There are no exceptions as there be no respecter of person in the earth, for all people stands before the judgments and justice of God except the elect Holy chosen people of God judging the people. The times are now times, don't let it be said that it is too late for you to enter eternal life. The Holy spirits of God makes certain all things are accomplished in the earth God hath called to be accomplished. The times are now times to take heed, in that ye see a straight path to follow the ways of God within your spirits in truth in all things said and done daily.

The new things of God are within the chosen elected anointed one's spirits anointed by God. The times are now times of the fulfillment of the millennial years. The new things of God are in the chosen elect Holy Christianity call by the Holy spirits of God upon the Holy people chosen by God a Holy land of people. The chosen people of God are paving the way to paradise heavens on earth. The anointed one the greatest Prophet of all times is in the heavens on earth making clear the way to eternal living eternal life within the spirits of God called by God in spirits in truth. It is through the spirits within is the only way to establish a relationship with God connecting you within your spirits to God spirits. There must be a connection between you and God that relates to the people of God. The spirits of God have motives that modify the mind into a spiritual mind set. The chosen people of God must have membership with God in the chosen elect Holy Temples of God. There must be faith and patience with God for God to operate in your life. The new things of God are prophesied in this gospel book of law by the Holiest Highest Priest Prophet ever walk the earth in your times of now times. The things prophesied come to pass on a daily basic where needed when needed.

It is within seven thousand years all unforgiving sinners will have passed away from every part of the earth. It is then the eternal paradise heavens on earth appear within a peaceful world without sins, sickness, and death unto eternal living eternal life. The mainstream to God and God's chosen elect people are the truthful spirits within you. The times are now times to listen to your mind speaking good things to your heart paving the way to eternal life for you. When your mind speaks to your heart with good things for you to hear, it is God speaking to you to hear. The times are now times to listen to God without fail hearing from your most intellect spirits of your mind is God. The times are now times to separate the spirits of the devil from the spirits of God within your mind. The spirits of God tell you good things, the spirits of the devil tell you things that are not good. When you know the spirits of God are before you, ye are then caught up with God in spirits in truth.

The anointed spirits of God within the people of God is God operating within the people of God to get to the people who have a need to know the truth about God. The anointed ones called by God in the earth is God in the earth working through the people of God in the earth. The times are now time the people recognize the times are times people pay up for their iniquities through suffering ways and afflictions until they come to their self and stop lying and sinning causing sickness and death to flourish through the earth daily. The people have a need to quickly recognize the wrath of God prevails over the entire world of people daily without fail in all things said and done. The times are now times the people have a need not to forget, all people, places, and things of sins, sickness, and death are destroyed by fire, water, accidents and death in every part of the earth. The anointed one the Holy one having seen many things enter the earth she had prophesied have already taken place in every part of the world upon the people. It is the most anointed one is highly favored with God with great wisdom and knowledge writes this gospel book of law to you call by the inspired spirits of God within her. It is the mysteries of God unfolding in every part of the world God had inspired her to call, saying to the people in every part of the world, ye must repent and come to yourselves in wisdom and knowledge of the eternal ways of God. The ways of humankind are temporary without fail in every part of the world, but the ways of God are eternal living eternal life in every part of the world.

The anointed one the Holy one continues to prophesy the new things of God unfolding in the entire world upon the people. The anointed one the most Holy one has already overcome the world in spirits in truth. The call of eternal visions and eternal dreams has taken place in the heavens on earth as the Holy righteous spirits of the people descend out of the midst of the heavens on earth operate to the good of eternal living eternal live. The anointed one the Holy one knows all the spirits of God operating in the heavens on earth. The brightness of wisdom and knowledge has come down from the spirits of the heavens on earth dwelling in the earth went forth in the chosen elect Holy Temples of God is God. The times are now times to remember the seven seals of God have been poured out into the heavens on earth reaching the spirits of the people dwelling in the heavens which is on earth.

The seven seals have been poured out upon the seven churches in Tallahassee, Florida saying hear what the spirits of God is saying to the seven churches in the heavens which is on earth. I say to you, woe be unto the people in every part of the world, for I God have seen you in the abominations of sins, sickness, and death receiving your punishments for unforgiving sinners who refuse to stop sinning and repent unto Holy righteous minds. The times are now times ye that have lost the way to eternal life show up on you quickly without fail in every part of the world. The times are now times ye have refuse to be Holy in all things said and done long enough, it is now your time is up as judgment and justice prevail over you in all things said and done. The times are now times to take heed in all things said and done in that ye fall not by the wayside loosing eternal life.

The times are now times like never in the history of life eternal life prevails over the entire world daily finishing all people, places, and things have a need to be finished. The times are now times the angels of God are singing and praising God in the chosen elect Holiness Temples of God. The great movement of God's Holy sprits spread over the entire world bringing the people to grips with the spirits w thin them of God. The marvelous works of God's almighty powerful acts are seen and heard spread in harmony within all people, places, and things called for the purpose of

139

eternal living eternal life. The times are now times to become on one accord in all things said and done daily.

The times are now times as the world turns there are many people still asleep in the things of God and are blind to the ways of eternal life as death takes its toll on many lives all over the world. The people in the earth are in a great mourning grieving the loss of love ones from passed up unto now as time slips away from them leaving them with the loss of eternal life. The people are living in a dying world of people until the people stop sinning in all things said and done as the people give an account of all things said and done unrighteous daily. The world has become a fearful place to live if you do not have God in your life. The times are now times disaster has struck in every part of the world in every family as many things are happening quick and fast without warning. It is without fail many people in the world quickly awaken unto the ways and spirits of God to serve God in spirits in truth leading to ways of eternal living eternal life. The times are now times to endure all things happening around you with much truth, faith, and patience within you knowing ye are standing before God and God's chosen elect people calling judgments and justice daily.

The times are now times to rise and be made whole by the renewing of your mind unto the powerful spirits of God. The times are now times to hold firm to your faith in God knowing God is the spirits in the waves of the air over all souls in the entire world. The time is time to make full account of all sins surfing the earth until all sins perish from the earth. The times are now times to know that sins cause sickness and death upon the people in the world. The times are now times to know the wicked sins of the people are for sex and monetary reasons have ruined the minds of the people. It is redemption with obedience to God is in the world is plainly in view in the people of God. The command from God is for the Prophets of prophesy in spirits in truth the things of God called unto the people.

The times are now times to build the alter of God in the elect chosen Holy ministries continually showing the foundations of Holiness Temples firm steadfast unmovable keeping the gospel laws of God in mind in all things said and done. The stiff necks of the people have passed away from the face of the heavens on earth perishing away with the sins of the people. There are many people lay down to sleep never to awake from their sleep but have perished in their sleep. There are many people perish from a lack of wisdom and knowledge because of the foolish imaginations of the heart. The religious style of Pentecostal Holiness Temples is the only acceptable religion with the stamp of approval from the spirits of God. The religious styles of the people are not approved of by God without Holiness in all things said and done no one can enter eternal life. It is for this reason many people die in sins unforgiving because they knew not the ways of God leading to eternal life. The many traditions cause many people to lose out on eternal life for a lack of understanding of wisdom and knowledge in the ways of God has already gone forth.

The spirits of the Holiest Highest Priest Prophet are exceedingly great making known the manifestations of the spirits of God unto the people as the mysteries of God unfold. It is made known those who endure until the end of all sins, sickness, and death are saved unto eternal life. All things made known come to pass instantly and quickly as the Lord speak to the people face to face through the chosen elect people of God. It is thy faith in the gospel of Holiness makes you whole. It is the imagination of the heart fool many people because of a lack of knowledge many refuse to live in the spirits of truth, faith, Holiness, and patience, causing themselves to lose out on eternal life. It is for those who follow in the spiritual words of God continue to prosper in the promise lands. It is those who have rebelled against the words of God are cursed with a curse and cut off from eternal life.

The times are now times to walk by faith in the spirits of God by allowing God to renew your mind daily in truth in spirits of God. The way to God the way to eternal life has been prepared for you in this gospel book of law. Behold are these words spoken and written unto you in spirits in truth. The Prophet speaks and writes as she is moved by the Holy spirits of God to do so in this present time of now times. The restoring of the earth is forming daily to the dedicated people that have commit themselves to God in spirits in truth in all things said and done. The chosen elect Priesthood glorify God in paving the way for the Holiness followers of God to be saved unto eternal life as the spirits of God continue to stretch forth into the people of God.

I the Lord your spiritual God say to the people in the heavens which are on earth, behold the Holies Highest Priest Prophet in whom I God am well pleased is the most Holiest One an angel of God in spirits of God in truth of God in whom I God have imputed all spirits to lead the way to a paradise heavens on earth. The Prophet of the Highest always hears my voice writing and speaking as I God call her to do. The times are now times to see the evidence of judgments and justice being fulfilled upon a world of people in all the heavens on earth. The times are now times; all things written and called by the mouth of the Holiest High Priest Prophet are fulfilled over the entire earth.

The violent people of the earth are uncovered and judged with justice in every part of the heavens on earth. The people with violent hearts cannot enter eternal living eternal life on a paradise earth, for the paradise heavens is a peaceful place. The work of violence is stoned in judgment. The people in the heavens on earth see the work of God prevail in the wrath of judgments and justice working to the good of the people who inherit the paradise heavens on earth. The times are now times every leader in leadership lying to the people. ye profit not from the people, but are brought to shame in all things said and done in all things hid from the sight of the people uncovered. The times are now times all leadership untrustworthy uncovered to their shame. The days are the last days of the sinners as many unexpected things uncover their sins without warning without fail right before them in all kinds of diverse manners.

The destructions of the wrath of God come without warning without fail as the years and seasons make known the wrath of God in the earth. The times are now times to remember the judgments and justice of God are before you daily calling into account the unrighteousness of the people. The brightness of God spirits leads to the righteous flock of God as there are no flock left in the stalls of the ungodly religious congregation using the people for sex and monetary reasons. The days are days that the herds of the unrighteous leaders in leadership are cut off from the folds, but them that are chosen people of God come out of the unrighteous folds rejoicing in the salvation of God with the strength of God in them in all things said and done. The uncertain paths of the people cease in the

143

judgments and justice of God. The times are now times to hear the voice of God direct your path to eternal living eternal life. The times are now times to stray not from the eternal words of God sent to lead and guard the people to eternal life. The times are now times you need God in your life more than ever before in times like these upon the people. The times are now times to know when the dust clears from all things said and done in the earth the people of God will be still standing, but the wicked cease.

The times are times to know the things of God are accomplished in all things said and done daily in every part of the earth. The times are now times to know the people of God have wisdom and knowledge in all things pertaining to being saved unto eternal life. The times are high times with visions from God performing the promise of the promise lands to the people of God. The times are times God make eternal ways performed through the people of God. The times are now times to know for sure you hear from God in that ye fall not on stony ground losing the way to eternal living eternal life. The times are now times to know eternal life is not for those who do not believe but is for those who believe in receiving eternal life. The times are now times to fix your spirits on the eternal things of God for the purpose of eternal living eternal life. The times are now times to believe in these words written and spoken unto you in that ye loose not the way to eternal living eternal life knowing ye are daily in the present eternal spirits of God daily.

10

The Paradise Heavens without Focus on Gender, Race, Creed, or Color

The focus of God is on the people with intentions of crossing-over into eternal living eternal life in the heavens which is on earth. The promises of God are not focus on gender, race, creed, or color. The focus of God is for the people to turn from their sins as God heals the lands. The people are commanded to be Holy followers of God hearing and doing the deep things of God heard from within them. The paradise heavens are formed without gender, race, creed, or color without prejudice gathering holiness Christianity as servants and disciples of God. The powers of the Holiness leaders in leadership lead the people to cross-over into the power eternal living eternal life. The spiritual ways of God are scattered upon all the face of the heavens on earth. The chosen elect Holy Temples are spirit to spirit with God face to face in spirits in truth.

The chosen elect Holy Priesthood help the people to cross-over into the power of eternal life. There is 2 Holy Priest over one COGIC Temple, a Bishop and Apostle over one Temple over one congregation of people. There are only10 males Elders there is only 6 Prophets, males and\or females there is only 6 Evangelist females only, assigned to each chosen elect COGIC Holy Temple Incorporated. These are they which are the 24 chosen elect Holy Priesthood assigned to sit in the judgment seat of God with power to judge the people and guide them to eternal life. The chosen followers of God are commanded to be hearers and doers of the deep things of God in spirits in truth.

The times are now times to build up the chosen elect COGIC Holy Tabernacles of God over the entire heavens on earth. The times are now times to hear the voice of God by fasting and praying, ye then become humble unto the spiritual voice of God in all things said and done according to the spirits of God. The spirits of God went forth into all the chosen elect Holy COGIC Tabernacles. It is I; God take all spirits of the people by force. It is I; God take all the lands of the people by force. The heavens which is on earth uncovered by the mouth of the Holiest Highest Priest Prophet ever to walk the heavens on earth in your time of now times. The Holiest Highest Priest Prophet stood and measured all things said and done in the heavens on earth writing them down according to measures in the seven seals pouring them out in the wrath of judgments and justice of God. The fig tree does not blossom for the unrighteous neither does there be any

146

fruit in the vines of the ungodly. There is no escaping eternal judgments and justice for the unrighteous.

The times are now times all things said and done ungodly in the earth are in failure, all people, places, and things yield to the spirits of God and God's people. The spirits of God and God's people are in all high places calling judgments and justice. The times are now times all people, places, and things are measured calling all ungodly deeds forth. The powerful spirits of God have struck forth in every part of the earth striking unrighteousness in a whirlwind scattering all people, places, and things said and done ungodly. It is I, God say to you, take heed in that ye are not lost by the wilderness of your mind. It is I; God call all things that needs you in the heavens which are on earth. It is I, God say to you, take heed to all things written and spoken unto you in this gospel book of laws.

It is I, God say to you, there is no females own a chosen elect Holy Temple of COGIC Incorporated. It is I, God say to you, there are no females over the congregations of the chosen elect Holy Temples of COGIC Incorporated. It is I God say to you, male is always the head of the household of the chosen elect Holy Temples of COGIC Incorporated. It is I; God say to you all congregations are under the leadership of the Bishops in the chosen elect Holy Temples of COGIC Incorporated. It is I, God called males to Preach; it is I; God call females to speak and not Preach. The females are Evangelist or Prophets; the males are Bishops, Apostles, Prophets, and Elders, in the chosen e ect Holy Ministry Priesthood of COGIC Incorporated. It is I, the Lord your spiritual God say to you, females are not called to Preach at any time. I, God say to you, the men take over the authority of the chosen elect Holy Temples. It is I, God say to you,

147

women take heed to these things written and spoken unto you in that ye loose not eternal life on a paradise earth at the end of all sins, sickness, and death cease when all judgments and justice are finished in the heavens which is on earth. I, God say to men, there is no male Evangelist in the chosen elect Holy Temples of COGIC Incorporated.

It is I, God say to you, take heed to these things written and spoken unto you in that ye loose not eternal life cast beneath the earth. It is I, God say to you, all chosen elect Holy Priesthood of COGIC always sit in the pulpit in that ye watch over the people spirits in the congregation. I say to you, there be no chosen elect Holy Priest Ministers men and women sitting in the congregation interfering with the spirits in the congregations, for the Holy Priest have a need to watch the spirits in the congregations at all times in that ye distract not the spirits have need to be heard and seen. It is I, God say to you, make room in my house for my people. I, God say to the people in the heavens which are on earth, all people are walking spirits in the heavens on earth. All visiting Priest Ministers sits on one side of the church for Priest Ministers only.

I the Lord your spiritual God say to you, there is no-one over the Holiest Highest Priest Prophet that has ever walk the heavens on earth in your time of now times. I, God say to you, the spirits of God are over the Holiest Highest Priest Prophet to lead the chosen elect Holy Priesthood in all things said and done by the way of Holy inspired spirits of God. The times are now times to see to it that ye be called by your God given name as Prophets, Bishops, Apostles, Elders, and Evangelist in Ministry. I, God have a need for you to be known to help my people cross-over into eternal life. The times are now times to keep standing when the dust clears

148

knowing it is not race, creed, or color that is important to God; it is saving souls of the people that are important to God.

The new creations of things promised from the beginning of times are now here prophesied in spirits in truth. The words of God are written and spoken that has been reserved for such times as these now in judgments and justice all things said and done in the heavens on earth. All spirits of God the people have a need for have gone forth in all the heavens on earth unto all nations, kindred, and people. The joy of the people is the strength of the Lord God's glory and honor in the chosen elect Holy Temples COGIC Incorporated. The people living in the wilderness of their mind refuse to accept the truth.

Behold the strength of Holiness is in all the heavens on earth accomplishing the purposes of God through the spirits of the Highest angel of God writing the Revelations of God. The Revelations of God written and spoken brings fear and understanding of the ways of God called unto the people in the heavens which are on earth. The spirits of God are in control in all the heavens on earth. The spirits of God and God's people are quickly destroying all unrighteous spirits in roaming the entire world.

The times are now times to give full account of deeds done continually as time as grown to be too late upon many people and grown to be not too late for others. The times are now times the Holy Ministries have grown to reign in the now eternal life Ministries of God. It is I; God have commanded the COGIC Incorporated to lead my people into eternal living in all things said and done. I, God say to you forget not a Prophet has been raised up as the Greatest Holiest Priest Prophet in the world in your times of now times leading and guiding the people to cross-over into eternal living eternal life in the heavens on earth. I, God say to the people in the heavens which are on earth, the people are in a falling state of mind have a need to rely on the Holiest Highest Priest Prophet ever to walk the heavens on earth in your times of now times.

The times are now times to remember the Prophet of the Greatest the Prophet of the Holiest the Prophet of the Highest make straight the prepared way to eternal living eternal life in the heavens which are on earth. The people, places, and things pertaining to God are at hand standing before the face of the people. I, God say to you the Prophet of the greatest bear record of the greatest spirits to ever walk on the planet of the heavens which are on earth. I, God say to you, I, God stand before the Greatest Prophet of all times, at all times planting her feet on higher grounds for the leading of the sheep in that no sheep be lost without a trail to come back to God. I, the Lord your spiritual God say to you, the spirits of the Holiest Prophet have been scattered over the entire heavens on earth. I, the Lord your spiritual God say to you, the knowledge and wisdom of the Highest Prophet have been spread over the entire heavens on earth.

The true Prophet with the spirits of God speaks and writes the spirits of God unto the people in the heavens which are on earth. The spirits spoken into the heavens on earth by the Greatest Prophet are scattered in spirits in truth unto whom and where it belongs. The powerful spirits of the Greatest Prophet are standing before the people daily over the entire world of people without fail. The spiritual heavens on earth are ruled with powerful spirits of God and God's people. The chosen elect meek inherit the earth taking it by spiritual forces from God. The promises of God are fulfilling the earth forever is God's glory and honor.

The angels of God watch over the people of God. The paths of God's people are marked by the spirits of God directed by the spirits of God. There is no one that can contain the people of God from the works of God at no time. There is no one who can escape the spirits of God's eternal judgments and justice prevailing in the heavens on earth. The presence of God's spirits daily meets the people face to face in the heavens on earth. The presence of God's spirits brings about a change in everyone's life. All things work to the good of the people cross-over into eternal living eternal life. The present spirits of the people are like a see-through glass to the Holiest Highest Priest Prophet. There is nothing un-notice in the spirits of the people by the Holy one. The Holy one detects all things said and done in spirits in truth in the heavens on earth. The times are now times to take heed to what is written and spoken to you in this gospel book of laws, in that ye are not cast beneath the earth.

The power of the Holy one is manifested to the people diligently through the mysteries of God unfolding before their eyes. The powers of the people of God brought forth the eternal judgments and justice of God upon the unclean hearts of the people. The chosen elect people of God speak with all authority of God in their spirits in truth holding back nothing without respect of person. The cleansing of the heavens on earth has already descended from the heavens on earth. The spirits of God have descended from on high in every corner of the heavens on earth. The spirits of the Holy one is fountains of living water unto eternal life on a peaceful earth. The chosen elect people of God represent God in power in

151

flesh in spirits in Holiness in truth in strength in faith in peace in trust and in love already gone forth in all the earth.

The heavens now opened on earth with great multitudes of people gathered in the heavens in the COGIC Holy Temples of God. There within the multitudes of people are the chosen elect people of God judging the people in the cross-over to eternal life. The chosen elect 24 Holy Priesthood in each COGIC Temple pave the way to eternal life as commanded by the Holy spirits of God. The chosen elect Holy Priesthood speak exceedingly great things in their spirits in truth. The chosen elect Holy Priesthood speak exceedingly great judgments and justice in their spirits in truth. The Holy One perceives all spirits near and far in heavens on earth. This is just another day the spirits of the Lord have kept the people of God from all hurt, harm, and danger because their minds continue to stay on the Lord.

The rumors of the Holiest Highest Priest Prophet ever on earth in times of now times among the people has spread reference the Holiest Highest Priest Prophet is a woman speaking and writing the revelations of God in her spirits in truth walking on the face of the heavens on earth. A genuine author of the new laws of God has written the revelation of times the people has been looking for a long time is now here. These things written are Holy and true paves the way to eternal living eternal life on a paradise earth. The quick boldness of Holiness instantly rebukes the people standing before the chosen elect people of God. The multitudes of Holy people inherit all the promise lands of unrighteous people. The times are now time to behold the deep-dept thereof God's eternal justice operating in the heavens on earth. The Holy One bear record of the deep spirits of God dwelling within her. The deep spirits of God over power the people in the heavens on earth. The deep spirits of Holiness are gone forth in all the heavens on earth in every land. The times are now time of the latter days of the Holy gospel building highways to eternal life heavens on earth. The times are now time the heavens on earth form one big Holy land within the cross-over into eternal living eternal life.

The wholeness of the chosen elect Holy Temples has built the Holy gospel of God through inspired spirits of Holy people of God. The world of people discovers God's chosen elect Holy people worshipping in the COGIC Temples has been brought forth in all the heavens on earth. All the nations in the heavens on earth become as one in one big Holy land. The spirits of God and God's chosen elect people have brought the people into captivity of the new things of God in their spirits in truth. It is in the waves of the air the spirits of God's covenants contain prophecies proceed forth from the Holy One. The fullness of the Holy gospel is within the COGIC Holy Temples as all other denominations fade out. The times are now times only the chosen elect Holy Temples stand in the heavens on earth.

The times are now times the people see the things of God standing in the plain open wide spaces of the heavens on earth. The times are now times of all things ye have need of are standing open in plain view written and spoken unto you. The times are now time the Holy gospel is exceedingly great. There are many people wish to see what the Holy One see and hear but will never be able to see and hear what the Holy One see and hear. The many things forming has been manifested unto the people from the Holy One. The voice of the Holy One is the voice of God scattered upon all the face of the heavens on earth. The times are the now times

God specializes in the impossible through the chosen elect people of God in the heavens which is on earth.

The established Holy gospel of God is seen among the chosen elect people of God. The times are now times the first be last and the last be first in all things said and done in the heavens which is on earth. The spiritual forces of God and God's people achieve all things through the purity of pure clean spirits in faith in truth. The Holiness believers unfold in all the heavens on earth. The power of the Holy spirits of God is poured out in all the heavens on earth. The power of the Holy One prevails fulfilling all people, places, and things in the heavens on earth. The words of God are written and spoken in easy plain and clear words for the people to understand the ways of God's eternal purpose from the beginning of times up until this very day. The times are now times all nations have humble themselves under the mighty hands of God.

There is no one certain race judged more than the other; all people are one and the same before God in the spirits of the chosen elect people of God judging all people, places, and things said and done in the heavens on earth. The times are now times to behold the inspired anointed versions of ordained powerful spirits of the Holy One writing the true words of God called from spirits out of the original King James Holy Bible in this gospel book of laws. The due season of people, places, and things come forth at the appointed times and seasons without fail. The call of the spirits from the King James Bible original verses are imputed in these gospel book of laws with clear understanding dividing the wicked from the righteous. This gospel book of laws interprets visions speaking judgments in the eternal justice of God. All people, places, and things of God are in the spirits of the

Holy One written and spoken unto you in truth in inspired ordained spirits of the Holy One.

There many great things spoken and written plain unto you ye now easily understand. The writing of this gospel book of laws is plain that ye can speak with clear understanding. The times are now times that the people hearts are grieved with many people, places, and things cause grief in their lives. The people have been divided up into groups of cultural poor culturally rich standing in judgments before God and the chosen elect people of God. The people have cause themselves many sorrows by their own inflicted cultural greed. A great destruction has failed upon the people of cultural greed in every corner of the heavens on earth. The times are now times the people have a need to see each other as one and the same as people of God. The prayers of the righteous are being answered at appointed times in seasons and out of seasons in the blink of an eye in the instant quickness of God.

The times are now times that the fullness of God and God's chosen elect people nourishes the people crossing-over into eternal living eternal life. The true promise hope is unfolding daily before the eyes of the people in the heavens which are on earth. The hope of a better world is forming during the people without notice as the spirits of God and God's people take all people, places, and things by force. The ways of God are scattered upon the face of the earth among the people. The powerful spirits of God are standing over every person in the heavens which is on earth. The times are now times the latter-day saints are in the chosen elect Holy Temples called by the spirits of God to inherit the paradise heavens on earth at the end of all sins, sickness, and death cease in the heavens on earth. The

155

spirits of this gospel book of laws are before the spirits of the people in the heavens on earth. The new creation of God great works forming daily are before the people of God in their spirits in truth. The reward of the heavens on earth is here standing before the people in the heavens on earth.

The promise to wipe away every tear is here forming all things to the good of the people. The times are now times bringing fellowship in the chosen elect Holy Temples. The times are now times the people tremble at the present spirits of the Holy One in respect for the powerful spirits of God standing before the Holy One. The sharpness of God's powerful presence over-powers the spirits of the people. The manifestations of the spirits of God are boldly present standing before the people. The people feel the effect of the bold powerful spirits of God operating in their presence. The people, places, and things in the heavens on earth have been gathered under feet of the chosen elect people of God.

The things are written unto you in this gospel book of laws are faithful and true leading to eternal life on a paradise heaven on earth. The faith of the people is tested by the least things they expect. The times are always now times to be aware of all things happening around you. The people have a need to live according to the spirits God are calling upon them to receive eternal life. The times are now times to be open to the spirits of God in your spirit now more than ever before in that ye not miss what ye have a need for, in your spirits in truth. The times are now times ye have a need for all these things written and spoken unto you.

11

The Voice of God Lights the Minds of the People

The spirits of God are in the I ght of the world confronting the minds of the people. The signs and wonders of God and God's chosen elect people have confronted the people spirits of those who are in disbelief God is operating the world in people, places, and things. The signs of the times form mighty miracles as well as the wraths of God over the entire world have showed up in every part of the earth. The resurrection of spiritual minds is for the people who have forgiving sins among them. The times are now times all people, places, and things not eternal fade out from eternal living eternal life. There is no peace in the heavens on earth until all sins have been judged finished and the paradise heavens appear.

157

The people in the dark are brought to the light of all things they have a need to know concerning eternal living eternal life. The fruit of the spirits of God dwell in the heavens on earth. The deep voice of God has come out in the minds of the people in every part of the heavens on earth.

The latter day chosen elect Holy Priesthood has all wisdom and knowledge you have need of in the new things of God. The people have been called under the mighty acts of the laws of God without fail. The traditional mind set of the people have already been over-thrown by the spirits of God and God's chosen elect people. The people have over-come traditional ways of doing things as traditional ways fades from the minds of the people. The times are now times behold the words of God have manifested in the gospel laws of God. It is from generation to generation the words of God written and spoken prevails bringing changes to a dying world of people. The new level of respect for God and God's chosen people has formed among the people in the heavens which are on earth. The times are now times to live eternal life with equal living conditions and justice for all people in every part of the heavens which are on earth.

I, God say to the people in the heavens which are on earth, become strong in your faith by the powerful acts taken place in your life. I, God say to you, I bring you restoration in every part of the heavens on earth. I, God say to you, the generations of now and the generations to come see my mighty works done in all the heavens on earth without fail. I say to you, all things are happening to the good of those who love the Lord your spiritual God. I the Lord your spiritual God say to you, spirits of death grieve every family in the land in every part of the heavens on earth. The times are the now times the earth is being rebuilt to accommodate eternal living eternal life paving the way for a paradise peaceful earth.

The people in the heavens which are on earth hearts ponder after seeing and hearing these things written and spoken appearing in the heavens on earth. I the Lord your spiritual God say to you, the Holy One has already condemn the earth in the eternal judgments and justice of God in all things said and done in every part of the heavens which is on earth. The light of spiritual Holiness allows the people to see clearly that they have been living in the process of eternal death within the general traditional practices instead of in the process of eternal life. The traditional practices in the system of govern laws of politics which have no favor with God and without trust in God as stated on federal funds, in God we trust.

The times are now times to take away the obvious doubts that exist about God and live in the good spiritual mind set of self-trust. The mind set of trust self is to believe in God because God is within your heart and mind working all things to the good of you. The things that come to mind and work to the good of you is God speaking to your mind in your spirits. The works and character (activities and actions) of a person are the spirits of that person that stands before God in spirits in truth. The wise judgments of God judge the works of the people which stands before God daily in all things said and done. The times are now times to let not your works and living be in vain with God and the chosen elect people of God. The awful fear of guilt and misery expediently awake all people of this world to the true reality of God and God's chosen elect people. The expedient consequences of ungodly behavior face the unrighteous every day.

The light of God shines upon the face of the heavens which are on earth, behold the people in the land of the living continuously. The light of the world is God operating in the heavens which is on earth. The new creation of a new world is in the fullness of the heavens on earth. The times are now times to realize death and life is in the power of each responsible individual. The times are now times to make good choices knowing right choices from wrong choices. The times are now times to lift your hearts and rejoice over the new creation of a new paradise world. The unrighteous stout hearted evil wicked people are brought low in judgments and justice of God and God's chosen elect people. The chosen elect Holy Temples of COGIC are the light of the world "house of God" exalted above all the mountains and hills.

All nations worship God in Holy COGIC Temples merging with the chosen elect Holy people of COGIC all over the world. This I, God say to you, this is commanded to enter eternal life; ye must worship in spirits in truth as one big Holy Land. The gospel laws of God have gone forth into all the people of the world in the heavens which is on earth. The generations of now and the generations to come, learn to walk in the light of God's new creations without fail. The unrighteous people are forsaken by the light of God as evil, wicked, prejudice, un-equal, sins, sickness, and death are destroyed perish from the new world order.

The judgment call of perilous times stands daily before God and God's chosen elect people. In the light of the world all people, places, and things are on one accord according to the will of God's purpose for the people since the beginning of times. The times are now times all people have gone into captivity because of a lack of wisdom and knowledge as hell on earth has enlarged as death beneath the earth has enlarged. The times are now times God is saying woe unto al evil wicked unrighteous prejudice people, woe unto you who call evil good and call good evil putting bitter for sweet and sweet for bitter. The light of God's words written and spoken unto you is exalted in every high place in every part of the heavens on earth. There is no judgment stone left un-turn.

The times are now times behold the Holiest Highest Priest Prophet has risen in the spirits of God in the truth of God. The chosen elect Holy COGIC Temples are near and far among the people operating in the marvelous works of God's Holy spirts in truth accomplishing God's purpose for the people crossing-over into eternal life. The people in the heavens on earth are convinced nothing but Holiness stands in the spirits of God and God's chosen elect people of COGIC. I the Lord your spiritual God say to you, it is I the Lord your God have called the chosen elect COGIC forth to the judgment seat of God to judge the people in the heavens which is on earth. I, God say to you, stop looking for me to come; I, God am here in spirits in truth within you and have not ever left the earth as I, God have watched all things said and done in the heavens which is on earth.

The times are now times; nothing in the earth will be left standing that is not in the will of God. The times are now times; all people, places, and things in the heavens on earth judged unforgiving come forward instantly quickly in judgments to the eyes and ears of the people. The judgments of God and God's people are not far off neither far away from all people, places, and things judged unrighteous. The times are now times all things hid in every situation are uncovered and touched in judgments by the spirits of God and God's chosen elect people. I, God say to the people in the heavens on earth, take heed that ye stumble not at these things written and spoken that are before you. I, God say to you, all these things written and spoken unto you are true and righteous revelations prophesied.

The times are now times in the eyes of the people supernatural being of powerful acts of God and God's chosen elect people powerfully judging the people in all things said and done in the heavens which are on earth. There be no one can touch the anointing spirits of God's people that have over-powered the people in the heavens on earth in spirits in truth. The chosen elect people of God see through the people as clear as looking through a clear glass. The mighty miracles of God and God's chosen elect people are signs and wonders in the heavens which are on earth. The mission of the chosen elect COGIC disciples is to pave the way to eternal life baptizing the people in Holy water teaching and preaching eternal living eternal life according to this gospel book of laws of God called unto them in spirits in truth.

The sacred spirits of God are within the chosen elect people of God. The people in the heavens which are on earth reap the benefits of the end of all sins, sickness, and death at the end of the last judgment call and the paradise heavens on earth appears. The times are now times to repent quickly before it is too late. The times are now times for the den of thieves with groups of support to repent and reframe from using God as a forefront for monetary reasons of self-gain before it is too late and you lose the way to eternal living eternal life along with the groups that support you. These things ought not to be done have set themselves up for eternal judgments with the loss of eternal life. Wherefore ye people call your self-

Ministers labor for money using God in vain as a forefront for self-gain have stored up riches in vain I, God say to you.

I, God say to you, ye have use the name God to bless your sins in the midst of the followers the people you have misled in your congregations that are eternally judged with you if they do not repent before it is too late and they lose their way to eternal life. I, God say to you, ye are curse with a curse for these things of self-gain and ye have not helped my people whom ye have continuously robbed before their faces. I, God say to you, all religious Ministers and their congregations have strayed away from Holiness for self-gain are daily standing before the judgments of God and God's chosen elect people. The times are now times ye under-cover thieves give an account in an instant in a blink of an eye eternal judgments are upon you as ye know who you are using God for a forefront for monetary reasons. I, God say woe to you who have made the house of prayer Temple a den of money thieves' money changers.

It is I; God say to you, the time is now up for monetary self-gain off the people who have trust you only to be robbed. I, God say to you, there is no other side beyond the graves beneath the earth. There be no one escape the righteous judgments of God and the chosen elect people of God. The times are now times to pray calling out to God; not calling out to Jesus, not calling out to the father. The times are now times to know God is not Jesus, God is not the father. The times are now times to know God is a spiritual being within you in spirits in truth. It is I; God say to you, I am God all by myself. I, God have told you before, ye have been misled by your forefather since the beginning of times added and took spirits from the Bible doing things I, God told them not to do, the same as Adam and Eve

163

did what I, God told them not to do. I, God say to you, no prayers are answered in Jesus name no prayers are answered in the name "father" for I, God have told you, I am God at all times all by myself in spirits in truth. All prayers in names other than God are in vain; your prayers are always prayed to God.

It is I, God say to you, take heed unto these things written and spoken unto you, in spirits in truth. I, God say to you, ye must pray in the spirits of God and no other names hindering your spirits. The praying of prayers to Jesus fades out from the face of the heavens which is on earth. The praying of prayers to the father fades out from the face of the heavens which is on earth. It is I; God have mercy unto them that repent of these things and pray unto me in the Holy spirits worshiping in the chosen elect Holy Temples. I, God say to you, take heed in that ye fall not by the wayside in all things said and done. I, God say to you, behold I do a marvelous work in your times among all nations in the heavens on earth. I, God say to you, I, God have made covenants with the chosen people of God have proceeded forth out into all the heavens which are on earth. I, God say to the people in the heavens which are on earth, my words are many, saying out with the old and in with the new people, places, and things of eternal living eternal life.

I the Lord your spiritual God say to you, ye now read all comprehendible words in plain easy to read words in that ye make no mistakes becoming perfect people of God as I God had plans for you from the beginning of times. It is I; God have come to you with more directions and instructions than ever before in that ye understand for the benefit of eternal life awarded to the people who endure until the paradise earth appears. It is I, God say to the people in the heavens which is on earth, take nothing for granted from day to day, for you do not know ahead what a day will bring you in an instant. It is I; God say to you; be careful about nothing in that ye be not misled by the wilderness (mental illness state of mind) state of mind. I say to you, there are many people living in the wilderness of their mind with no way out even with guidance, for they are too far gone in the deep wilderness (mental illness state of mind) of their mind.

I the Lord your spiritual God say to you, ye have been warned of many things as you know destructions of judgments stands before unrighteousness without warning in all things said and done in the heavens which are on earth. It is I, God have called a set order of things unto you, in that ye take heed without fail knowing there be no judgment stones left un-turn for the benefit of eternal life The times are now times the unrighteous quickly feel the effects of powerful actions of eternal judgments and justice of God. I, God say to the people in the heavens which are on earth, pray much, for ye have a need to hear from me in spirits within you in spirits in truth in all things said and done in the heavens which are on earth. It is I; God say to the people in the heavens, my words written and spoken unto you are Holy, faithful, and truth. It is I; God say to you; my chosen elect Holy people are, spiritual, faithful, and true. It is I, God say to the people in the heavens, when I God call my chosen elect people; they hear me call and they answer me. I, God say to you, the labor of the chosen elect people is heavy within clearing the heavy hearts of the people. It is beholding these things written and spoken unto you are already operating upon you.

I the Lord your spiritual God have brought forth all things written and spoken unto you. I, God say to you, receive these things written and spoken unto you within your spirits within truth within you. I the Lord your spiritual God say to you, I have sent you a comforter in flesh in body are my word written by the Holy One the Holiest Highest Priest Prophet to ever walk the heavens on earth in your times of now times. I, God say to you, these words are direct from me in spirits in truth in Holiness in the Holy One that was promised would come to you from the beginning of time for such times as these.

It is I; God say to a dying world of people, I speak my words forth of mind own pleasure according to my will for the people seeking eternal life. I, God say to a dying world of people, my work is not finish henceforth in that ye follow instructions given you in this gospel book of laws in all things said and done in that ye fall not by the way side into the wilderness of your mind. I, God say to you, at the end of the last judgment call appear the paradise heavens on earth. I, God say to a dying world of people take heed that ye endure in all things said and done in these latter days now upon you. I, God say to the people in the heavens, the unforgiving sinners continue to sin is because they know they have unforgiving sins among them as they have loss eternal life because of their unforgiving sins among them.

I the Lord your spiritual God say to you, I am within the chosen elect People of God speak my words according to what I God have called unto them. There are many people have suffered in ignorance of wisdom and knowledge even at this present time. There are many things happening must happen paving the way eternal living on a peaceful earth. There are

166

many stiff neck people in the world who have refuse the Prophets from the beginning of times. There are many people who say there is no modern-day Prophets in the world. It is I the Lord your spiritual God say to you, I send the Prophets whom I, God choose, when I choose, and where I choose. I say to you, there has always been Prophets among the people in the heavens which are on earth. The people must serve God in spirits in truth to know real Prophets from false Prophets to know real religion from false religion to know real Ministers from false Ministers.

I the Lord your spiritual God say to you, I am good spirits within you; I am truth within you working all spirits within you to the good of you. I, God say to you concerning the Holy Prophets sent unto you, ye have harden your hearts and understood not, but have lean to your own understanding without wisdom and knowledge in the spiritual realm of the things of God. I the Lord your spiritual God say to the people in the heavens on earth, I, God have been among you always without notice as I, God continue still among you without notice within the people of God within spirits of people who believe in the spirits of God. I, God say to you, ye having no acceptance to the spirits of good things within you is God, ye are misled by foolish spirits within you. The things written unto you are the plain and simple truth about God advising you to follow the truth making straight your pathway to eternal life.

I the Lord your spiritual God say to you, there is no one over the Holiest Highest Priest Prophet but the spirits of God within her. I the Lord your spiritual God say to you, the spirits of God and God's chosen elect people reign in the heavens which is on earth. It is with expedient recovery people come back to God are caught up with God in spirits in truth in faith

167

within self. The times are now high times of God's eternal judgments operating in the heavens on earth. The chosen elect Holy Priesthood Ministers must be ordained on paper and ordained by the Holy spirits of God spiritually hearing from God in spirits in truth within self before being over the congregation of people. All chosen elect Holy Priest Ministers must be inspired and anointed to preach eternal life from this gospel book of laws call according to the will of God. The duty of the chosen elect Holy Priest Ministers is to watch over the souls of the people, help the people to cross-over into eternal spirits of eternal living eternal life. The chosen elect Holy Priest Ministers keep the people nourished in spirits in truth enduring the latter day's judgments of God.

The times are now times for the people to realize they are governing under the mighty spirits of God's sprits of eternal living eternal life. I the Lord your spiritual God say to you, all these words written and spoken unto you have already went forth in the heavens on earth. I the Lord your spiritual God say to you, all these words of this gospel book of laws have went forth in spirits in truth in every part of every land. The times are now daily signs of the times calling to judgment all unrighteous living conditions and unrighteous ways of the people. It is I, God say to you, make no mistake by these things written unto you. The spiritual words of God are spoken into existence spreads over the entire earth.

The signs of the times are written in words called into existence are the signs of the Prophet here in the presence of the people in the earth. The signs of the times are now times to listen to the words of God written unto you are valuable to you for crossing-over into eternal life in that you lose not the way to eternal life. The chosen elect Holy COGIC Temples is the way to guidance of eternal life. The times are now times the gospel laws of God are put into action quickly without fail. The chosen elect Holy Priesthood do not pay tithes and offerings of any kind. The single parents with under age children at home pay no tithes; the elderly pay not tithes, the widows pay no tithes, anyone with eternal injuries or eternal sickness pay no tithes, and those who do not have enough for their cost of living for the month do not pay tithes. The times are now times to be not dismayed, but endure until the end of all sins, sickness, and death cease keeping a sound mind in all things said and done. The times are now times of, in with the new things call by the spirits of God according to the need of the people. The people must endure trying times like these with much faith and patience holding out until the end of all judgments and justice of God as the paradise earth appears at the end.

The times are now times the work of God is at hand in every part of the earth. The times are now times to pray much, attending the chosen elect Holy Temples staying among the chosen elect saints of God in that ye receive much strength to endure. The times are now times ye have a need to find yourselves among the chosen elect saints of God where the spirits of God are always working according to the will of God. The chosen elect Holy saints are strong in the will of God speak strength to the weak saints. I the Lord your God say to you, take no thought of your own, but read the books of the Holy One for strength and truth in crossing-over unto eternal life. I, God say to you, ye have need to be strong for it will be alright after a while as I, your spiritual God stands daily during all things said and done in the heavens which are on earth.

I the Lord your spiritual God say to you; endure, for there are brighter days ahead at the end of all these things happening. I, God say to you, all things happening have a need to take place clearing the path to eternal living eternal life. I say to you, behold the prayers of the people are being answered according to the will God for the purpose of eternal life on a paradise earth. I say to you, the people are brought to the knowledge of the truth as God brings all things forward showing the power and authority of God's purpose for the people. The spirits of God cannot be touch by the thoughts of the people at any time. The spirits of the chosen elect people of God cannot be touched by the thoughts of the people at any time. I the Lord your spiritual God say to you, according to your faith ye receive understanding and knowledge in this gospel book of laws in all things ye have a need to know in times like these. I, God say to you, ye must be born again receiving the Holy spirits in that ye hear from God in spirits within self in truth within self. The spiritual rebirth renews your mind to the spiritual things of God reframing you from the lust of the flesh.

I say to you, unless ye are born again in spirits in truth, ye cannot in no wise way inherit eternal life. I say to you, allow the light of God to shine in your life leading you to eternal life. I, God say to you, every tongue openly confesses the eternal powers of God are operating calling the everlasting eternal judgments in the heavens which are on earth. The spirits of God and God's chosen elect people travel the heavens on earth accomplishing the purposes of God according to eternal living eternal life. The trials and tribulations of the people are not eternal. The Holy spirits of God snatches the people of God from danger saving them unto eternal life. The times are now times to have the religion of the Holy spirits of God dwelling on the inside of you eliminating foolish thinking of the mind. The Holy spirits of God want dwell in a foolish mind. The mind must be free to hear the spirits of God speak to you within the mind. The mind must always be open to true good spirits receiving what God speak unto you in spirits within in truth within.

It is I, the Lord your spiritual God say to the people in the heavens which are on earth, I, God am in every land seeing all things said and done daily. I, God am among the people in the world reigning zealously restoring earth bringing all people, places, and things into subjection of the Holy spirits of God. I, God say to you, there be no one depart from this gospel book of laws and receive eternal life. I the Lord your spiritual God say to the people in the heavens on earth; all people, places, and things in the heavens on earth are brought unto the subjections of the spirits of God and God's chosen elect people, in that is eternal living eternal life appearing on a paradise earth. I, God say to you, a people in the heavens on earth, I, God are spiritually dwelling during all things said and done in the earth daily destroying all sins. The times are now times all sins must give an account of the seen and unseen unrighteous actions of sinners refuse to stop sinning. The unrighteous sinners with unforgiving sins have failed to hear the spirits of God during them because their sins have blocked their hearing way to eternal life

The times are now times the voice of God speak all things the world have a need of to be cleansed into pureness destroying all people, places, and things not needed in eternal life. The times are now times; one God one faith one chosen elect Holy gospel religion anointed people stands before the spirits of God to judge the people and one chosen elect Holy baptism stands before the spirits of God. The unforgiving sinners are roaming to and for in the earth not knowing which way to go because the wrath of God has destroyed their minds. The unrighteous unforgiving sinners who continue to sin stands during much suffering until they are no more in the heavens on earth; are you one who continues to sin until it is too late to enter eternal life.

The vain prayers and vain cries of the unjust are not heard in the spirits of God as they see their troubles have increased upon them much more in a quick instant more than ever before. There be many of the unjust wanting to die and cannot because they have some suffering to do standing in the just judgments of God and God's people. The unjust stands during much hell cursed with a curse until buried beneath the earth turn to dust with no return to eternal life. The times are now times dead bodies beneath the earth quickly turn to dust and fade away beneath the earth. The times are now times the dead quickly fades away from the grieving memory of the people in the heavens which are on earth. The times are now times all people, places, and things perish from the earth quickly turn to dust beneath the earth. The times are now times the earth is cleansing itself from dead corpse on the grounds of the heavens which are on earth now turn to dust quickly in every part of the heavens on earth. The times are now times all people, places, and things take place in every part of the earth different than before. The times are now times all things said and done are clearing the way to a paradise heavens on earth even though it may not look like it to the naked eye; it is only in the spiritual hearing and seeing ye recognize the paradise heavens appearing hence forth forever more eternal life is appearing right befcre the eyes of the people without notice.

The times are now times to lel the" joy bells" ring in your soul crossing-over into eternal life. The peorle are the sheep of the pastures of God being shepherd into eternal living eternal life as the hypocrite goats committing iniquities sin of all kinds are separated from the sheep of God. There are many people in the world continue to sin continue to be in failure of receiving eternal life. There are many people lose the way to eternal life because of false congregations cropping up all over the world. The people fall in the same tracts as their false leaders over them having a form of religion that is false. The times are now times false religion are on false grounds are on stony grounds stoned by the spirits of God and God's chosen elect people called to judge the people in all things the people say and do in every part of the world. The people sitting under false leadership inherit the troubles of the false leader they are under.

It is I; the Lord God say to the people in the heavens on earth, the false leaders in leadership have use God as a forefront for monetary reasons long enough now give an acccunt in a quick blink of an eye. The times are now times for the people to turn around and deviate from false religious leaders before it is too late. There are many false Teachers, Prophets, Preachers, Bishops, Elders, Apostles, and Evangelists judged false separated from eternal life-giving account of deeds done refusing to stop misleading the people for monetary reasons. The times are now times the false religious leaders in the synagogues give an account quickly in every part of the world heavens on earth. The times are now times the eternal judgments of God are upon all unrighteousness. The labor of

173

unrighteousness unfolds before the people quickly in the judgments and justice of God.

The times are now times are all false religion pass away from the heavens on earth except the chosen elect Holiness people of God. The highways to the heavens are for the pure-hearts of the righteous people crossing-over into eternal life. The highways to the heavens are the chosen elect Holy Temples of the COGIC Incorporated. It is I, the Lord your spiritual God say to the people in the heavens which are on earth; all my words of this gospel book of laws are already operating in the entire world of heavens on earth. I, God say to you, there are many no-good seeds cut off from the land of the living. I, the Lord your spiritual God say to you, all leaders in every area of leadership have a need to repent making sure ye have crossed over into righteousness in the right leadership. The times are now times all false leaders in every area of leadership are brought low giving account of deeds falsely done.

I, God say to you again, all leaders must be ordained inspired and anointed by the Holy spirits of God. The Holy Priesthood of God must have a call on their life having been called to preach or speak by the Holy spirits of God. There are no false Holy leaders in leadership at any time. The false leaders in leadership must be removed from leadership quickly without fail. I, God say to you, all false leaders in leadership for money of self-gain, power, and authority give a quick account of vain deeds done misleading the people. There are many people dying in the world for a lack of wisdom and knowledge. The times are times to not put off until tomorrow what you can do right now. The times are now times to get your soul blessed right now before it is too late. The times are now times the sanctified

174

people are all on one accord in the will of God crossing-over unto eternal life identified by God as the Holy chosen people of God right now.

The doors of the chosen elect Holy COGIC Temples are open to the people of God with forgiving sins crossing-over into eternal living eternal life. The times are fixed times of what God shut no one can open; what God open no one can shut. The spirits of God and God's chosen elect people are beyond the spirits of the people in every part of the world. The times are now times all people, places, and things having no value to eternal life are cast beneath the heavens. The windows of every living soul must be opened to spiritually living eternal life. The times are now times all useless people in the heavens on earth have already lost the way to eternal living eternal life. It is I, the Lord your spiritual God say to the people in the heavens on earth, I am a just God make no mistakes in eternal judgments and justice upon the people in the world. The times are now times all things end formed from the lust of humankind; renewed by the spirits of God and the chosen elect people of God.

The times are now times to realize unforgiving sinners receive much hell on earth condemned according to judgments and justice of God and God's chosen elect people. It is eternal judgments eternal justice eternal sickness eternal deaths puts an end to sins of people who refuse to stop sinning. The judgments and justice of God are upon the unjust everyday as the unjust has harden their hearts they are afflicted with the wrath of God upon them until all sins, sickness, and death cease in the earth. It is the majesty and power of God shine forth among all people in the heavens on earth saying unto the people repent without fail and cross-over into eternal living eternal life. The proud and stout hearts of the

175

people have set their affections on the fleshly-people fleshly-places, and fleshly-things of this world. The lust of riches in material things ye suffer having no money to buy are not for you but are for you at an appointed time. The jealous hearts incubate sin bringing on trouble and hardships to many people.

The times are now times to set your hearts on the people, places, and things of God without fail before it is too late. The times are now times to walk according to the eternal will of God eternal purpose for eternal life. This gospel book of laws is written unto you according to the eternal purpose of God. The eternal purposes of the chosen elect COGIC people are to preach, speak, and judge all things within the minds of the people that work to the good of eternal life. The eternal purposes of the chosen elect COGIC people are to gather the people unto repentance with sanctified works according to eternal life.

The times are now times there are many forgiven sinners in the world of people in the heavens which are on earth saved unto eternal living eternal life. The times are now times of God's powerful acts brought forth in an instance without warning in many situations. There are many things have already manifested itself in the earth without notice to the people. There is no-one in the world that can escape the powerful actions and spirits of God in the world heavens which are on earth. The times are now times of preaching in the land to be over are drawing nearer when the just judgments of God are finished. The times are now times to know the eternal gospel laws of God are daily upon the people judging them in all things said and done in every part of the earth without fail. The times are now times the kingdom people of God take all things by forceful spirits of

176

God called in every part of the heavens which are on earth. The times are now times to know the people of God are not in bondage to the ways of humankind.

12

The Gospel Laws of God Exist Upon the People

The gospel laws of God exist upon the people God commanded all people, places, and things in the heavens which on earth renewed in the minds of the people. The destroying of sins has already taken place over the entire world. The secret works of God explore on the minds of the people. The spiritual presence of God has showed up over the entire world. The chosen elect COGIC people of God are seen and heard over the entire world. The times of serious difficulties exist upon the people. The unforgiving sinners are condemned as not receiving eternal life in the heavens which are on earth. The new dentities of a renewed lifestyle are upon the people. The times are now times all people in the heavens on

179

earth greatly fear the actions of God controlling the people have over-powered the people in every land. The call of the chosen elect Holy Priesthood is upon them as the gospel laws of God are fulfilled upon the people.

It is I, the Lord your spiritual God say to the people in the heavens which are on earth; all things said and done by the people keep the prophecies of this gospel book of laws written and spoken unto you. The times are now times to have more faith and love than ever before abounding in works in all things said and done daily. The times are now times to keep your garments of the heart spotless without wrinkles seeking God in all things said and done. Remembering the chosen elect Holy Priest Ministers baptize all people crossing-over into eternal life. The chosen elect Holy Priest Ministers always speak repentance to the people. It is I, the Lord your spiritual God say to you, ye have a need to accomplish all things written and spoken unto you in this gospel book of laws called according to the will and purpose of God leading to eternal life. Thus I, God say to you, perform all things according to the will of God called unto you. The times are now times the custom and traditions of the people continue to fade away from the face of the earth.

The times are now times all people, places, and things hearken to the voice and spirits of God. The times are now times the people have a need to know all spirits of God and God's chosen elect people are accomplishing God's eternal heavens on a paradise earth. The times are now times all people in the earth are under powerful actions of God called unto where and whom it belongs to. The times are now times all people living in the heavens on earth has a need to make the spiritual connection with God understanding all things written and spoken in this gospel book of laws of God. The times are now times all people living in the earth awaken to the spiritual presence of God standing before them daily in all things said and done.

The unrighteous are spiritually cead even though they are alive in the flesh. The righteous are resurrected unto the spiritual things of God through faith in God speaking to their spirits within them. The spiritual air waves of God are over the entire earth with control over things where there is a need to control for eternal living according to the will of God. There are many people standing before the judgments of God without notice in the earth misusing and abusing their authority used against the people. The times are now times the sacred works of God are being revealed to the people fulfilling all things called unto the heavens which are on earth. The works of God are too high to comprehend. The ways of God are pass finding out unto the people. There more and more good things of God to come to the people in the heavens which are on earth from generation to generation.

The ascension of God's spirits in the heavens revealed to the people. It is written and spoken all things in the spirits of God must be renewed. The times are now times all eternal righteousness shine forth over the entire world. The resurrection of eternal life is all people, places, and things are restored to its proper order according to the eternal purpose of God. The people in the heavens on earth see God face to face working within the spirits of the chosen elect people of God. There are people with spiritual hearing ears hear God within their spirits to spirits. The spirits of God and God's chosen elect people knows all hearts. The

181

wrath of God's anger is in judgments is a cloud in the day and fire by night upon the people dwelling in the heavens which are on earth. The times are now times the grieving rich cry and the grieving poor cry now more than ever before. The spirits of God's justice are making judgments on all things said and done in the earth. The justice of God is upon the people without notice because of their disobedience to God and the lust of their hearts. There are many people brought to repentance seeing God's judgment on sins brings death in every part of the heavens which are on earth.

The wages of sin are death is weighting heavy over the entire world of people in the heavens which are on earth. The revelations of God are now in force over the entire earth more than ever before. There be many people pass away from the earth in great numbers more than ever before because of the wages of sin. There are all manner of things happening all around the earth because of the wages of sin. There are many people sinning have been turning over unto their reprobated minds have no control over their mind to sin. The times are now times for the people to humble themselves under the mighty spirits of God asking God for wisdom and knowledge in the eternal things of God before it is too late. The call of judgment has speedily overtaken all unforgiving sinners who have refused to stop sinning in every part of the world.

The times are now times all unforgiving sinners answer to the judgment calls of God. The spirits of God are saying to the people; come unto me and I, God will give you rest. All people have come short of knowing the presence of God is operating before them in spirits in truth. It is I; God have all power in the heavens which are on earth has been written and spoken unto you since the beginning of times. There is no-one in the

182

heavens which are on earth that can stay the spirits of God operating in the earth. The spirits of God have bind up many people, places, and things in the earth. The spirits of God have loosed up many people, places, and things in the earth. It is written, all people living in the earth is call to repentance without fail. It is I, God that is angry with the people who continue to sin every day without notice standing before the wages of sin is death. The people who continue to sin have harden their hearts against righteousness losing the way to eternal living eternal life. It is time to give up sin for what is right in the cross-over to eternal life.

The spirits of God are saying take no thought for tomorrow; all things ye have need of for eternal life are added unto you in due time in due season. The times are, let each day speak for itself for you know not what a day may bring. The times are now times of new earth forming new life new equal living conditions new birth new identities new lifestyles new faith new trust new thoughts new times new seasons new food new drinks new places appears in the paradise heavens which are on earth. There are many things are happening because people believe their sins are covered and no one sees them commit their sin. The sins of the people are not committed in secret because they do not see anyone looking.

The people must realize the spirits of God see through people as God's chosen elect people see through people in the earth committing sins. The sins of the people are not covered as all hidden sins are uncovered and judged daily until all sins, sickness, and death has cease from happening in the heavens which is on earth. The secret ways of God judge all seen and unseen sin committed by the people. The people have a need to be taught their sins are not covered their sins are not unseen but are seen because the spirits of God tell spiritual mind people among them what they have done. The people a need to know spiritual mind people see right through them hearing and seeing the sins they have committed. The people must understand all hidden sins come forward in spirits in truth unto the spirits of the spiritual mind people in the heavens which are on earth. There are people in the heavens on earth live in spiritual minds live in truthful minds.

The times are now times of the people sinning in the earth come forward without fail. The times are now times the people with secret sins come forth without fail. The times are now times all people, places, and things come forward judged by the judgments and justice of God and God chosen elect people judging by spirits judging by truth. The people are troubled by many things happening in their life. The people face their troubles face to face with much endurance and faith in God. The people must realize all people, places, and things give an account in judgments whether good or bad. The spirits of God always stand over everyone touching all things said and done bringing to judgment all unrighteousness. The people must realize the wrath of God are among all unrighteousness calling judgments and justice where needed when needed. The spirits of God are a dangerous thing to not trust just because you cannot see God. The times are now times to know that God walk with you side by side and never leave you.

There be nothing left untouched in the heavens on earth as all people, places, and things give an account daily in all things said and done in the world. The minds and souls of the people are touched by the spirits of God in one way or another. The people realize the spirits of God are operating in the earth more than ever before. The people realize God is close upon the people more than ever before. I, God say to the people in the heavens on earth; times are now times to come to yourselves and stop sinning and having hate for one-another. I, God say to you, the times are now times all people "shall" know that I am God in the earth calling forth wrath on all sins big or small; sin is sin in judgment daily. The times are now times all people must seek the righteous ways of God standing in the earth.

The times are now times of all witchcraft brought forth are the things said and done by evil wicked people for the sake of self-gain are standing during judgments and justice daily in every part of the earth. The times are now times to know God have zero tolerance for sin. The times are now times to know God has over-come the world of sinners who continue to sin in all things said and done. The wrath of God has smitten the earth with famine, pestilence and destruction according to the wickedness of the people within eternal judgments of eternal justice upon unforgiving sinners who continue to sin. The times are now times to make this world a better place to live.

Behold are all people, places, and things God hath called to be sealed until the end of all sins, sickness, and death cease in the heavens on earth. Behold are all people, places, and things in the earth have been smitten with the spirits of repentance in every part of the heavens on earth. I, God say to you, all these words written and spoken unto you in this gospel book of laws are scattered over the entire world in every part of the heavens on earth. The wages of death stand upon all people, places, and things processing sin in things said and done. The times are now times I; God say to the people in the heavens on earth; everyone in this world "will" hearken unto these spirits written and spoken unto you in this gospel book of laws without fail.

It is I the Lord your spiritual God say to you; all these spirits written and spoken in this gospel book of laws are in spiritual force upon the people without fail in every part of the earth. The times are now times the forces of God slay the people quickly in an instance for lack of repentance. The people must repent and stop sinning to be saved unto eternal life. The times are now times for the last judgment call of God upon the people. It is I; God have the spiritual plans to eternal living eternal life spread to the spiritual minds of the people willing to live eternally.

The times are now times for the people to realize the Messiah the Anointed One the Holy One the Holiest Highest Priest Prophet lives among the people in the heavens on earth in flesh in body in soul in heart in Holiness in righteousness in spirits in truth in God. The times are now times for the people to realize a greater than Jesus is here a greater than Moses is here a greater than them all is here in the heavens which are on earth. The cleansing of the hearts of the people in the earth are spirits called by the Messiah according to the spirits of God within the Messiah. It is I, the Lord your spiritual God have called the promised Messiah to the people to lead them to eternal life in the promise lands appearing in every part of the earth.

The times are now times it came to pass in the latter day's judgments; people without count people without number as the sands of the sea gathered to see the Messiah televised in the lands of the living. The people in a great astonishment in the heavens on earth witness these saying in written and spoken in this gospel book of laws written under the anointing of the Greatest Messiah of all times in the times of now times. The times are now times the ascension and manifestation of the Messiah spirits are in the world heavens which are on earth. The times are now times the presence of God is within the Messiah called into existence according to the spirits of God within her.

The people see with their eyes the Messiah the Anointed One the Holy One the Greatest Prophet ever wa k the heavens on earth in the now times. The times are now times the spirits of the Messiah stirred up the hearts of the people went forth in every part of the earth. The times are now times the people are inspired by the Messiah in the heavens which are on earth. The times are now times the people are Holy and righteous in all things said and done because of the Messiah being viewed in flesh in body in soul in the heavens on earth. The times are now times the people see in natural view the presence of the Messiah. There are many people faint at the presence of the Messiah; fo the spirits of the Messiah are very powerful in spirits in truth in the heavens on earth. The Messiah in the heavens on earth is exceedingly great and powerful with mighty acts in the heavens on earth controlling the deep sacred people, places, and things in the heavens on earth.

The times are now times when the Messiah stands to speak in the chosen elect Holy COGIC Temples everyone is quite governing themselves according to what has been spoken. There is no back talk to the Messiah at any time as known all spirits are subject to the Messiah having the last say so in all situations. The chosen elect Holy Priest Ministers must take orders from the Messiah at any given t me. The times are now times there is no arguing among the chosen elect Holy Priest Ministers at no time remembering the call of judgments are upon all things said and done daily without fail. The times are now times there is no backbiting in the chosen elect COGIC Holy Temples at no time remembering the call of judgments comes in an instance at any given time.

The times are now times to remember the Messiah is the light of the world shining bright by day and by night. The times are now times to walk in the light of the truth and nothing, but the truth sent unto the people by the spirits of God in the heavens on earth. The times are now times to remember the utterance of God is upon the Messiah at any given time God speaks through the Messiah. The times are now time to remember a Prophet may speak at any given time called by the spirits of God without fail in the Temple. The Prophets only show up in the chosen elect Holy COGIC Temples when led by the spirits of God at any given time in any service. Behold a Prophet raised up Messiah in the heavens on earth have been living among many

People surround her without notice. The Messiah in the heavens on earth declaring all good spirits belong to God in all things said and done in every part of the earth. The eternal discipline of God is in every part of the heavens on earth. The transfiguration of the people happens as an individual affair in the twinkling of an eye ye are changed to the good of eternal life. The chosen people of God inherit the heavens on earth according to the will of God's purpose since the beginning of time. The spirits of God are sealed up in order in every part of the heavens on earth. The people from generation to generation who refuse to stop sinning will pass away from generation to generation until sins, sickness and death have ceased in the heavens on earth. The times are now times, blessed is ye who are not offended by this gospel book of spirits spread over the entire earth. The times are now times according to the promises of God all things promised are happening according to the will of God. The forces of God take every land have a need to be cleanse by force.

It is I; God speak all things commanded for eternal life for justice will have been served on the unjust at the appearing of a paradise earth when there will be no need for Bibles. I, God say to you, the Bible days since the beginning of times has been contradictive, for these things ought to not have been done. I, God say to you, for this reason, I have sent the Messiah to guide my people to eternal life. It is I, God say to the Messiah, write these things down in a book I, God speak unto you thus and go tell my people what I, your spiritual God have spoken unto you in spirits in truth. It is I, God say to you, the people of the past generations from the beginning of times strayed from the spirits of God for self-gain as the people of today have strayed from the Holy spirits for self-gain. I, God say to you, these are reasoning the world of people are face with the call of wrath, destruction, judgment call and justice without fail in every part of the heavens on earth.

I the Lord your spiritual God say to you, the Ten Commandments has not been lived neither followed from generation to generation. I, God behold all people have sinned and come short of respect for the good prosperous spirits of God within them. It is I the Lord your spiritual God say to you, the times are now times ye are raise in resurrection according to these prophecies written and spoken unto you in this gospel book of laws for the cross-over into eternal life forming in every part of the earth. I, God have prepared for the people in the heavens which are on earth, a straight path to eternal life as my judgments and justice are fulfilled in every part of the earth. I, God say to you, all things ye have need of for eternal life appears unto you in spirits within in truth within in every part of the earth. I, God say to you, all things written and spoken unto you are brought forth by way of eternal judgments leading to eternal life. I, God say to you, my powerful actions are at hand in every part of the world heavens on earth. I, God say to you, all my purposes are accomplished dwelling during the heavens on earth.

It is the eternal discipline of God in the earth leading to eternal life. It is the reinforcement of righteous paths that leads to the eternal spirits of God. It is the resurrection of just judgments of God leads to renewed heavens on earth. It is the things the people have a need of are expediently made manifest unto the people in the heavens which are on earth in every part of the earth. There are many people of this world have condemned themselves unto eternal death by continued living in sins in the wilderness of their minds. It is the true Holy gospel lifted in every part of the earth. The times are now times all other denomination fades out in the call of judgments and justice of God. It is I; God have drawn all seasons unto me in actions of wrath and judgments on a dying world of people as the times are now times of hope for eternal life. I, God have always been lifted in the earth in spirits in truth operating within spirits of the believers with hope of the resurrection of eternal life which is now here.

I, God say to you, all things are happening according to that which I, God have called. It is for the call of eternal life forming in the earth I, God cleanse the earth of all people, places, and things related to sin. The times

190

are now times the people of God stand before God with clean eternal Holy hearts without spot without wrinkle. I, God say to you, ye must live Holy leading to eternal life to be received in peaceful paradise heavens on earth. I, God say to you, be blessed lifted within spirits in self unto all things ye have need of on a paradise heaves on earth. It is I; God behold all people, places, and things in the earth. It is I, God sent unto you the Messiah whom have no respect of person as all people in the heavens have a need to be Holy and righteous. I, God say to you, all things written and spoken by the Messiah unto you in this gospel book of laws are quickly upon the people without fail.

This I, God say to all people in the heavens on earth, all people in this world that receive eternal life enters in at the straight gate, discipline in the Holy spirits of God within self. It is I; God say to you, I hold all powerful actions in my spirits always spread over the entire heavens on earth. It is I; God am that I am in spiritual truth without fail. I, God say to you, every thought in the heavens on earth stand before judgments daily in all things said and done in every part of the earth. I, God say to you, behold in the heavens on earth, I, God pour out blessings upon blessing within the call of just judgments that eyes have not seen neither have ears heard enter into the hearts of humankind the things I, God have already prepared for eternal life.

A transfiguration of the people heart, mind, body, and soul being caught up with God in spirit in truth in all things said and done is required at the hands of the people. The times are now times the transfiguration of God takes place within the heart, mind, body, and soul of the people in the heavens on earth. The transfiguration veil of protection surrounds the

191

people of God in every part of the heavens on earth. The spiritual angels of God are in the waves of the air in every part of the heavens on earth. The physical spiritual angels of God are in every part of the heavens on earth. The chosen people of God are converted to complete spiritual minds worshiping God in spirits in truth in the chosen elect Holy Synagogues of righteousness. The marvelous works of God are in the spiritual body of Holiness. The times are now times of eternal change unto eternal life unto eternal people in the eternal heavens on earth. The eternal change of the people is in the force of the air waves taking place in every part of the heavens on earth. The times are now times without count without measure in seasons out of seasons all people, places, and things change eternally are in the spirits of the people that are caught up with God in spirits in truth in the heavens on earth.

The people of God in the heavens on earth are known by their fruits of labor in Holiness chosen elect Temples of God. The people in other denominations other than the COGIC Incorporated chosen elect Holy Temples are out of order in false forms of religion having no hope in eternal life. The times are times of eternal latter day's eternal judgments and eternal justice of God over the entire world of people in all things said and done in the heavens on earth. The powerful actions of God are everyday upon the sinful nations of people. The eternal signs of the times are upon the people without fail in all things said and done. The people yield to the eternal signs of the times upon the chosen generations of people. The times are now times for the people to give eternal reference with respect to God and the chosen elect people of God in every part of the heavens on earth without fail.

The signs of the Messiah are upon the people without notice as the people live in the wilderness of their minds from teaching of their forefathers looking for the return of Jesus, a false teaching from the beginning of times. I, God say to you the people in the heavens on earth, I, God pointed out the Messiah before and after birth to many people surrounding her mother during these times as these Christians professing to have spiritual mind sets. It is my spirits surrounds the Messiah this very day have been over look by people who profess to be spiritual mind people surrounding her in Holy Temples she attended up to this very day, she have walk the earth without notice upon the people watching all things said and done in the earth. I the Lord your spiritual God say to the people in the heavens on earth, ye are a generation of people like the generations of people of past generations since the beginning of times profess to have spiritual minds; yet ye refuse the anointed Prophets I, God sent to you in spirits of God in spirits of truth. I, God say to you, the times are now times to repent realizing ye must be born again in spirits in truth within self. I the Lord your spiritual God say to you, ye are a people blind to the ways and spirits of God.

I the Lord your spiritual God say to you, ye that have rejected the Messiah I, God sent to you have rejected me (GOD) in spirits in truth in flesh in body in the heavens on earth. I, God say to you, ye have rejected the spiritual being of the Messiah as ye have not realize there is no return of Jesus which ye have been falsely taught by your forefathers. I, God say to this people, ye have a need for eternal change in spirits in truth within self. It is true that everyone has been blind in the eyesight of the Prophet Messiah before them without notice. I the Lord your spiritual God have brought you up to the conscious of your spiritual mind in spirits in truth reference the Messiah before you. I the Lord your spiritual God say to you, there is no return of Jesus at no time in the heavens on earth.

I, God say to you, everyone surrounding the Prophet Messiah has been blind in the eyes of the Messiah in the places she has travel and lived. It is I; God do all things according to the fit of eternal life fulfilling upon all people, places, and things in the heavens on earth. I say to you, the justice of God prevails over the entire earth without fail in all things said and done by the people. It is the power of God daily standing before all people, places, and things. I the Lord your spiritual God say to the people in the heavens on earth, the heavens on earth is mine and the fullness thereof. I, God say to you, these are critical times, much prayer is needed. I the Lord your spiritual God say to the people in the heavens on earth find yourselves among the chosen elect Holy Saints for truth in true spirits, faith, and strength leading to eternal life in the elect chosen Holy Temples of God. I the Lord your spiritual God say to the people in the heavens on earth, endure until the end of people, places, and things cease in the earth that are not eternal.

I the Lord your spiritual God say to you the people in the earth, all people, places, and things that have been stoned by the powerful eternal spiritual judgments and justice of God come forward in all things hidden in the earth are rooted up by the wrath of God. I the Lord your spiritual God say to you with a loud voice; all my words written and spoken unto you in this gospel book of prophecies are loud, plain, and clear to you in that ye understand without fail. It is I the Lord your spiritual God say to you the people in the heavens which are on earth; from the foundation of things

194

of the beginning of times up until the foundations of things of this very day are the things in the spirits of God still stand without fail are not void.

I the Lord your spiritual God say to you the people in the heavens on earth, whosoever hear these things written and spoken in this gospel book of prophecies and do them continue "wise" leading to eternal living eternal life. It is I God say to you the people in the heavens on earth, the renewed eternal foundations of life have been laid for you to build thereof without fail. I, God say to you, thereon in spirits in truth, the things of God revealed and manifested in the spirits of the people in the heavens on earth. I, God say to you, all things in spirits in truth accomplished in every part of the earth without fail. I, God say to you, all things in the spirits of the people have a need for rebuild in all things said and done daily. I, God say to you, all things called in the spirits of the people work to the good of the people for eternal living eternal life.

I the Lord your spiritual God say to you, behold, are the discipline people of God in every part of the earth I, God say to you, forget not the Holy Priest Ministers calling the repentance to God in the elect chosen COGIC Holy Temples of God in every part of the heavens on earth. I the Lord your spiritual God say to you, receive the spirits of God with open hearts leading to eternal life. I, God say woe to them that deny these revelations of God written and spoken unto you for the sake of eternal living eternal life. I say to you, these are the latter day's end of all sins, sickness, and death in the heavens on earth. I the Lord your spiritual God say to you the people in the heavens on earth, hearken unto these words ye have read in spirits in truth in that ye comprehend all things written and spoken. I say to you, turn to the spirits of God and repent of all things said and done that ought not to be said and done.

I say to you, continue not in sin, for the wrath of God is upon you daily in judgments of all things said and done. I say to you, remember the latter days of God are in the spirits of God without number without count. I God say to this people, take heed to these prophecies ye read. I the Lord your spiritual God say to you, ye have need of these things happening around you clearing the way to eternal heavens leading to eternal life on a paradise earth. I, God say to you, all things happening come like a thief in the night continue to take place in every part of the earth. I the Lord your spiritual God say to you, the wages for sin is death; when the people stop sinning death then is finished when all sins have finished in the earth. The times are now times, the divine revelations of God are fulfilling upon the people daily in every part of the earth. The people continue to pass away unto eternal death until sin is finish in the earth. I, God say to the people in the heavens on earth, there is no other way around sin; the people must stop sinning in the earth for death to cease in every part of the earth. The times are now times to give up sinning and return to God in spirits within self in truth within self.

The times are now times more than ever before are divisions spread among the people upon the face of the earth in every part of the earth. The people continue to perish in the earth for lack of wisdom and knowledge in all things said and done as the destructions of God call wrath before all things ungodly said and done. The times are now times more than ever before to be real with God in all things said and done daily knowing the judgments of God are before you daily. I the Lord your spiritual God say to you the people in the earth ye are many people teaching and preaching without being inspired by God in spirits in truth as the judgments of God are standing before you until ye cease from unrighteousness' losing your way to eternal life. I the Lord your spiritual God say to you teaching and preaching without being inspired; the synagogues sins committed are wages of eternal death saying step down while you have a chance before it is too late and the wrath of God have covered you up in eternal judgments.

I the Lord your spiritual God say to you people who refuse to hearken unto these words written and spoken clearly unto you, ye are not able to stand the eternal judgments and justice of times. I the Lord your spiritual God have spoken you, women are not Bishops, Preachers, Elders, and Apostles; women are only Prophet Ministers, and Evangelist Ministers called to speak not Preach with a loud voice; only men preach with a loud voice in the chosen elect house of God. I, God say to you, men are not Evangelist; only women are Evangelist in the chosen elect house of God. The times are now times to pay up wages of sin for denying the spirits of God called unto you now written and spoken in easy to read and understand prophecies. The times are now times many people pass away in their sleep never to awake again. The times are now times to feel God deep down in your spiritual soul as you awake to the spiritual truth of God and Gods people. I the Lord your spiritual God say to the people in the earth, blessed, is ye who are not offended by the truth of the Holy gospel of God.

The chosen elect Holy gospel of God is in all the heavens on earth fulfilling the things which are written and spoken unto you in these

197

prophecies of this book. I, God say to you, behold this is the chosen generation of people in captivity of eternal judgments of God leading to eternal living eternal life without fail. The times are now times of the first are last and the last be first fulfilling in all things said and done in every part of the earth. It is I the Lord your spiritual God say to you, the Holy Priest Ministers are ripe in the presence of God's Holy spirits with power and strength from on high in the chosen elect Holy Temples building things from the manner of the spirits of God within self. I say to you, there are many people in battle with the Holy spirits of God lose their way to eternal life slain by the Holy spirits of God. The times are now times, it is not good to grieve the Holy spirits of God, for God change not; neither bear down to sorrow and grieving spirits of the people. The times are now times many people are slain in the Holy spirits of God are saved unto eternal life.

The times are now times more than ever before the people are in distress heavy burden by bereavement of disaster causing much suffering within severe depression with serious mental and emotional disorders upon the people. The times are now times more than ever before every families in the heavens on earth mourn the loss of love ones in every part of the earth. The times are now times more than ever before to dwell in the chosen elect Holy Temples not by clock time, but by the Holy spirits of God saving the souls of the grieving people. It is I the Lord your spiritual God say to you, always allow the spirits of God to have free course in the Holy services of God. I, God say to you, it is not time that is by your side, but the Holy spirits of God is by your side. The times are now times more than ever before the chosen Holy people are brought forth to be saved in the presence of God in spirits in truth.

I the Lord your spiritual God say to you, the times are now times more than ever before; those that are not worthy of leadership in Ministry, time to step down from Ministry. I, God say to you, all people of God are nourished by the Holy spirits of God in all things said and done. I the Lord your spiritual God say to you, the Holy Priest Ministers are in strict observance of the people in the congregation at all times removing people who come to interrupt the service at all times being led by the Holy spirits of God in all things said and done. It is I the Lord your spiritual God say to you, times are times more than ever before to teach, speak, and always preach eternal living eternal life in the chosen elect Holy Temples of God.

It is I the Lord your spiritual God say to you the chosen elect Holy Ministers, miracles come by faith within the person you touch they are healed according to their faith in God. The people must trust and have faith in God in all things said and done for the land to be healed. The times are now times more than ever before the chosen elect Holy Priest Ministers must have faith and trust in the spirits of God and faith and trust in self in all things said and done. The times are now times more than ever before the chosen elect Holy Priest Ministers must always please the presence of God without fail remembering what is too hard for you is just right for God. The times are now times to remember, there is no failure in God. The times are now times to remember more than ever before; the spirits of the people are renewed daily in faith in spirits in truth in God.

The times are now times according to the promises of God; the promises are appearing in every part of the earth. The times are now times the people have a need to quickly humble themselves under the mighty hands of God. The times are now times according to the will of God infants

199

and children that do not have sin among them inherit from their kindred in their seed inherit eternal life. I the Lord your spiritual God say to you, there is no baptism acceptable to the spirits of God for infants and underage children; the acceptable age of baptism is 7 years old and older. I the Lord your spiritual God say to you, many things have been said and done that should not have been said and done in every part of the earth. The times are now times things are made known clearly with understanding are the things called unto the people seeking eternal life. I the Lord your spiritual God say to you, all sins in all things said and done have been eternally condemned in judgments and justice of God.

The times are now times of faith, hope, and patience with much endurance is a great reward of eternal life. I, God say to you, ye must confess openly that ye believe and understands all things written and called unto the spirits of the people for the sake of eternal life. The times are now times to confess openly ye believe in the Messiah I, God sent to lead the people to eternal life through all things written and spoken by her. I, God say to you, the promise of eternal life is now before the people. The times are now times to confess the heavens are being restored on earth to paradise heavens on earth. I say to you, open confessions of God are real in your life brings much comfort to the soul.

The times are times to heed to the voice of God leading you to eternal life. The times are times to not get discourage because of things happening around you but continue to trust in God in spirits in truth within self. The times are times to know all things of God are accomplished upon the people for eternal purposes as promised from the beginning of time. The times are times to let go and let God take charge of your life in all things said and done daily. The times are forming the renewed heavens on earth through all things said and done daily in every part of the earth God's words written and spoken in this gospel book of law prevail. The times are now times to detour your lifestyle for the chance of receiving the gift of eternal life. The times are now times to thank God for the promise of eternal life forming in every part of the heavens which are on earth.

13

Woe unto You Who Deny the Prophecies of the Messiah

The times are now times of all things are standing before the judgments of God said and done. I the Lord your spiritual God say; woe unto you who deny these prophecies written and spoken by the Messiah of God's spirits in the heavens which are on earth. I, God say to you, repent and live eternally in the heavens on earth. I, God say to the people in the heavens on earth; the spirits of the Messiah are dwelling deep within the heavens on earth. It is I the Lord your spiritual God within the Messiah speak through the Messiah.

The times are now times to labor in the chosen elect Holy Temples learning of me, your eternal spiritual God within you. The unbelievers who seek to destroy the Holy kingdoms of God are converted by the Holy angels of God. The times are now times of one religion one gospel; for it is written all religion are false except the elect chosen Holy Temples. I, God say to you, one God one religion one chosen elect Holy gospel people of God. It is written the people have been misled by false leaders in leadership not inspired by the Holy spirits of God neither ordained to be in Ministry.

I the Lord your spiritual God say to you, the Messiah speak with boldness and all authority from God with strength and power from on high in spirits in truth. It is I, God say to you, ye see and hear much more than a Prophet is the Messiah in the earth; for this is she, of whom it is written promise to come. It is I the Lord your spiritual God say to you, behold I God send my messenger the Messiah before thy face which prepares the way to eternal life making straight the pathways to a paradise heaven on earth.

It is I; God say to the people in the heavens on earth; among those born among the living women and men; there is not a greater Prophet Messiah ever walk the heavens on earth in your times of now times. I the Lord your spiritual God say to the people in the heavens on earth; this is the first in your times of now times and the last in your times of now times; for there will never be another with the mind set as the Highest Holiest Priest Prophet Messiah of all times. I the Lord your spiritual God say to you; I am God the beginning and the end of all people, places, and things in the earth I God call into existence. I am God unto all eternity have sent the Messiah to lead a dying world of people out of the wilderness of their mind set. I, God say to you, all people, places and things that are alive and well are alive because I God has mercy angels before them protecting them in times like these upon the people. The times are now times are worse critical times of more than ever before upon the people of the chosen generation of people.

The times are now times to repent more than ever before; woe unto all people in this world in that ye repent of your thinking within things said and done ought not to be said and done. The times are now times to fulfill the meekness and lowness of heart in that the remissions of sins brings comfort unto the people within their self from the spirits of God seeing that ye are in spirits of repentance. The times are now times more than ever before the people who repent behold the power of God's authority over their life with joy and hope leading to eternal life. The fulfilling of the prophecies of God are written and spoken unto you, in this gospel book of eternal laws of God. The times are now times more than ever before to choose life eternal or death eternal.

The times are now times more than ever before the wages of sin is death upon the people who always refuse to stop sinning knowing the difference between right and wrong choices ye make in life daily stands during God's judgments and justice. The times are now times more than ever before; all things that are not acceptable unto God are standing before the judgments and justice of God daily in every part of the earth. It is I; God have spoken through the Messiah saying sickness and death stops when sins stop in every part of the earth. I, God say to the people in the heavens on earth, the more sins in the earth, the more sickness and death in the earth. I, God say to you, death stops sins at the root. I, God say to the people in the heaven on earth; at the end of all sins, sickness, and death cease, appears a peaceful paradise earth. I, God say to you, all sins and sinners must be judged the wages of sins is the loss of eternal life from every place in the earth, in that there be peace in every part of the earth. The times are now times woe unto all people in this world in that ye repent of your thinking in all things said and done ought not to be thought or done.

I, God say to this people in the heavens on earth, the spirits of death and fear are upon the people who continue to sin. I, God say to this people in the heavens on earth, the spirits of death and fear takes its toll on the people in all denominations until all denominations cross-over merging with the acceptable chosen elect COGIC Incorporated Holy people of God. It is I the Lord your spiritual God have deemed all denominations false accept the chosen elect COGIC Holy people of God. I the Lord your spiritual God say to you, take heed to all things seen and unseen I, God have called into judgments against the people in every part of the heavens on earth. I, God say to you all people, places, and things called come forward in judgments without fail.

I the Lord your spiritual God say to you, behold I am God exhorts the Messiah daily in wisdom and knowledge in all power in all strength in all things said and done without fail. Behold it is I the Lord your spiritual God know all things said and done in every land; I, God speak these things to the Messiah as there be nothing hid from the spirits of the Messiah. I, God say to you, I am God within the spirits of the Messiah as the spirits of the Messiah dwell over the entire heavens on earth without fail. I the Lord your spiritual God know the truth of all things said and done. I, God say to you, without fail all things said and done in the heavens on earth are in the eyes and ears of the Messiah in spirits in truth. I, God say to you again, all things hidden in the heavens which are on earth are revealed without fail.

I the Lord your spiritual God say to the people in the heavens on earth; I am God in the heavens on earth saying all ye that labor with the chosen elect people of God learn of me as ye inherit eternal life on a paradise heavens on earth. The times are now times more than ever before; women are called as Prophets and Evangelists to speak the word of God called unto them in spirits in truth. The women Priest Ministers are not called to preach but are called to speak by inspiration ordained by the Holy spirits of God within them. I, the Lord your spiritual God say to you; women preaching have not ever been acceptable spirits of God and the chosen elect people of God.

I, God say to you, women use loud voices to sing in spirits in truth in the chosen elect Holy Temples of God. I, God say to you, women are not given heavy voices to preach at no time as men has been given heavy voices to preach sermons of eternal life in times like these upon the people. I, God say to you, the men are to show authority as they always speak or preach to the people. The soft voice of women is not in power over men in the chosen elect house of God with exceptions of the Messiah. I the Lord your spiritual God say to you. see to it that ye abide by these things written and spoken unto you; in that ye fall not by the wayside on stony ground in all things said and done.

The times are now times the people dwelling in the Holy spirits of God acknowledge God has sent the Messiah in the earth dwelling in the earth with majesty worthy of glory and honor from the elect COGIC Holy people of God. It is I, God say to you, the city of Tallahassee, Florida behold the greatest woman ever walk the heavens on earth in your time of now times. I the Lord your spiritual God say to you, the presence of the Messiah

207

spirits is continually before the people with great desire to feed the people all things God have called unto her hearing. The spiritual realm of the Messiah lifts the people up on high receiving revelation, faith, and strength to endure the signs of the latter-day times. The times are now times to be on one accord in spirits in truth in the chosen elect house of God. The people in the heavens on earth are exhorted by the spiritual presence of the Messiah in the chosen elect Holy Temples of God. I, God say to you the peace of God rests upon the people seeking eternal life on a paradise earth.

The gifts of God are many in the spirits of the people manifested to the people. It is the spirits of God teach you wisdom and knowledge in all things said and done. I the Lord your spiritual God say to the people in the heavens on earth, I am God and I the Lord your God lie not. I, God say to you, many things come upon the people they have need for eternal life; ye then recognize the spirits of God in the presence of the people in their spirits within self are spirits of truth in all things written and spoken unto you in this gospel book of prophecies. I, God say to the people in the heavens ye have declared my words written unto you.

The times are now times the chosen elect Holy Priests Ministers preach The Holy gospel in every part of the earth according to spirits of eternal life. The times are now times the chosen elect ordained Holy Priest Ministers speak and preach with joy sanctified in Holiness inspired by spirits of God within self. The times are now times ordained Ministers have a quick need to repent unto the realness of Holiness inspired spirits of God. It is now; many ordained Ministers of God are raised up in the chosen elect COGIC Holiness Temples to help Shepherd the people into eternal life. The times are now times the spirits of Holiress are established and stirred up in the people seeking righteousness leading to eternal life. The times are now times the people are stirred up in righteous spirits within by the prophecies of the Messiah written and spoken unto them.

The times are now times all people, places, and things in the earth are defeated by the spirits of God in every part of the earth. The times are now times the rebuke of all people, places and things ungodly are defeated by the people of God in every part of the earth. The times are now times all the beasts in the earth are defeated by the spirits of God's people. It is I the Lord your spiritual God say to you, all things written and spoken unto you by the Messiah have already defeated the people according to the purpose God hath called in every part of the earth. I the Lord your spiritual God say to you; the Messiah cannot will not have not lied about all things written and spoken unto you in this gospel book of prophecies.

There is no one the same neither equal neither greater than the Messiah I, God have sent to lead the people out of the wilderness of their mind. The times are now times every person lives in obedience unto the spiritual voice of God without fail losing not eternal life. The times are now times all righteous spiritual minds hearken unto the eternal spiritual voice of God without fail. The times are now times the eternal ways of God are in the heavens on earth in all things said and done in the eternal spiritual minds of the righteous people of God. The times are now times for the people to reap their harvest of righteousness taking the righteous ways of living by spiritual force within. The times are now times all chosen elect COGIC Incorporated Temples gather the people according to the will of

God unto one religion one gospel one big Holy land as one and the same over the entire earth against spiritual wickedness.

The chosen elect COGIC Holy Temples of God remain the eternal chosen elect people of God to lead the people to eternal life obliged to abide by the gospel laws written and spoken unto them by the Messiah sent by God. The times are now times in every part of the earth to face the things of God call by God without notice without warning. The afflictions of the unrighteous are upon them seeing money is not the answer to all things said and done; a righteous heart treating all people equal is the right way to eternal living eternal life as the paradise earth forms from these things written and spoken the Messiah unto the unrighteous. The times are now times all things call by God cleanse every land in every part of the world. The times are now times the things of God are upon the people daily are parable situations the people do not understand the ways of God. The ways of God are not comprehendible. The times are now times the people faith requires actions leading to eternal life. The times are now times all people must be in right standing with God. The times are now times to yield to the spirits of God within self. The people must have belief and trust in God by hearing the words of eternal life.

The people must remember faith is divine time accomplished individually without fail. The people must build and grow into their own faith receiving instruction from God within self without fail. The times are times to remember life and death is in the power of the tongue. The lands of plenty are upon the people without notice without fail. The break-through of eternal life is here upon the people without notice without fail. The people must decree their faith trusting God with expectations. The

210

times are now times to stay connected to the spirits of God within self-trusting yourself without fail. The times are now times to remember the earth is the footstool of God; meaning all people, places, and things are under the spirits of God are under the spell of God. I say to you, spells of God are good minds or reprobated minds without fail. The times are now times to remember the laws of mankind perish from the face of the earth as the paradise earth forming appears.

I the Lord your spiritual God say to you, many leaders in ministry in leadership have called them-selves unto ministry have a quick need to step down from ministry; ye are not led by the Holy spirits of God standing before the judgment call of God without fail ye are judged for misleading the people. The people have made ministry a common thing for monetary reasons and power over the people. The times are now times I the Lord your spiritual God say to you, it is time for the people to realize different religious congregations were not called; it is one big Holy land called since the beginning of times. I, God say to you, one big Holy land is forming in the heavens on earth called by the spirits over the entire earth without fail. The judgment seats of diverse religion are in judgments and justice of God. I say to you, there are many people grieving the Holy spirits of God fail by the wayside onto stony ground stoned by the spirits of God.

It is I the Lord God say to you, all my words fulfilled instantly in every part of the earth without fail. The times are now times for the people to be caught up with God in spirits in truth within self. The people have wax cold unto all Ministers but accept the chosen elect Holy Ministers. It is all denominations have denied the boldness of Holiness; accept the chosen elect Holy Temples. It is I the Lord your spiritual God say to the

211

people, ye have denied and reject my messages from the Prophets long enough; it now ye give an account before the latter-day judgments in every part of the earth.

It is I the Lord your spiritual God say to the people in the heavens on earth fulfilling; many people in every part of the earth in other denominations other than the chosen elect Holy Temples are given a chance to convert to the chosen elect COGIC Incorporated Temples of God called by God to judge the people. The times are now times to come to your-selves and know Jesus Christ is not God; but Jesus Christ was a Prophet called by the spirits of God to lead the people. The times are now times to know God is spirits that were within Jesus led to comfort the people. It is I, God say to you, the people have been in a fallen state of mind ever since the Prophet Jesus transgressed against the words of God in spirits in truth from the beginning of times which fell on generations of past unto generations of today as the line judgments call is drawn on the chosen generations of today.

The times are now times for the people who do not believe in God are in a fallen state of mind turn into a reprobated mind. The evil wicked doers have no power effect on the people of God in every part of the earth. The times are now times the spiritual dead minds seeking the spirits of God are resurrected. The people who refuse the gospel truth about God are in a fallen state of mind in the wilderness of their mind.

The times of now times the people of other denominations quickly congregate with the chosen elect COGIC Incorporated Temples of God praying that God not destroy them and their Temple but allow them to merge into the righteous ways of God leading to eternal life. The people now know they must be obedient to the words written and spoken by the Messiah to be acceptable unto the spirits God call by the spirits of God within the Messiah. The people know not to let it be too late to enter the kingdom of God. It is I God calling the pecple to merge as one big Holy land in spirits of God in truth of God without fail. I, God change not from the things called in spirits in truth already in the earth accomplishing its purposes.

The times are now times all people in the heavens on earth confess the Messiah of God is in the earth among the people face to face in the body of Holiness. It is I; God have no respect of person at no time testified in all the earth. The times are now times the works of God are the heavens on earth among the people as the hidden things among the people is revealed in the opened by forces of utterance upon the people. The people that are hidden in the earth committing secret unrighteousness come out with forces upon them confessing and asking the people for forgiveness. It is I, the Lord your spiritual God have spoken all things plain that was hidden from the minds of the people until such times as these showing forth all things the people have a need to know. I, God say to you, all people, places, and things that are lies hidden in the earth show up quickly that are working against the people.

The times are now times the words of God accomplish its purposes quickly upon the people. The call of prepared ways, times, and seasons of God are before the face of the people in due seasons in due times. There are many people in the earth with iniquities of hidden treasures are cursed and condemned already in the judgments of God. The times are now times

213

the truth has come out about God spiritually descending judgments and justice over the entire earth upon the people. The times are now times the days of the unrighteous are numbered in the wrath of God roaming the entire earth. The times are now times the wrath of God cleanse the entire earth of unrighteousness. The times are now times; ye that contend against these written words of God seeking your own power are cursed and condemned in the wrath of God upon you.

The times are now times in the earth the wages of sin are death angels released in the wrath of God until all sin are finished in the earth. The times are now times the wrath of God releases many disastrous accidents of nature without fail over the entire earth. The people committing unforgiving sins cannot hear in the spirits of God because of their evil hearts, they only hear evil spirits within leading them to destructions in the wrath of God. The times are now times many people perish are swallowed up in sink holes in the depths of the earth because the unrighteous refuse to stop sinning in the earth. The times are now times; the loss of love ones grieve many people to death is over the entire earth.

The times are now times the ways of God no-one know the paths of God which come in many ways as a thief in the night. The times are now times; you are here today and maybe gone tomorrow in the wrath of God clearing the way for a paradise earth. The times are now times to get right with God in that God is on your side and will never leave you guiding you to eternal life. The times are now times, tomorrow is not promised; for many people are in the wrath of God as their punishments are upon them because of their sinful hearts refuse to stop sinning while they have a chance. The times are now times of all s ns are cut off from the roots never to return in the paradise heavens on earth. The times are now times to change your ways to the righteous ways of God loosing not the way to eternal life before it is too late.

The times are now times to recognize who God is in your life leading to eternal benefits. The times are now times to know God is not Jesus Christ as many people have professed to think this which is not true. The many false religious leaders in leadership in the world have misled the people. The false religious leaders in leadership have not heard the voice of God call them to preach. I the Lord God say to you whom have misled the people, if I the Lord God had call you to preach ye would not have misled the people into false beliefs. I am God in spirits in truth all by myself; I am not Jesus I am not your father I am not Jehovah; I the Lord God is always God all by my-self. I the Lord God am always spirits of truth within you.

I the Lord God say to you whom have misled the people, ye have not heard from me, ye have spoken of your own heart and have cause the people to error with hearts far from me. The people misled have for-got I am God all by my-self within your good spirits leading to eternal life. I the Lord your spiritual God say to the people in the heavens which are on earth many of you in numbers without count have denied the Holy Spirits of God as ye teach and preach within other denominations other than Holiness denominations. I God say to you, if there be no spirits in the mind of the people then there would not be wisdom and knowledge in the mind of the people. It is I the Lord your God say to you; all good promising spirits are mine within the people of wisdom and knowledge.

215

It is I God in control possess all good souls full of all wisdom and knowledge in every part of the earth. I God say to you, if there be no spiritual God within you, there are no creations of things replenishing the earth as needed. I God say to you, the spirit of God is open to all people who receive it within. I the Lord your spiritual God say to the people in the heavens on earth, all hypocrisy and deceptions stand before eternal judgments in the justice of Gods Holy spirits. It is through transgressions human beings mistook the spirits of wisdom and knowledge of God as knowledge of their own spirits. The people are looking at self-gain in all things said and done in pass generations and generations of today. It is I God now draw the line with this chosen generation of people face to face in all things judged said and done in every part of the earth. I the Lord your spiritual God say to you, take heed that ye are not on stony ground in the spirits of God. I God say to you, the people of this world have no respect for God in all things said and done. I God say to you, the people left in the earth after sins are finish have much respect for God in all things said and done.

It is I God say to you, humankind has been in a fallen state of mind ever since the people of the beginning of times transgressed against the words of God in spirits in truth Adam and Eve has fell on every human being born from generation to generation. The people of the beginning of times disobeyed the words of God as do the people of today's generation of people disobeys the spirits of God heard within them. It was the days of Jesus the Prophet disobeyed God when God told him to write and prophesy what he hear and tell the people thus what God said neither adding nor taking from the spiritual words given him to tell the people thus what God said. It was then Jesus the Prophet allowed the people to add and take from the spiritual writings given him. It was then God turn Jesus and the people into reprobated minds because the people saw spiritual gain for self in all things they said and done. The Prophet Jesus disobeyed God's orders allowing the people to continue self-gain leaving the people of God they dishonored out of their plans.

The Prophet Jesus disobeyed God's orders to write what he heard within his spirit neither adding nor taking from what he heard neither allowing anyone else to neither add nor take from what he heard in his spirit. The Prophet Jesus disobeyed God's orders allowing the people to add and take from what he had written as the people told Jesus God did not tell him these things he had heard and written as they said to Jesus God told them to write the things Jesus allowed them to write. The disobeying of Jesus allowed the people to be in a state of confused mind set about the Bible as the people are in a confused mind set today about the Bible as the people add and take from the Bible today. It was then God allowed eternal death spirits of judgments to enter among all humankind and beast in the earth.

It is the disobeying of the Holy spirits of God within self-cause disastrous spirits to enter the earth. The people are in self-gain spirits for monetary reasons and sexual favors imposing control power over the people causing spirits of reprobated minds condemned in judgments by God for transgressions against the spirits of God within self. Prophet Jesus and the people went beyond limits of God's divine laws heard within as they transgressed against the spirits of God for self-gain as the people do today. God had warned Jesus no-one hears these things he hears in his spirits so that there would be no confusions of spirits within.

It is I God say to you the pass generation of people did not take heed unto my spiritual words within them as do this people of today the same sins has continued in the reprobated minds of the people claiming the good wisdom and knowledge spirits of God as their own spirits. It is I the Lord your spiritual God in-control of all wisdom and knowledge spirits within the people. It is I the Lord your spiritual God put a stop to all sins committed in the earth are in judgments daily until all sins in the earth cease. It is I the Lord your spiritual God change not but show the people among the living my words prevail in the heavens which are on earth in every land without fail shoot forth accomplished.

It is always I God have come to the people in plain words that ye now have more understanding than ever before in that ye lack not wisdom and knowledge of the things of God ye have a need to comprehend knowing judgment is upon you. It is I the Lord your spiritual God say to you, nothing is impossible or too hard for God in all things said and done. It is I the Lord your spiritual God have the first and the last say so in all things said and done. There be nothing left undone leading to eternal life, for all things have a need to be done prevail in every land. It is I God say unto you people in every part of the earth who deny the powerful spirits of God, are part-takers of forbidden fruit in all things said and done in the earth as Adam and Eve was.

The times are now times to come to yourselves giving thanks to God for your well-being giving thanks to God for wisdom and knowledge giving thanks to God for fame and giving thanks to God for your wealth. It is time-out for playing with God in all things said and done in the earth knowing the wrath of God's judgments are daily in every part of the earth. I say to you, many people in the earth have failed to realize God is spiritually in control of all good accomplishments. I the Lord your spiritual God say to you, it is I who has given humankind spiritual wisdom and knowledge to replenish the earth from the beginning of times the same as today humankind has a spiritual mind to restore and replenish the earth to the need of the poor, sick, afflicted and the people having hard times and tribulations.

These things were always the original plans of God, so that the people could learn to trust their wisdom and knowledgeable spiritual instinct which is God within. The people has refused sound mind (spiritual mind) forming ways to do and say things that benefit self-gain in all things said and done in the earth. These are reasoning the world of people are in a worse shape than ever before in history. It is for these reasons the call of judgments is upon this chosen generation of people. The ways of self-gain are unrighteous self-gain for money and sexual favors are the root of much unrighteous ways of humankind. The fall of humankind revolves around lust, sex, money, and pride denying the Holy spirits of God. It is the now times the earth is in a fallen state of being cleansed unto a paradise earth. It is the now times after all forgiven sinners have endured the wrath of God and the end of sins cease in the earth will live forever without sins, sickness, and death in the earth. The times are now times all things work together to the good of those who endure until the end of all sins perish in all the earth. The earth is then pure and clean with the love of God's Holy spirits in every part of the earth. The times are now times ye have a need to take heed to all these things written and spoken unto you.

The people have a need to know that evil cannot overpower the people who hearken unto the powerful spirits of God within them. It is the afflictions of God overpower the unforgiving sinners in the earth robbing them of their unrighteous self-gain strength and power for self-gain have slacken down to no-power at all and no self-gain at all. The judgments call of God has visit their sins with eternal destruction upon them of unrighteous self-gain. The unrighteous self-gainers are now powerless within their evil spirits as their pride turns into suffering in many ways. The people against the eternal spirits of God are stoned with many afflictions. The times are now times God is calling for eternal organization of all things said and done leading to eternal life.

The times are now times the earth is renewed daily by the eternal spirits of God. The spirits of God and the people of God spirits are renewing the earth to one big Holy land. The things call by God renew the earth are called to the spirits of the people in the earth. The people of God see and hear all things called unto them from the spirits of God. There is no misunderstanding in the spirits of the people of God calling things as though they were, and they appear. The times are now times of God and the people of God inherit the earth as promised. The people of God have always listening hearing ears ready to hear from God.

14

The People Have Deliverance Faith in God

The times are now time the people continue to be delivered by their faith in God as the chosen people of God are in the spirits of God. The people living by faith in God endure all things happening around them. The times are now times the Preachers preach repentance and eternal life to the people. The times are now times the forgiving sinners receive deliverance of eternal life within baptism of Holy water with Holy hands. It is I the Lord your spiritual God say to the people; all things written in this gospel book of laws are the gospel truth unto you unto eternal life. It is I the Lord your spiritual God say to you; all things are judged according to the things written in this gospel book of laws guiding you to eternal living eternal life. It is I the Lord your spiritual God say to you; take heed to these things in this gospel book of laws written unto you is the way to eternal life. It is I the Lord your spiritual God say to you; this book has been written for your deliverance according to the will of God for eternal life within a paradise heaven on earth.

The times are now times you are delivered by the renewing of your mind daily in all things said and done. The times are now times a great light of God shines all over the earth. The times are now times the anointed Prophets of God are Holy inspired revive the people of God by delivering the words of God to the people. The great wickedness of the people is before the synagogues brought to the light spoken in open judgments of the chosen Holy Priest casting all evil wickedness out of the chosen Holy Temples. The times are now times all denominations are destroyed except the chosen Holiness denomination of God called by God. The times are now times the Prophets speak forth the revelations of God manifested by the power of God. It is I the Lord your spiritual God say to you; it is the responsibility of the Prophets to make known the foreknowledge of God calling unto the people the eternal words of God in all things said and done. The times are now times all spirits of God and God's people pave the way to eternal living eternal life. The times are now times all things said and done are standing before judgments of God and God's people dwelling in every part of the earth. The times are now times all things written and spoken establishes a pure heaven on earth.

The times are now times the Holy Priest Prophets of God speak in the chosen Holy Temples of God at any given time called of God. The times are now times when the Prophet stands to speak in the chosen Holy

Temples; the people are silent as the words of God spoken in spirits in truth. The times are now times the Prophets are not on a timely schedule to come to the chosen Holy Temples of God. The times are always now times all chosen Holy Priest operate soulfully by the spirits of God. The times are now times the chosen Holy Prophets and Priest are always granted wisdom and knowledge to labor in the chosen Holy Ministry by the Holy spirits of God. The times are now times the congregation have need to direct their attention to the Prophets and Priest with all due respect.

The times are now times the words of God must go forth in spirits in truth during the same hour at any given time God call it forth to the spirits of the Prophet and/or Priest. The times are now times all things are said and done with much affect and respect for God. The times are always now times to give much respect and order in the chosen Holy Temples of God. The times are now times the dead minds of the people are called to resurrection by the spirits of God. It is yet ye live; your body and soul are dead to the spirits of God. The times are now times the restoration of the dead bodies (dead minds) are resurrected to open spiritual true minds. The times are now times to hear God speak eternal life to you. The body dies that hear not the spirits of God speak life into your body reviving you unto eternal life on a paradise earth as promise from the beginning of times. The people are in a temporal death state of mind with a will to die without return of eternal life; for death is eternal without return to life. The body is in a sinful fallen state of mind without will to live eternal life. The times are now times to revive the mind from the fallen state of mind to the eternal living state of mind awakening to the spiritual state of mind in the eternal spirits of God.

The spirits of God are in the waves of the air spread over you daily to receive spirits of eternal truth awakening you to eternal truth. The times are now times for the people to gather in the chosen Holy Temples of God to hear the truth about eternal God eternal living eternal life. There be many people not receive eternal life because of their unforgiving sins among them; there be many people receive eternal life because they have forgiven sins among them; but they must endure until the end of all sins, sickness and death has cease in the heavens which are on earth. The times are now times the government of all things is over-thrown in all the earth. The times are now times the towns and cities rebuild to the standards of God ordered by the spirits of God within them. The times are now times many spiritual leaders convert to the chosen Holy Temples of God to receive eternal living eternal life.

The times are now times the people are slain and overthrown by the spirits of God are revived and stirred up instantly according to the spirits of God eternal ways for the people. There are many people in failure enraged over the defeat of God's Holy spirits in the earth showing all power over all things said and done in the earth. There are many people judged have lost the way to eternal life overthrown hath denied the spirits of God's power in the earth. The times are now times the people having listen hearing ears hear what the eternal divine spirits of God said to the people. The times are now times the divine spirits of God deliver the people to eternal equal living conditions. The times are now times the people see the works of God delivered in every part of the earth.

224

There are people who refuse to be Holy in spirits in truth attacked by the wrath of God are faint in mind without eternal life. These are they living in the wilderness of their mind die because of lack of knowledge as they are condemned by the spirits of God. The times are now times the people of God are distinguished from the people who refuse eternal life. The people who refuse eternal life desire the lust of the flesh focus on the things of mankind which are temporary. The things of God are eternal forever as the people of God inherit eternal living eternal life take all things by force from the people who living temporary. The times are now times the people of God are the forgiven sinners living by faith enduring times like these standing before them.

The people of God are miraculously saved from eternal death beneath the earth. The people of God have entered the covenant of God; be ye Holy in all things said and done daily. The times are now times the wrath of God's destruction is upon all people, places, and things said and done unholy untruthful to the people. The times are now times of all things written in this gospel book of laws are fulfilling its accomplishments upon the people already. The people in the earth know the spirits of God are planted in all the earth accomplish its purpose. There be nothing left undone; for all things called eternal in the earth be accomplished daily until finished in every part of the earth. The times are now times all things be accomplished the people have need of for eternal living eternal life. It is I the Lord your spiritual God say to you; the spirits of the Messiah are in the earth in spirits in truth accomplishing God's purposes.

The times are now times the people of God serve God in spirits in truth dwelling on the inside of their hearts daily hearing the voice of God

225

lead and guide them. The times are now times God speak to the eternal need of the people in all things said and done daily. It is the ways of God is past finding out as the things of eternal life appear into existence over the entire world the people have eternal need of. The times are now times all things said and done ungodly give an account in judgment to God quickly in an instant. The times are now times of judgment daily until all sins have perished from the face of the earth. There are people giving an account of their sins in judgment quickly, not seeing the wrath of God before them with much destruction upon them. The times are now times the people must realize Jesus Christ is not God, whom many people have openly confess false beliefs. The people have been in a fallen state of mind ever since the Prophet Jesus transgressed against the words of God to please the people that denied him. The transgression of Jesus and the people fell to every generation of people as the people of today still transgress against God and God's people. The times are now times out for playing with God as God has drawn the line with many judgments upon this generation of people having much focus on the things of God.

The times are now times all confusions about the ways of God are done away with as this gospel book of laws lead the way to eternal living eternal life. The chosen Holy Priest are gone forth with power from on high in every part of the earth. The times are now times the resurrections of eternal judgments are gone forth in every part of the earth until all humankind believe and worship God in spirits in truth. The times are now times every leader in leadership in the chosen Holy Temples exercise authority with power from on high in the proper manner and disturb not the Holy spirits of God operating in the chosen Holy Temples of COGIC

Incorporated. The times are now times the Messiah in the earth is not touched mentally and physically by spiritual wickedness.

The times are now times the eternal Messiah eternal spirits in the earth call eternal things as though they were, and they appear in the earth according to the eternal spirits of God in the earth. It is I the Lord your spiritual God say to you; seek my eternal spirits and find them within you and all eternal things ye have need of be added unto you eternally according to eternal life. The times are now times all things said and done hide in every part of the earth are eternally uncovered and judged in spirits in truth in the people in the earth called by the spirits of God. The times are now times the many written Bibles will perish from the earth without fail clinging to this gospel book of laws in spirits in truth in God in the earth. The times are now times for instructions on eternal living eternal life on a paradise earth. It is I the Lord your spiritual God has revised the spirits of the people to eternal living spirits eternal life spirits within the paradise heavens on earth at the end of all sins, sickness, and death without fail.

The times are now times the stiff-neck people quickly give an account in judgments lose the way to eternal living eternal life. The times are now times these things written unto you are the signs of the times already upon the chosen generation of people as sins perish from the earth daily until finish in every part of the earth. The times are now times the people with hardened hearts repent of their mischievous ways of doing and saying things are not proper eternal ways of God. The times are now times the proper eternal ways of God defeat the people in all things said and done daily in the earth. The times are now times the chosen Holy

Prophets with spirits of revelation of God in spirits in truth defeats the people in all things said and done before them.

The times are now times all denominations become as one big Holy land in God in spirits in truth in Holiness in the chosen Holy Temples in every part of the earth. The times are now times all denominations except Holiness ye who refuse Holiness are driven to desolation lose the way to eternal living eternal life. The times are now times the power of God work through the people of God restoring the eternal future of the people. The times are now times God is spiritually paving the way to eternal life working spiritually through the people as there is no way to escape from the wrath of God roaming the earth seeking spiritual wickedness within the hearts of stiff-neck people. The times are now times seeking those people whom have profess to have known God's Holy spirits working in your life but ye have walked away from God unto the things ye lust in the flesh in the world; it would have been better if ye had not known and profess the spirits of God working within you and then walk away as the times are now times of destructions of judgments upon sinful fleshly life styles.

The times are now times to spiritually wake up seeing and hearing the promise eternal things of God daily forming in every part of the earth until all eternal things are finish. The times are now times the spirits of God and the Messiah are accomplished upon the people daily. The times are now times the spirits of the people are renewed daily in the likeness of God in the image of God in the eternal truth of God. The times are now times the new heavens on earth are appearing daily before the people without notice, and without fail in every part of the earth. The times are now times the words of God are instantly quickly gone forth operating in every part of the earth in all things the people say and do. The times are always now times to take notice of all things said and done surrounding you in every part of the earth.

The times are now times have gone forth in the Holy Synagogues the chosen Holy Priesthood speak and preach eternal living eternal life to the people without fail. The times are now times no female have power to preach but have power to speak as Prophets and Evangelist in the chosen Holy Temples of God. The times are now time no male is called to be an Evangelist as women are called to be Evangelist in the chosen Holy Priesthood of the Holy Temples. The times are now times females are not Bishops, Apostles, Elders, and Preachers and do not Sheppard the chosen Holy people of God. The times are now times the males are always the head of the household of God. The times are now times to cross-over into the spiritual message called by the spirits of God in every part of the earth. The times are now times to know God for your-self as God shake away the hands of death from your life according to your faith in God. The times are always now times for the duty of the Prophet to hear from God at any given time. A female Prophet can own a Temple, but the Temple must be Sheppard by a male always chose Holy Priest. The times are now times the female Evangelist cannot own a chosen Holy Temple of God at any time.

The times are now times all things take place in every part of the earth called by the spirits of God and the Messiah in the earth. The times are always now times to make room n the Holy Temples to receive the chosen people of God. The times are now times there must be 24 Holy Priest in the Holy Temples to over-see the congregations at all time

229

without fail. The times are now times there must always always be 6 Elders and/or 6 Apostles to equal 12 males 6 Prophets and 6 Evangelist to over-see the congregation. The Bishops must always be the over-seers of the chosen Holy Temples. The times are always now times for the chosen Holy Priesthood to be open to the Holy spirits of God without fail.

The times are now times to be out with the old traditions of mankind and in with the renewed eternal Holy spirits of God without fail. The times are now times to make provisions for the new arising of the new world order arising of the paradise heavens on earth at the end of all judgments, sins, sickness, and death in every part of the earth. The times are now times no-one can live eternal life on the earth without instructions and guidance that leads the way to eternal living eternal life. The times are now times of every word that proceed out of the mouth of the Messiah are from God with truth with eternal spirits without fail spread over the entire earth. The times are now times I the Lord your spiritual God say to you; take heed to all things written in this gospel book of laws without questions without fail without your soul being lost to eternal living eternal life.

The times are now a time the resurrections of eternal judgments are in all the earth bringing eternal justice until all sins in the earth is finished. The times are now times sins continue to bring death upon the people until all sins are finished in the earth. The times are now times the people are continually destroyed more and more by fire, water, and accidents in every part of the earth until sins are finished in the earth and the people are worshipping God in spirits in truth in Holiness in every part of the earth. The times are now times the people pray for togetherness of all people. The times are now times all people, places things ungodly come forward. The times are now times things ungodly in the earth are in judgments daily swallowed up in the wrath of God without fail. The times are now times the people are called in spirits in truth to stray not from this gospel book of laws called unto you from the spirits of God.

The times are now times I God say to you; see to it that ye not add neither takes from these prophecies of mine at any time. It is I God say to you; in the same hour ye add or take from these prophecies of mind, ye receive the loss of eternal life as destruction is upon you instantly. It is I God say unto you consider all things are done ye have eternal need of by the Holy spirits of God within you. The times are now times the truth prevails quicker than ever before. The times are now times all things said and done must be in agreement with the Holy Priesthood calling a conference with those in leadership away from the congregation of people in that all things be kept in conference in confidentiality away from people who have no need of knowing the information discussed between the people in leadership. I God say to you; always see to it that ye abide by these things without fail losing not the way to eternal life standing before you.

The times are now times I God say to you; the Bishops and Prophets change things quickly where there is a need to change things for the benefit of eternal life. I God say to you; times are now times all things are done in the chosen Holy Temple are descent and in order as required by the spirits of God. The times are now times I God say to you; there be no meetings of arguments at no time; as you know God is not a God of confusion but a God of all thing's descent and in order in all things said and

231

done. The times are now times all things said and done in the earth are done in a descent order that brings peace to a world of people seeing eternal living eternal life.

The times are now times of true light of the world is in the earth within the Messiah eternal life dwells in the earth as the Messiah is never touched by sickness never touched by death never touched by evil wickedness never touched mentally never touched physically never touched by talk never touched by letter and never touched by evil wicked spirits. It is I then your spiritual God say to you; these things are already operating in the earth without fail standing before you. The times are now times I God say to you; it is time to take God serious in these words written and spoken unto you without fail take heed and question not the eternal work of God. The times are now times I God say to you all leaders in leadership unfaithful to the people destruction is upon you as ye have lost the way to eternal life.

The times are now times I God say to you; the ministering angel of God the Messiah is in spirits in God in truth is eternally in the earth. It is I God say to this people in this world ye doeth many things should not be done ye say many things should not be said. It is I God say to you all things said and done are judged daily until all sins perish from the earth and eternal life appears in the earth. The times are now high times the Messiah in the earth speak eternal spirits into the air of the earth. The times are now times anyone believes not the Messiah is in the earth, ye have lost the way to eternal life. The times are now times I the Lord your spiritual God say to the people in the heavens on earth; my words are accomplished all over the world without fail the resurrection of eternal life shines in all the

232

earth. The times are now times to choose this day eternal life or eternal death. The times are now times ye must have the Holy spirits within to inherit eternal life. The times are now times appearing peace on a paradise earth rings out in every land after all sins, sickness and death have perished from the earth. The times are now times no human is always wise without the spirits of God dwelling on the inside of you. The times are now times the people are failures without God's spirits dwelling within the hearts of the people. The times are now times to know God specializes in all things said and done in the heavens which are on earth.

The times are now time the choice is yours to accept or reject the Holy spirits of God within you already as the times are now times to find God within you. The times are now times I God calls all things unto the people ye have an eternal need for, according to the spirits of God. I God say to you; seek my spirits and find them and all things be added unto you ye have need of for eternal life. The times are now times for the people to have faith in God in all things said and done in their daily lives. The times are now times the people are failures n things said and done because of lack of wisdom and knowledge in the eternal things of God. The times are now times the people must confess their sins and repent one to another in all things said and done. The times are now times the eternal spirits of God are loosed in the earth judging all things said and done daily.

The times are now times without the resurrection of the Holy spirits of God in your life ye are open to wrong spirits directing you to stony ground as you lose the way to eternal life. The times are now times to renew your mind by transforming your mind unto the spirits of God; ye then receive the light of God unto eternal life in heaven which is on earth

233

as ye then lose yourself from the pains of hell on earth as failures in all things said and done daily. The times are now times the wrath of God is hell on earth as failures in all things said and done daily in the earth. The times are now times the people have a need to take possession of their soul and have faith in the spirits of God within them to receive eternal life on a paradise earth as sins, sickness, and death cease at the end of all judgments finished in the earth. The times are times to realize ye are deceived by the wilderness of your mind leading to stony ground losing the way to eternal life.

The times are now times the spirits of the Messiah uncover all things said and done in the earth called by the spirits of God according to eternal purpose. The times are now times the people more and more journeys through the wilderness of their mind filled with hatred, murder, sexual wickedness of evil desires with strong wrong thoughts of lusting for money and worldly desires leading to the destruction of their lives daily in every part of the earth as they lose the way to eternal life. The times are now times showing all things said and done covered in secrets are uncovered and revealed to the people who have a need to know. The times are now times the actions of God's spirits are upon the people in the earth.

The times are now times showing the people in the earth that have refuse the righteous spirits of God are over-powered by evil wicked spirits of their own as their minds weaken causing them to lose the way to eternal life. The times are now times the people in the earth that hear not the words of God called unto them are journeying through the wilderness of their mind filled with hatred, murder, sexual wickedness of evil desires with wrong thoughts lusting for money and worldly desires leading to

234

eternal death. The times are now times of all things said and done in the earth that covered in secrets are uncovered by the actions of God's spirits upon the people in every part of the earth. The people in the earth refuse the righteous spirits of God are instantly over-powered by their own evil wicked spirits of their reprobated minds weakened in spirits in truth causing them-selves to lose out on eternal life.

The times are now times no-one can live in this life now and the renewed life appearing without the spirits of God dwelling on the inside of you. The times are now times the Holiness Ministers in leadership must be spiritually ordained in the spirits of God without fail inspired in the Holy spirits of God. The times are now times ye must have been baptized in Holy water filling the Holy spirits of God as ye are baptized in Holy water; otherwise ye are not to preach and teach the people in the chosen Holy congregations or ye see quickly see destructions of God upon you. It is I God say unto you; ye must abide by this gospel book of laws in that ye loose not eternal life in the heavens which are on earth.

It is I the Lord your spiritual God say to you; all things written and spoken are regulated by the gospel spiritual truth guidelines written unto you according to inspired spiritual truth. It is I the Lord your spiritual God call all these things into existence according to eternal need on a paradise heaven on earth. The times are now times ye have a need to be careful following the ordinance of the Holy spirits of God within you directing all things you say and do. The times are now times ye are commanded by the spirits of God to take heed to all things I God speak to you within. The times are now times to lean not unto your own understanding knowing these are the latter-days of judgments upon the people dwelling in every part of the heavens which are on earth. The times are now times to forget not all things said and done in the earth in secret are uncovered without fail in spirits in truth in every part of the heavens which are on earth. The times are now times to know that ye are being watched by God and the people of God in all things ye do and say daily in every part of the heavens on earth. The times are now times to know God is before you.

15

The Times Are Now Times for Instructions on Eternal Life

The times are now times to believe the laws of this gospel book of laws are laws and orders of God commanded by God unto all the people of this generation and the generations to come. The times are now times to know accidents, pain, sickness, crime, and death continue in the earth until all people in the heavens which are on earth hearken unto the voice of God in every part of the earth. The times are now times for the people to comprehend instructions given them leading the way to eternal life. The times are now times all Temples are built on the Holy grounds promoting the Holy spirits of God leading to eternal life. The times are now times I your spiritual God say to the people in the heavens which are on earth;

unless you believe in the spirits of your mind that are good spirits leading you to eternal life; ye lose out on receiving eternal spirits leading you to eternal life in all things said and done daily.

The times are now times for the people to abide by the Holy spirits of God written and spoken unto you as ye hear the spirits of God within you speak guidance unto you. The times are now time to study true words of God to show yourself approved in the spiritual sight of God; knowing in much study and instructions from God, ye loose not eternal life. The times are now times the people must always be in the will of God. It is I the Lord your spiritual God say to you; it is my will that no souls be lost from eternal life as the constitution of eternal life guidance are written and spoken unto you in the gospel book of laws written unto you. It is I the Lord your spiritual God say to the chosen appointed anointed gospel leaders in leadership; the times are now times to preach and teach eternal life and eternal death to the people. The times are now a time the people must know death is eternal with no return from beneath the earth.

The times are now times I the Lord your spiritual God call all eternal things forward as all ungodly deeds being committed in every part of the earth are judged daily brings destruction upon the people. The times are now times leaders in religious leadership not preaching and teaching eternal life are failures in all things said and done because of a lack of spiritual wisdom and knowledge from God. The times are now times religious leaders in leadership without the Holy spirits of God dwelling within you quickly see destructions of God upon you and your congregation without fail. The times are time is out for self-gain in unrighteousness imposed upon the people. The times are now times these things written and spoken unto you prevail quickly as the laws and justice of God calling eternal judgments upon the people in all things the people say and do in every part of the earth.

The times are now times eternal judgments are called daily by the chosen people of God until all things are with eternal purpose surface with eternal appearance in every part of the earth in all things the people say and do. The times are now times eternal judgments have quickly spread over the entire earth. The times are now praying times in every part of the earth more than ever before. The times are now times I the Lord your spiritual God say to you; pray that you are in the will of God daily without fail knowing your prayers are answered according to the will of God. The times are now times preparing ways to eternal living on a paradise earth are comprehended by the people in every part of the earth. The times are now times the people must quickly hearken unto the eternal spirits of God within self.

The times are now times the people in the earth who receive eternal life continue living in eternal spirits of God daily giving counsel to those in need of eternal guidance. The times are now times all people are treated equal and fair in all things said and done in the earth as the forces of God and God's chosen people dwell in the spirits of the people calling evidence of one-accord according to the will of God in eternal spirits in eternal truth. The times are now times the chosen people of God take all things said and done by eternal forceful spirits. The times are now times to know the greatest abomination to God is unequal living of unequal

239

treatment in the miss-leading of the people by those in leadership in every part of the earth are in eternal judgments of God and God's chosen appointed people. The times are now greater times are showing the people without spiritual Holiness are in the dark wilderness of their minds losing the way to eternal life. The times are now greater times are showing there be no denominations left standing except the appointed anointed chosen Holiness people of God whom have already inherit the earth as promise by the eternal spirits of God.

The times are now times are showing those who are in leadership for self-gain in all things said and done quickly fail without self-gain imposed on the people. The times are now times the people must take the eternal path to eternal life within spirits within truth. The times are a time that shows up on the people who takes the wrong path of life. The times are times the people have lost their sense of directions from God saying be ye Holy in all things said and done for I God am Holy in spirits in truth. The times are now a time that shows up on a stiff-neck people who refuse to hearken unto the direct eternal spiritual guidance of God and God's appointed and anointed chosen people of God. The times are now times shows up the corrupt denominations impose on the people for monetary reasons of self-gain without saving souls unto eternal life.

The times are now a time to be led within self by spirits of truth in all things said and done daily knowing the judgments of God are upon you without fail in all things said and done. The times are now a time shows up on the people in leadership have failed the people as a failure one toward another to each other in all things said and done without equal treatment to all people dwelling in the earth. It is I the Lord your spiritual God say to

240

you; come out of the wilderness of your minds and take heed unto all eternal things I God have called unto you that are written and spoken in this gospel book of laws in that ye fall not on stony ground in failure of all things ye say and do in leadership in every part of the earth. The times are the now times I the Lord your spiritual God say to you; no denomination is built on the rock of Holiness unless it is an Holiness Temple in the name of the Holy Temple of God chosen, anointed, and appointed by the eternal spirits of God. It is I the Lord your spiritual God say to you; the times are times the people are enlightened by the eternal spirits of God in that ye transgress not against the eternal words of God written and spoken in this gospel book of laws guiding you to eternal living eternal life in all things said and done in every part of the earth.

The times are now a time shows up on the people who have harden their hearts against the words of God causing themselves to fall on stony ground in the wilderness of their minds. The times are now a time shows up on the people who are in great errors stoned by eternal judgments of God in all things they say and do. The secrets of God are hidden in the earth accomplishing its purpose of eternal living eternal life upon the people in every part of the earth. The times are a time shows up on the so-call religious denominations having a form of godliness have become proud doers of wickedness imposed on the people as the people cannot determine what denomination is wrong and what denomination is right. The times are now a time to know Holiness is right.

The times are a time shows up on the people of many are called, but few are chosen in numbers as the sands of the sea without count. The time shows up false religious leaders in leadership who have departed

241

from the ways of God to their own ways of the gospel seeking money and not seeking to save the souls of the people. It is I the Lord your spiritual God say to you; these things done are daily in eternal judgments for miss-leading the people under false religion. I God say to you; I never called any denomination, but Holiness saying be ye Holy for I God am Holy. The times are ye have a need to receive the eternal spirits of Holiness knowing I God come to you within spirits within truth leading and guiding you to all eternal righteousness preparing you for eternal living eternal life on a paradise earth appearing in the heavens on earth in every part of the earth. The times are now times I God say to the people; it is time to come to your-selves in faith in truth in spirits in God in all things said and done daily. The times are a times that were appointed for such times as these of the latter day's judgments and justice of God in every part of the heavens which are on earth.

The times are It is I God say unto the people in the heavens which are on earth; I God have not call for different denominations as the people has formed a great fall away from the truth and build false Temples, Churches, and Synagogues misleading the people under a false form of religion in every part of the earth. These things were foretold from the beginning of Bible days formed corrupt religion entered the minds of the people reprobated minds. The times of reprobated minds were the times the people disobeyed the spirits of God from the beginning of the creation of the world. The reprobated spirits of the people from the beginning of times entered the minds of the people from generation to generation up to this very day as people form false religions misleading the people in every part of the heavens which are on earth.

The people are in a frame of mind to disobey the spirits of God to please people for self-gain monetary reasons and sexual favors leading to a loss of eternal life for many people. It is I the Lord your spiritual God said to you from the beginning of times; I God put my spirits in all humankind as I God put my spirits in all humankind this very day; for all humankind are made in the image of God in body in spirits in truth in the heavens which are on earth. It is I the Lord your spiritual God say to you as I said to the past generations of people from the beginning of times; ye now give an account for the refusal of my Holy spirits I the Lord your spiritual God hath given you. The times are a time to change in the twinkling of an eye into the eternal things of God. It is I the Lord your spiritual God say to you; see the vision, only the chosen appointed Holy gospel prevail in every part of the heavens which are on earth. The times are a now times; if anyone refuse the Holy gospel, ye have already been condemned unto eternal death beneath the earth turn to dust shortly their after without return to the heavens which are on earth.

The times are a now times all things said and done having forgiven sins are judged forgiven sins in the heavens which are on earth. The times are a now times all things said and done having unforgiving sins are judged unforgiving sins in the heavens which are on earth. It is I the Lord your spiritual God say to you; the Holy gospel is gone forth in all the heavens dwelling on earth are a chosen people of God in Holiness gospel of God in spirits in truth in God. The times are a now times the mighty miracles of God have showed up dwelling in every part of the earth without fail. The times are a now times eyes have not seen neither have ears heard the things of God prevailing in the Holy lands of God in every part of the

243

heavens on earth. The times are a now times to walk the highways of the heavens with a pure heart. The times are a now times the people of God prevail in all things said and done leading to eternal living eternal life.

It is I the Lord your spiritual God give you instructions for eternal living eternal life. It is I the Lord your spiritual God give you all things cometh forth I God have eternally called unto you, ye have a need on the paradise earth appearing before the people as the people keep on toiling through the storms of life. The times are a now times God knows how much you can bear as the words of God prevail have already come to pass in every part of the heavens which are on earth. The times are a now time all things I the Lord your spiritual God have spoken are in place accomplishing its purpose of eternal living eternal life. The times are a now times all things eternally are spoken into existence in every part of the heavens on earth through the spirits of God and God's chosen appointed and anointed people in every part of the world. The times are a now times there be much more destructions upon people, places, and things destroyed in the heavens which are on earth until all people, places, and things perish that have a need to perish in every part of the heavens cleansing the world of sins, sickness, and deceases. The times are a now times forming the worry to be at rest and be bless with the promises of God in every part of the heavens on earth.

The times are now times for the people to change their ways of thinking in this world of people who are proud because of costly churches, costly temples, costly synagogues, costly houses, costly cars, costly buildings, diamonds, and other costly things that are really no value in the eye sight of God. There are many deceived by the appearance of others because of the outer appearance as the times are more and more God judge the heart and not the outer appearance. The times are now times ye must appear unto God Holy and sanctifed dwelling in the spirits of God in all things said and done. The times are now times ye must appear unto God in spirits of God in truth of God. The times are now times the resurrection of the anointed COGIC appear unto all people a chosen people of God in every area of life and style of life.

The times are now times for the wise people of God to fulfill the messages of God sent unto the people of God. The wise people of God are anointed by the words and spirits of God in every part of the earth. The times are now times to know God's eternal justice are in every part of the earth. It is I the Lord your spiritual God say to you; ye must apply your heart to understanding the words of God as ye know these are the days of the appointed times for such times as these that are upon the people today. It is I the Lord your spiritual God say to you; these are the appointed times prophesied from the beginning of times past. The times are now times to live in the promises of God showing forth all things promise by God. The times are now times the people give an account of all things said and done standing before judgments daily. The times are now times to resurrect from dead minds unto the spiritual minds. The times are now times to show forth the spiritual things of God called to mind by the spirits of God as ye know these things were already spoken of in the Holy Bible. The times are now times the people of God inherit all things called unto them for eternal living eternal life.

The times are now times all things appointed to happen in times and seasons appears in the times and seasons appointed by God in spirits

245

in truth in every part of the world. The times are now times all things are appointed to happen by the spirits of God call to the Messiah in the heavens which are on earth. The times are now times to know there be known stones left un-turn in the earth. The times are the latter day times the people must bear their own cross called and appointed for such times as these today. The times are times to know all things happening in the earth pave the way unto a paradise peaceful eternal earth for the chosen people of God to inherit the goodness of God in all the earth in peace in spirits in Holiness without fail show forth all things being done called by the spirits of God without fail appear as God called it to be. The times are now times the people inherit the goodness of God in every part of the earth without fail in every part of the earth.

The times are now times ye must trust in the spirits of your mind God is with you in all things said and done daily or ye cannot be saved unto eternal life. The times are now times ye must trust and prove ye believe in the spirits of God within you to be saved unto eternal life. The times are the now times all people see the visions of the Messiah go forth in all the earth. The times are now times gone forth unto all forgiven sinners the resurrection of the spiritual mind set unto those who have eternal life receive the spiritual mind set of the things of God leading to eternal life. The times are now times the resurrection of eternal death is gone forth in every part of the earth unto all unforgiving sinners who receive not eternal life. It is the justice of God in all the earth calling all things happening into existence cleansing the earth of sins, sickness, deceases, and death. The times are now times the mercies of God leading to eternal life are extended unto all forgiven sinners in every part of the earth. The times are now times to repent armed with righteousness in that the spirits of God direct you daily unto all righteousness as ye live forever in the heavens which are on earth.

The times are now times the COGIC people of God put on the whole armor of God in all things said and done without fail. The times are now times the people are changed in the twinkling of an eye to the eternal ways of God. The times are now times the people receive all that they have eternal need of believing by faith receive the kingdom of God that is here forever without fail. The times are now times it is too late for the unforgiving sinners to repent as their sins are too great and they refuse to stop sinning. The unforgiving sinners have fallen on stony ground stone by the spirits of God un-forgiven by the spirits of God without fail in all things said and done. The times are now times take not a day for granted for ye know not what tomorrow will bring you in judgments daily. The times are now times to know your soul is at stake for eternal life or eternal death without fail. The times are now times to quickly choose this day which path ye will take without fail.

The times are now times to know that everyone quickly give an account in judgments of daily deeds done. The times are now times to know those with unforgiving sins are quickly giving accounts daily destroyed in the spirits of judgments of God and God's people calling for righteousness in all things said and done daily by the people in leadership in every part of the earth. The times are now times to know the people of God continue to prosper in all things said and done daily without fail. The times are now times to fear the Prophets of God and know who the real Prophets of God are, without fail. The times are now times to know who the strangers are with strange behavior having a form of religion. The wicked evil behaviors of the strangers in the land are brought to the light of the world without fail. The times are now times there are no hidden sins in the earth. There are many people in the earth shame to trust the spirits of God within them as God deny them who are shame to receive eternal life. The people of God see and hear all the sins of the unforgiving sinners are not hidden in every part of the earth.

The times are now times I God quickly answer the prayers of the righteous people. The times are now times the good news spread of the Messiah speaking the words of God calling a thing as though it were, and it spread in places where the eternal need is according to the spirits of God. The times are now times the people thirst for righteousness finds the words of God spoken are written true spirits of God called unto the people to take heed in this gospel book of laws of God. The times are now times the people on stony ground are quickly stoned by the spirits of God in every part of the earth. The times are now a time of blessed is ye who repent with forgiven sins among you in every part of the earth. It is I God say to you, the prayers of the righteous are quickly heard in holiness in truth in spirits in all eternal things said and done daily in the earth.

The times are now times the wicked are brought under by their sins committed. The times are now times the righteous is over the wicked in all eternal things said and done in the earth. The spirits of God have already overcome the people in the earth overpowering them in all eternal things said and done in the earth. The times are now times to have faith asking God for eternal needs as God bless you according to eternal needs in every part of the earth. The times are now times to believe God blesses you

248

according to the eternal will of God's blessing of eternal life spreading over the entire earth. The times are now times to understand the spirits of God as God bless and grant you with whatsoever is right according to the eternal will of God. The times are now times to know God does not grant what is contrary to the will of God. The times are now times to know God knows your eternal needs within the eternal plans for your eternal life.

The times are now times God has an appointed time for all eternal things in every personal life in the heavens which are on earth. The times are now times the lust of the heart is disposed as the trying of your faith hath weaken needs more renewed faith and strength daily from God. It is the people tempt themselves with lust and greed. The times are now times for the chosen Holy leaders in leadership to teach the people eternal life with peaceful living on a paradise earth. The times are now times for the people in other denomination to count it a privilege to be given the chance to become Holy because they were misled and did not fully understand the will of God is be ye Holy in all eternal things said and done. The times are now times to know the glory of God is in the earth spreading over the entire world within the chosen righteous people of God.

The times are now times to know the glory of God flows within the chosen Holy Temples of God. The times are now times to know the Messiah of God is in the earth according the promises and will of God eternal purpose for the people in the heavens which are on earth. The times are now times to know the wicked stout hearts have lost the way to eternal life. The times are now times the righteous people of God are restored daily in eternal spirits in eternal truth in every part of the earth having forgiven sins with eternal needs. The times are now times to know

249

God's words fail not and heavens which are on earth pass not away as the chosen people of God has eternal favor from God in the earth. The times are now times to know the eternal spirits of the people is God in the earth for God is eternal spirits in eternal truth calling all eternal things forward.

The times are now times to know the denominations have gone astray from the spirits of God unto their own belief for self-gain in lust and power over the people leading to a narrow road of destruction quickly upon the people without notice. The times are now times to know all unholy deeds ought not to be done quickly give an account in judgments and justice of God and God's people. The times are now times to know only the chosen Holy Temples of God continue to stand in the earth. The times are now times to know many leaders in a form Christian leadership have led the people astray from the eternal Holy ways of God in the earth. The times are now times to discern who God is speaking to in eternal spirits in eternal truth. The times are now times the people need spiritual mind eternal shepherds to guide the eternal sheep to eternal life.

The times are now times to stop worshiping leaders in leadership and worship God in spirit in truth in Holiness leadership. The people in the world have gone astray for lack of wisdom and knowledge. The times are now times to know the people have been sinning since the beginning of times as the wrath of God has been upon the people in just judgments of God. The Holy Bible has caused the people to go astray as they have not honored neither followed the Holy Scriptures. The times are now times to know without Holy spirits within, no-one can enter eternal living eternal life. The times are now times to sift out the true spirits in the Holy Bible from the untrue spirits in the Holy Bible. The times are now times to know

250

the Holy spirits of God in the Holy Bible has been blaspheme by generations of people since the beginning of times bringing about many confusions of all scriptures as the people have not stood the test of times labeled in the Holy Bible.

The times are now times I your spiritual God call all eternal things forward in the earth as needed for fulfill eternal life. It is I the Lord your spiritual God is supreme in every part of the heavens which are on earth. The times are now times to know the signs of the Messiah are in the earth as the promises of God are fulfilled upon the people eternal needs in every part of the earth. The times are now times I your spiritual God are calling for the people to hear in spirits in truth the words of God spoken to you in spirits in truth is God within you. The times are now times for the people to stop living in the wilderness of their minds facing the reality of God is real in the earth blessing the people according to eternal needs in every part of the heavens on earth. The times are now times to know that I the Lord am just in all judgments upon the people in every part of the earth clearing the way to eternal living eternal life forming a paradise earth at the end of all sins, sickness, and death.

The times are now times ye that thirst for righteousness in the Holy spirits of God ye quickly find it within yourselves; it is the spirits of God ye hear speak to your mind daily within you. The times are now times to discipline your mind listening to the good eternal spirits of God within you. The times are now time to know righteousness are in the Holy COGIC appointed chosen Holy Temples appointed by the Holy spirits of God. The times are now times it is I God say to you time is out for playing with God; the time is time to go to the chosen Holy Temples of God seeking the

251

eternal Holy spirits of God until ye find it in spirits in truth within self. It is I the Lord your spiritual God say to you, ye have need of the chosen COGIC people to strengthen and guide you into all righteousness leading to a saved eternal life for each person dwelling in the chosen Holy Temples.

The times are now times to know and sift out the wicked people whom are authors of confusion in the earth. It is I the Lord your spiritual God is the author and finisher of your eternal spiritual faith spoken and written within self. The times are now times to know I the Lord your spiritual God have called unto this world the chosen Holy COGIC elect Priesthood charged with the judgments of judging the world in eternal spirits in eternal truth in the heavens which are on earth. The times are now times to know there is strength and power in Holiness for you to be strong in all things happening before you daily. The times are now times to know the chosen elect COGIC Holy Priest reigns in all eternal things said and done over all Holiness gospel in the world of Holiness going in and coming out in every corner of the heavens which are on earth. The times are now times to know the chosen Holy Priest are inspired by the holy words and holy power of our eternal God. The times are now times to know the eternal God is calling the freedom of all nations over the entire world.

It is I the Lord your spiritual eternal God say to the people in the heavens which are on earth; I God am the eternal author of all eternal spirits dwelling in the earth with eternal authority and eternal power over all eternal ruling spirits in the eternal heavens which are on the eternal earth. It is I the Lord your spiritual God are present near and far in ruling spirits of the people calling all things forward near and far said and done

252

in the heavens which are on earth. The times are now times to know there is no-one in the heavens on earth quest on the powerful work of God near and far as the mysteries of God unfolds in every part of the world in daily judgments and justice of God and God's chosen elect people.

The times are now times to know the lands of sin has brought terror to the world of people in every part of the heavens which are on earth. The times are now times to know the chosen elect Holy Priest have authority to baptize the people whom have forgiven sins among them receiving eternal life. The times are now times to know the people with unforgiving sins among them have already been condemned by the eternal Holy spirits of God. The times are now times to know the eternal people of God receives eternal life never die but live eternally on a paradise earth forming daily before the eyes of the people. The times are now times the ordained chosen elect Holy Priest of God are educated with much spiritual experience inspired with the words of God deep within feel with eternal Holy spirits of God. The times are now times I the Lord your spiritual God say to you; ye have a need to pray worshiping in the eternal Holy spirits in that ye receive eternal life. There are many people as the sand of the sea choose to go down the wrong path receive not eternal life.

The times are now times the people know ye have been misled by a form of religious congregational Preachers must quickly turn to the chosen elect Holy congregations before it is too late. The times are now times all forms of false religions quickly give an account in judgments and justice of God. The times are now times to know ignorance to the words of God is no excuse; saying I did not know is not forgiven but judged in the loss of eternal life. The times are now times God and God's elect people see beyond the hearts of the people according to eternal judgments and justice of God. The times are now times to accept the true facts about God and God's eternal words written and spoken unto you in this eternal gospel book of God's laws called unto the people residing in the heavens which are on earth. The times are now times God are moving on the thoughts of the righteous people residing in the heavens which are on earth.

The times are now times all baptisms are performed only if the chosen elect Holy Priest is given permission to do so by the eternal Holy spirits of God saying that individual have forgiven sins among them with permission from the Holy spirits of God to receive eternal life. The times are now times all chosen elect Holy Priest speak with eternal boldness having eternal authority from the eternal Holy spirits of our eternal God within self. The times are now times to weather the storms of life believing God is making everything alright within judgments and righteous justice in every corner of the earth. The times are now times to know many people are turn away from eternal life because their sins are unforgiving sins that are too great for God to forgive them.

The times are now times ye must show yourselves approved of by God to receive baptism leading you to eternal life. The times are now times to pray to enter the eternal spirits of God that are already within you, ye then can hear God speak to your heart. It is I the Lord your spiritual God have sent the elect chosen powerful Holy COGIC Priest to lead and guide you to eternal life. The times are now times those who have a need to continue to seek the eternal Holy spirits of God are told by God to the elect Holy Priest this person is not ready for eternal baptism leading to eternal life saying this person have a need to pray much for directions within the Holy spirits within self.

The times are now a time to know eternal vengeance is in eternal judgments belongs to eternal God over all the eternal heavens which are on earth. The times are now times to know prejudice die quickly in eternal judgments of God and God's chosen elect people. The times are now times expedient many people awake to reality of these things spoken and written unto you in this God's gospel book of laws. The times are now times the people who do not awake to the written spoken words of God continue for a short while with empty souls have lost the way to eternal life on a paradise earth. The times are now times to awake and step into eternal spiritual reality of God in that ye awake from the dead mind unto the eternal spiritual mind seeing divine justice of God prevail leading to eternal living in the heavens which are on earth.

The times are now times to awake to the realness of God and repent from self-inflicted guilt. The times are now times prejudice cannot be hide facing the people face to face with the eternal judgments and justice of God in every part of the heavens which are on earth. The times are now times prejudice is called to eternal justice of God and God's chosen elect people. The times are now times people with prejudice hearts see eternal justice of God upon all nations of people in every part of the heavens which are on earth. The times are now times for the prejudice people to know their prejudice hearts have been judged and are in the wrath of God's just judgments daily until all sins, sickness, and death is finished in the earth. The times are now times all prejudice is revealed in every part of the heavens which are on earth.

255

The times are now times for the people to know ye that have fallen deep into transgression have fallen onto stony ground in just judgments of eternal God and God's eternal elect chosen people. The times are now times to awake to situations God have brought you out of spiritual wickedness in high place ye could not see. The times are now times the people are punished severely for their sins in every part of the heavens which are on earth. The times are now times many people awake to many troubles and hell here on earth because of sinful evil hearts in the earth. The times are now times the people who do not belong to a Holiness Temple indulge themselves in a sense of confusion and hell leading to the loss of eternal life. The times are now times to know the many people as the sands of the sea have lost the way to eternal life.

The times are now times of Holiness or hell on earth until ye perish from eternal life. The times are now time the people are carried captive by the foolishness of the wilderness of their minds. The times are now times many people pierce themselves over and over with many sorrows they have brought upon themselves because of their own wicked hearts. The times are now times to awake to the eternal spirits of God within self-bringing you pleasure in all eternal things said and done daily in your life. The times are now times many people inflict much hell upon themselves. The times are now times the people cause themselves much worry and excessive pain because of their stiff necks doubting the eternal spirits of God. The times are now times many people recognize and witness the spirits of God, but still refuse the ways of God so that they may continue to say and do things their way that leads to the loss of eternal life. The times are now times the people torment their life blaming others for their self-inflicted faults and sins they repent not shows a loss of eternal life. The times are now times God hath given the people time to repent in past times that have refused as now times are too late for many, but not too late for others.

The times are now times the good vines are separated from the bad vines as the bad vines are sifted from the good branches the people of God. The times are now times the good people in the vineyards make a connection to good branches meaning the people in other denominations connect with the chosen elect people of God rather than lose out on eternal life. The times are now times the people in the vineyards are rewarded according to works and gifts in the Holy spirits of God. The times are now times the unforgiving sinners in the earth are encircled by eternal judgments and justice of God in every part of the earth.

The times are now times I the Lord your eternal spiritual God commanded the Messiah in the earth with eternal Holy spirits of God dwelling in the earth. The times are now times to be resurrected and lifted unto the eternal spirits of God in the chosen eternal Holiness elect Temples of God eternal COGIC Temples. The times are now times you are converted by the renewing of your mind daily in the eternal spirits of God; ye then hear God speak to you in the spirits of your mind dwelling in eternal spirits dwelling in eternal truth. The times are now times the people of God are saved from all hurt, harm, and danger living according to the eternal spirits of God. The times are now times the angels in the waves of the air protect the anointed people of God in every part of the heavens which are on earth.

257

The times are now times to break the yoke of sins as ye then are saved from the sins consequences of others committing sins within life difficulties. The times are now a time salvation is essential that ye are immerged in Holy water with Holy hands washing away sins with the blood of the Holy spirits is the Holy water of the chosen elect Holy Temples. The times are now times to be qualified to receive Holy baptism as a candidate for eternal life. The times are now times to be qualified as a candidate for Holy baptism ye must have forgiving sins among you. The times are now times the Holy chosen elect Priest knows those who are qualified candidates for Holy baptism as God speak to them by way of the Holy spirits of God. The times are now times the Holy eternal spirits of God require the people to repent unto Holiness in the chosen elect Holy COGIC Temples. The times are now times it is God eternal spirits in the waves of the air requires the people to be Holy to receive eternal life in every part of the heavens which are on earth.

The times are now times to know blessed is ye who repent having forgiving sins among you. The times are now times to know all things done and said explain why God sent the Messiah Prophet in the earth among the people un-noticed in the heavens which are on earth. The times are now times to know this thing reference the Messiah Prophet was prophesied in the beginning of times for such times as these for the sake of eternal life promise to the people. The times are now times to understand the eternal spirits of God like never as the Holy Bible have described the qualities needed to receive eternal life on peaceful paradise heavens on earth.

The times are now time to be only baptized in the eternal Holy spirits of God along knowing I am God all by myself in eternal spirits in eternal truth. The times are now times all people are invited to attend the Holy Temples as the unforgiving sinners are sifted out to leave the Holy Temple Holy grounds from among the people of God with eternal life. The times are now times there be no interruptions of the Holy spirits in the Holy Temples mentally neither physically. The times are now a time blessed is ye who repent who are not stubborn unto the eternal spirits of God in the waves of the air in every part of the heavens which are on earth.

The times are now a time blessed is the broken hearted with forgiving sins among them. The times are now a time to be saved is to have eternal life. The times are now a time to repent, be baptized worshiping God among the Holy chosen people of God in eternal spirits in eternal truth. The times are now times to know even after you are baptized ye are still judge daily until the end of all sins, sickness, and death is finished in eternal judgments and justice of God and God's elect chosen Holy COGIC Priest. The times are now times to see to it that ye are worthy to be baptized for eternal life. The times are now times to know Holiness is having the hold-part of God's image in eternal spirits in eternal truth in all things said and done daily in life. The times are now times to teach the children about God and God's eternal spirits that leads to eternal life. The times are now times the chosen elect Holy Priest does not baptize little children and infants. The times are now times children must not be baptizing until they understand right from wrong being taught to lead a good and righteous lifestyle leading to eternal life.

The times are now times for the elect chosen Holy COGIC Priest to carry out the orders of God leading the people to eternal life. The times are now times people stand face to face with God's eternal justice and judgments daily upon the people in every part of the heavens which are on earth. The times are now times everything in the earth is judged for eternal renewal of God's new eternal creation taking part in every part of the earth in the spirits of the people residing in every part of the earth. The times are now times the forces of God are spiritually in the air waves of the earth paving ways for eternal life on a paradise earth after all sins, sickness, and death have been judged finished. The times are times to be delivered from disbelief of God's eternal Holy spirits knowing God is in control of the whole earth and all people, places, and things within the earth. The times are now times to know you are one step away from receiving eternal life knowing you must build on these things written and spoken unto you for the purpose of eternal living eternal life.

16

The Times are Times to hearken unto Voices of God and God's COGIC People

The times are now times you see all cultures comes together in the spiritual beauty of Holiness went forth in all the heavens on earth in every land. These are days and times of seasons God spirits of justice invade upon the property of the prejudice unforgiving sinners by force lay during all things said and one are stone that are ungodly. It has been since the beginning of times humankind tell lies for monetary reasons, many reasons known, and reasons of uncertainty unknown to the people are all standing before the judgments of God and God's chosen elect COGIC people. The times are now times there are no petitons held before God as these are the latter days of justice and judgments standing before God and the elect chosen people of God judging the people daily by way of spirits and truth in all things said and done daily.

The times are now times to be steadfast unmovable in the renewed messages from God written and spoken in this gospel book of laws written for the good of the people crossing over into eternal life are gone forth in all the earth. The times are now times for the rising generations to automatically take part in eternal Holiness in the spirits of God and live forever after receiving eternal life under the leadership of the chosen elect people of God. These are times to realize the battles in the earth are not yours, but they are just right for the Lord in the call of justice judgments of the latter-day times of now. The times are now times the battles in the earth are not yours but the spirits of God paving the way to a paradise earth.

It is after this great battle with cultures in judgments for calling racisms to the attention of God, there is one thing for certain after Go's just judgments all people will become lovers of each other on one accord according to the prescribed ways of God, called by God. The times are now times one against the other have no place on the earth according to the just judgments of God and God's chosen elect people. The times are now times to bear the just judgments of God in the heavens on earth according to the spiritual ways of God and God's chosen elect people in the earth. The times are now times the false liars in the earth give an account daily. The times are now times all sins in the earth cease after all unforgiving sinners have perished cease from the heavens which are on earth. The times are now times blessed are the people who bear the Prophet Messiah in the heavens which are on earth. The times are now times to pray that ye can bear the things in the earth that are happening near and far in the earth. The times are now times to pray that ye are not afflicted by the wrath of God's judgments dwelling in the earth. The times are times to pray that ye repent in that your soul be cleansed and opened unto the eternal spirits of God.

The times are now times no harm come to the chosen people of God. The times are now times dead bodies beneath the earth are food to the beast beneath the earth until turn to dust eternally. The times are now times the people of God are blessed and healed from all sins, sickness, and death dwelling in the earth. The times are now times the unforgiving sinners are whip with many stripes within the wrath of God dwelling in the earth. The times are now times the forgiven sinners are healed with many eternal stripes of eternal justice within the blessings of God dwelling in the earth. The times are now times to know the earth is filled with the spirits of the Prophet Messiah dwelling in the earth. The times are a now time that shows up every evil under sun as there is nothing hid said and done in the earth.

The times are now times the spirits of the Prophet Messiah cover all the heavens which are on earth. The times are now times in all the earth rising unforgiving sinners' sins uncovered and judged by the wrath of God dwelling in all the earth. The times are now times all things are judged said and done in the earth as the spirits of God and God's chosen elect people send spirits over every part of the earth judging the people. The times are now times the spirits of justice of God and God's people invade upon the property of the prejudice unforgiving sinners in every part of the earth.

The times are now times by force all sins are stone in all things said and done ungodly. The times are now times to know God spirits of justice are in every of part of every land in all the earth. The times are now times all things said and done in the earth come forth out seen and heard unto the people who have need to know. The times are now times the hidden power of God is operating in the earth daily in all things said and done.

The times are now times the strength and power of God is prevailing in the chosen people of God as the Prophet Messiah comes in full force in spirits in truth. The times are now times all things the Prophet Messiah call in the earth takes its course when and where needed in all the heavens which are on earth. The times are now times the indignation of God's anger has showed up in the wrath of God dwelling in the earth. The times are now times the voice of the Prophet Messiah in the earth is made known within the things of God written and spoken unto you receiving eternal life. The times are now times all things ye have need of for eternal life are written and spoken unto you in this gospel book of God's laws.

The times are now times saying with all that ye have seek ye the eternal spirits of God and all eternal things be added unto you. The times are now times God have wrought judgments and justice in all the earth. The times are now times the days pass and days come of God's eternal judgments are prevailing in the earth until all sins are finished. The times are now times many things come upon the people unexpectedly as a thief in the night in the wrath of the judgments of God in every part of the earth. The times are now times it is I God say to this people in this world, ye are of blind minds and blind hearts doeth not comprehend the works of God in all the earth. The times are now times the great works of God are here in every part of the earth. The times are now times the mighty rich prejudice cry bitterly in every part of the earth.

The times are now times the prejudice people weep bitterly for the days of God's anger wrath bring troubles of distress and desolation and death to the people that are unforgiving sinners in the earth. The rich prejudice people see the wrath of God's destruction upon them in many things said and done daily in the earth. The times are now times there are many hell and death upon every part of the earth. The times are now times the prejudice hearts have already been judged see God's destruction of wrath upon them daily until they are no more spreading prejudice in the heavens which are on earth. The times are now times God put an end to wicked hearted people daily until finish in all the earth. The times are now times that are without count the ends of sins cease come in every part of the earth.

The times are now times before the day is pass the fierce anger of God comes upon the unforgiving sinners like a thief in the night casting many deaths and troubles providing hell is here in every part of the earth proving all these things written and spoken unto you in this gospel book of laws called according to the spirits of God imputed within the Prophet Messiah the greatest Prophet ever walk the earth in your times of now times. The times are now times to know that many things written in the original Bible back in the Bible days are not true and that is why the people have not lived the scriptures but have tried to abide by them as spiritual writings were added and taken from the original Bible.

The times are now times I God put an end to all liars in the earth writing words saying God said words I God did not say to them as I God call all things said and done to my eternal spiritual ways ye have eternal need of to live on a peaceful paradise heavens on earth. The times are now times it is I the Lord your spiritual God say woe unto a prejudice nation of people my words and spirits are against you in all things you say and do unrighteous to the people in every part of the earth. The times are now times to know the wicked rich that are against the people ye as a wicked rich have corrupt the earth with your wicked evilness for monetary reasons and power over the people; It is I God say to you your time is now up as there is no money needed in the paradise heavens forming in every part of the earth. The times are now times all power with monetary reasons imposed upon the people are called forward in eternal judgments and justice of God and God's chosen elect people. The times are now times evil wicked hearts now give an account for their wicked evil ways imposed upon the people in every part of the earth.

The times are now times the wrath of God upon the people complete its course coast to coast until all sins are finished in the heavens which are on earth. The times are now times all things said and done in the earth ungodly are rooted up from the roots and burn eternally from the face of the earth. The times are now times I the Lord your spiritual God has come operating in the earth in judgments and justice in times ye have not prepared for in every part of the earth. The times are now times I the Lord your spiritual God cause many things to happen around you near and far in the call of judgments and justice in every part of the earth. The times are now times many people are moping in self-pity saying and doing things should not be done in the earth.

There are some people saying things that should not be said as they say that God is unfair are their words that cause them more troubles of hell on earth leading to the loss of eternal life. It has been seen and heard that the mouth of humankind has no control of self-contain spirits from things ought not to be said and done in the heavens which are on earth. The times are now times I the Lord have call spiritual control within self within all things said and done in the heavens which are on earth and keeping in mind the paradise earth is forming. The times are now times to keep in mind ye give an account of all things said and done daily in the heavens which are on earth in every part of the earth. The times are now times to remember I, the Lord your spiritual God have called into account all things said and done daily in the heavens which are on earth. The times are now times to remember the ungodly mind speak according the flesh of un-eternal things that have no effect on eternal life. The times are now times to speak the effect of eternal life for self-gain of eternal life forming eternal heavens on earth. The times are now times I the Lord your spiritual God call a Holy land with a Holy people conscience of the eternal spirits of God in all things said and done in the earth.

These are times and seasons God has beautified the people of God for such times as these. These are times and seasons beautiful are the chosen elect people of God with wisdom and knowledge of God's words from this gospel book of laws call eternal life unto the people. These are times and seasons the chosen elect Holy Priest are led by the spirits of God in all things said and done daily. These are times and seasons the chosen elect Holy Prophets are led by the spirits of God in all things said and done knowing all things beforehand. It is time to realize from the beginning of time the Holy spirits bear record of God speaking to the people by way of the Holy spirits and through the mouth of the Prophets inspired by the Holy spirits of God.

It is I the Lord your spiritual God say to the people in the heavens which are on earth, the Holy spirits of God bear record of the Messiah Prophet in the earth speaking and writing things call to her spirits according to the spirits of God called to her by the spirits of God within her knowing all things in the earth. The times are now times all things are sealed within the spirits of the Messiah Prophet God hath called unto her in spirits in truth are the revelations of God within her saying the revelations of God is without void without end within her spirits within truth. The times are now times to know the Messiah Prophet without end is in the earth in flesh in body in spirits in truth in now times and seasons.

It is I the Lord your spiritual God say to the people in the heavens which are on earth, it has been since the beginning of times humankind has refused the spirits of God as do humankind do today bringing forth dead works from dead minds leading to judgment call of eternal death. It is I the Lord your spiritual God say to the people in the heavens on earth, the spirits of the people in the earth reveal the people in the earth has no knowledge of the spirits of God working through the Messiah Prophet call to the earth by the spirits of God. The times are now times all sins buried beneath the earth turns to dust shortly they're after leaving no return of the dead, neither tracks of death beneath the earth. The times are now times to acknowledge the judgments of God are daily upon the people in every part of the heavens which are on earth.

The days times and seasons are precious in the spirits of God are the people of God in the heavens which are on earth. The times are now high times and seasons to doubt not but believe in the eternal true spirits of God within you leading to eternal life by way of this gospel laws written and spoken unto you in spirits in truth. The times are now timing and seasons the eternal things of God are made known unto you in spirits within you in truth within you in that ye understand in the plain. The times are now times these eternal things written and spoken unto you warn the people in the heavens on earth there is no time left for confusion of the mind with self-inflicted stubbornness leading to loss of eternal life.

The times are now times to know ye are in the latter days of God's eternal judgments' daily until all things are finish and there be no more sins left in the heavens which are on earth. The times and seasons in the earth are now times the spirits of God and God's people destroy in every part of the earth, all unbelievers that disbelieve God is the owner of all eternal good spirits dwelling within the mind-set of rich thoughts within the people. The times are now times to know the people of God have already inherited the heavens which are on earth in every part of the earth. The times are now times to remember all religions are false except that of Holiness chosen people of God call by the Holy spirits of God in every part of the earth.

The times are now times to be steadfast unmovable in the new gospel laws of God written and spoken unto the people in the heavens which are on earth. The times are now times for you to even yourself with the eternal spirits of God lined up with the gospel laws of God, and know the whole face of the earth evolves around the eternal spirits of God and God's chosen appointed people in every part of the heavens which are on earth. The times are now times to know this is the latter times and seasons of the rain that wash un-cleanliness' from the heavens which are on earth. The times are now times to know the Lord your spiritual God cast all shepherds of the Temples that are not real but has a form of religion.

The times are now times have come to pass the unclean Temples in sin are crush from the face of the whole earth. The times are now times to know unclean spirits pass away from the whole face of the earth. The times are now times true prophecies appear as false prophecies are crushed with its maker eternally perish from the face of the earth. The times are now times crushed is everyone spirits who wear garments to deceive the people. The times and seasons are now times to remember all denominations are false except Holiness denominations. The times and seasons are times to hearken unto these words said believing in the eternal spirits of God that are in control controlling all things said and done working to the good of the people receiving eternal life.

The times are now times ye believe in these words believe in the Messiah Prophet in the heavens which are on earth. It is I the Lord your spiritual God say to you, it is the Messiah Prophet in the earth have written spoken and prophesied these things unto you in years pass unto this very day saying until all things are finished all things continue to happen in every part of the earth in every season. The times and seasons are now times the chosen Holy Priest teach the people to believe in the eternal God in

270

eternal spirits in eternal truth in eternal people in the eternal earth. The times are times to remember ye with forgiven sins are resurrected from spiritual dead mind to eternal spiritual minds saved by the eternal spirits of God in every part of the heavens on earth. The times are now timing and seasons all unbelievers of these words chance losing out on eternal life. The times are now high times there be no more persecutors of Holiness religion in the all the land. The times are now times and season the Messiah Prophet in the earth recreate all things said and done in the earth in eternal spirits in eternal truth.

The times are now timing and seasons the people of God benefit from eternal life are converted to the new spiritual eternal things of God. The times are now times all the people of God desire the eternal spirits of God casting out all doubt being steadfast and unmovable in the heavens forming on earth. The times are high times for the Holy and righteous people of God in every part of the heavens on earth. The resurrection of all things said and done in the earth are renewed daily cometh in the heavens on earth until all things are finished. The times are now high times Holiness reign in all the heavens on earth. The time is now high times and seasons the justice of God and God's people prevail in every part of the heavens on earth.

The times are high times the Holiness chosen Priest reign having all power to heal the sick and cast out devils in the chosen Holy congregations and in the heavens on earth. The times are now high times the chosen Holy Priest teach eternal life to the people in the chosen Holy Temples. The times are now high times the chosen Holy Priest are established in peace. The times are now timing and seasons all eternal things are gone forth in

271

the earth in eternal spirits in eternal truth. The times are now high times to see the kingdom of God operating here in the heavens which are on earth in every part of the earth. The times are high times to know the people of the kingdom take all things said and done by spiritual force operating in every part of the earth. The times are now times to remember God and God's people take all things said and done spiritually destroying all things ungodly by force bringing justice of God to the people in all the heavens on earth as unforgiving sinners perish daily without fail because of a lack of knowledge.

The times are now high times the rising generations understand spiritual Holiness automatically takes part in eternal Holiness in the eternal spirits of God live forever and never die. The time is now high times and seasons the rising generations understand spiritual Holiness automatically take part in eternal wholeness in the spirits of God live forever and never die. The time is now high times and seasons all generations now and to come enter a covenant with the spirits of God eternally without fail. The times are times to realize sins have so easily beset pass generations because of lack of spiritual understanding within self. The times are now times to come to the knowledge of spiritual understanding within self.

The rising times are all generations believe in the eternal Messiah Prophet in the heavens which are on earth. The rising times are all generations worship in spirits in truth in wholeness in Holiness in the chosen Holy Temples of God called by the eternal spirits of God. The times are high times all generations understand the good spirits within self-belong to God; it is God speaking to the inner spirits within the mind. The times are now times to lay aside the weight of every burden in that it is

272

well with you opening unto the spiritual mind within self in all things said and done daily. The times are now high times to realize there be no other denominations chosen by God other than Holiness denominations as all other denominations are false called by the spirits of God in every part of the heavens which are on earth.

The times are now times to know the chosen Holiness people of God inherit the promise lands in every part of the earth. The times are now times to prove ye are Holy in all things said and done as God said be ye Holy for I am Holy within good spirits of truth within one's self. The times are judgmental times the Messiah in the earth spiritually drive all sins from the face of the earth in every part of the earth establishing peace in all the heavens which are dwelling on earth. The times are high times Holy spirits of the people dwelling in the earth establishes peace in the earth. The times are times and seasons hope are in the world for a better world of people seeking eternal life. The time is now times and seasons, unclean spirits are washed from the face of the earth along with its maker in every part of the earth. The times and seasons are all people are made accountable for their own actions whether good or bad ye are judged according to the spirits of God and God's chosen people.

The times are now times and seasons to know without a doubt these words written and spoken unto you are for instructions leading to eternal living eternal life on a paradise earth within the promise peaceful lands call by the sprits of God and God's chosen anointed people in every part of the heavens which are on earth The times are times and seasons to know many people want make it to the promise lands in the heavens which are rising in every part of the earth because they are bound by the

273

foolishness of their reprobated minds with no hope and no future within the promise lands. The times are now times to see in the heavens which are on earth the righteous branch of religion is Holiness religion raised up in the heavens which are on earth. The times and seasons are now times to see all religions fade away from the face of the earth except Holiness religion remain in the heavens on earth.

The times are now times and seasons the spirits of God reserve the people of God dwelling in the eternal spirits of God as God's justice in the earth destroys the wicked every day until there are no more sins, sickness, and death destroying the people in the earth and the judgments of God and God's people ends. The times are now times and seasons God speaks to the people in visions and dreams destroying all false religions along with its makers. The times are now times to recognize the new rising appointed people of God appointed by the eternal spirits of God to judge the earth in eternal spirits in eternal truth in every part of the heavens on earth. The times are now times to acknowledge the eternal spirits of God awakening the human sense to a spiritual mind set in the greatness of God planting these words of God in the hearts of the chosen people of God in every part of the heavens on earth seeking eternal living eternal life.

The times are now times to possess the promise lands taking them by forceful spirits of belief in eternal spirits in eternal truth. The times are now times to hear nothing but the gospel truth about the promises of God forming in every part of the earth. The times and seasons are all holiness priesthood speak, teach, and preach according to the Holiness doctrine given in this gospel book of laws called according to the eternal spirits of God in spirits in truth unto all the people among the living in the heavens which are on earth. The times are now times all Holiness Temples must be on one accord according to the eternal spirits of God dwelling in the earth in spirits in truth. The times are now jucgment times and seasons dwelling in the earth daily forming the promise lands according to the eternal spirits of God for eternal living promise lands in every part of the earth.

The times are now timing and seasons the judgment call of God eternally root up all the temporary things of humankind renewed by the eternal things of God in eternal spirits in eternal truth. The times are now times to know the eternal spirits of the Messiah are in the earth prevailing in eternal spirits prevailing in eternal truth cannot be touched by spirits of the people in the earth. The times are row times to know all wicked spirits are being eternally washed from the face of the earth. The times are now times the eternal faith of the people show progression of eternal belief in eternal living dwelling in eternal spirits hearkening from the instructions given in this gospel book of laws called by the divine eternal spirits of God in spirits in eternal truth.

17

All Chosen Holiness Priesthood Preach According to These Eternal Gospel Laws

The times and seasons are the chosen Holy Priesthood preach according to this eternal gospel book of God's laws I the Lord your eternal spiritual God say to you in every part of the earth. The times and seasons are the people of God are nourished by the spirits of God in all things said and done. The times and seasons are to know the names of the wicked are not among the eternal names of the chosen people of God judged eternal life by the chosen Holy Priest. The times are now times to know the people who have no part in righteousness have no part in the eternal paradise earth with the eternal people of God. The times are now times to know the people that are not ordained by the Holy spirits of God are not to lay hands on the forehead of the people in the chosen Holy Temples of God. The times are now times to be careful about what you speak in the chosen Holy Temples of God.

The times are now times to know all chosen Holy shepherds are called and ordained in spirits according to the eternal spirits of the new renewed things of God to teach the people. The times are now times to teach the people, life is eternal, and death is eternal according to the eternal spirits of God dwelling in every part of the heavens which are on earth. The times and seasons are now times all Bible stories and Bible scriptures are fading away from the face of the heavens which are on earth. The times are now times and seasons forming the renewed things of our eternal God as promised in the Holy Scriptures. The times and seasons are performing the instructions given in this gospel book of laws as called according to the eternal spirits of our eternal God.

The times are now times I the Lord your eternal God spiritually say to the chosen Holy Priest, teach no other doctrine other than this eternal doctrine in this eternal gospel book of laws called unto you for the eternal purpose of the eternal promise lands promised to the people since the beginning of times for these things leads the people to eternal living eternal life. The times are now times to know I the Lord your eternal spiritual God have mercy on the chosen people of God with forgiven sins. The times are now times I the Lord your eternal spiritual God say to you; there is no Jesus to come, for I the Lord your eternal spiritual God have never left you, but has always been before you in spirits in truth without fail. The times and seasons are I the Lord your eternal spiritual God say to

278

you, ye praying in Jesus name in vain. I the Lord your eternal spiritual God say to you, it is not Jesus answering your prayers, but is I the Lord your eternal spiritual God answer your prayers in spirits in truth.

The times and seasons are I the Lord your eternal spiritual God say to you, see to it that ye walk according to these orders written and spoken unto you in this gospel book of laws for the purpose of eternal living eternal life in that ye fall not on stony ground losing the way to eternal life. The times are now times I the Lord your eternal spiritual God say to you, be not judged stoned by the eternal spirits of God because you fell on stony ground. The times are now times to yield to the eternal spiritual words of God called unto you for the eternal purpose of eternal living eternal life. The times and seasons are I the Lord your eternal spiritual God say to the chosen Holy Priesthood; it is time to rise knowing you were called from the birth of the mother's womb for such times as these of today.

The times are now times and seasons I the Lord your spiritual God say to you, see the visions praying that ye be not tempted by unsaved people above what ye cannot bear in that ye are strengthen daily bearing all things said and done in the earth until the day of judgment has finished its course in the earth. The times are times to remember ye are living in the great days of God's eternal judgments in the earth daily. The times are now times to pray that the eternal Holy spirits of God teach you all things ye have a need to know in eternal spirits in eternal truth. The times are now times to call on God more than ever before in faith in that ye receive eternal life having forgiven sins among you. The times are now times to stay in the will of God's eternal purpose for the eternal promise forming in all the earth. The times are now times to know the Holy spirits teach you

279

all eternal things ye have a need to know. The times are now times all chosen Holy Priesthood have a great work in the vineyard of the Lord.

The times are now times all chosen Holy Priesthood will perform the labor in which ye were called to perform without fail in all things said and done daily. The times are now times only true believers of God's eternal spiritual words are called by the sprits of God according to the eternal purpose of the eternal promise land. The times are now times forming there be no Bible colleges needed, for ye are inspired and ordained in the Holy spirits of God in eternal spirits in eternal truth leading to eternal living eternal life. The times are now times to know the inspiration of God is a gift from God and not an educated guess about the spirits of God. The times are now times ye must be inspired and ordained in the eternal spirits of God to be in the chosen Holy Priesthood of God's chosen people.

The times are now times to know being inspired and ordained by the spirits of God is to hear God speak to you in all things said and done. The times are now times true believers of God's inspired words are on one accord learning renewed inspirational eternal spirits of God. The times are now times of the Pentecostals in Holiness are all on one accord believing and hearing the same eternal spirits leading to eternal living eternal life on a paradise heaven which are on earth. The times are now times to be sure and very sure that you are hearing from God and not from self-dividing self-spirits to eternal spirits of God leading to eternal living eternal life. The true believers of God's eternal spirits are Holiness Christians crossing over into eternal spirits of God leading to eternal living eternal life.

The times are now times to do things the right way without fail according to the eternal spirits of God. The times are now times for the chosen Holy Priest to cross the people over into eternal living eternal life without fail. The times are now times all chosen Holiness Priest always sit in the pulpit strengthening the power of Holiness Priesthood overthrowing evil spirits that enter in the Temple in the congregation. The times are now times for the chosen Holy Priest to keep watch over the people in that ye loose not the way to crossing the people judged eternal life over to eternal spirits of God. The times are now times the forces of God over power the chosen Holy Priest in all things said and done daily.

The times are now times to take all things said and done by forceful spirits putting evil spirits out of the Temple as you know evil spirits are them to stop the work of God within the Temple. The times are now times to overthrow evil spirits within the chosen Holy Temples of God. There is no place for evil spirits on chosen Holy grounds of God and God's chosen people. It is I the Lord your spiritual God say to the chosen Holy Priest; these orders must always be followed in that the Holy spirits have free course in the eternal will always of God during services in the Temples. The times are now times the waves of the air protect the people of God by way of spiritual angels in the waves of the air in every part of the earth.

The times are now times for the chosen Holy Priests and Prophets to judge the people with forgiven sins among them eternal life. The times are now times I the Lord your spiritua God has called an order of twenty four chosen Holy Priest in each chosen Holy Temple to judge and cross over the people to eternal life of my people judged eternal life called by the Holy Priest and Holy Prophets. The set order in the chosen Holy Temples are 1 Priest, 6 Prophets, 12 Elders, and 5 Evangelist are of the chosen twenty four Priesthood appointed to cross the people over into eternal spirits of God leading to eternal living eternal life in every part of the heavens which are on earth. The numbers double in count for bigger chosen Holy Temple are 1 Priest, 12 Prophets, 12 Elders, and 10 Evangelist are of the chosen appointed Holy Priesthood to cross the people over into eternal spirits of God leading to eternal living eternal life in every part of the heavens which are on earth. The time is out for Ministers playing church for monetary reasons imposed upon the people. The times are now times all Prophets Males and Females are called Prophets there is no Prophetess I the Lord your spiritual God say to you. I the Lord your spiritual God say to you, see to it that ye a chosen Holy Priesthood follow these orders called unto you in eternal spirits in eternal truth.

It is I the Lord your spiritual God say to you, see to it that ye neither add neither take from these numbers called unto you keeping these numbers in order with the size of the Temple in that all chosen Holy Priest are counted for in all things said and done in an decent order called unto you in eternal spirits in eternal truth. It is I the Lord your spiritual God say to the chosen Holy Priest; see to it that ye have plenty good room in the chosen Holy Temples to receive my people I the Lord your spiritual God send to you. The times are times to remember these are the days of God's daily judgments are upon all the people dwelling in the earth without fail judging the good as well as judging things that are not good.

The times are the chosen Holy Priest must remember to never sit in the congregation in that ye keep good watch over the congregation of people. The times are times the chosen Holy Priest must remember Holy

282

Priest sitting in the congregation takes away from the operation of the Holy spirits operating in the Temple. I the Lord your spiritual God say to the chosen Holy Priest see the vision of the Holy spirits operating in the Holy Temple in a decent order called unto you in eternal spirits in eternal truth. It is I the Lord your spiritual God say to the Holy Priest; see to it that ye fall not on stony ground losing the way to eternal living eternal life in crossing my people over into eternal spirits called unto you to do for ye have good instructions in this gospel book of laws call unto you in eternal spirits in eternal truth. The times are now times to remember the chosen Holy Priests are in the presence of God's Holy eternal spirits face to face in all things said and done daily. It is I the Lord your spiritual God say to the chosen Holy Priest walk according to the eternal spirits of God without fail as Holy Priests in the chosen Holy Temples of God called unto you in all things said and done.

The times are now times to please God according to eternal spirits called unto the chosen Holy Priesthood without fail in eternal spirits in eternal truth. The times are now times it is well with you as chosen Holy Priests called to judge the people according to spiritual truth. The times are times to remember ye as chosen Holy Priests oversee many souls called to your charge to keep measuring all things said and done according to spiritual truth in righteousness. The times are now times all chosen Holy Priest must stay on one accord as there be no big I's and little U's knowing all chosen Holy Priesthood are equal in the presence of God's eternal Holy spirits at all times helpers to one-another in all things said and done in the chosen Holy Temples.

The paradise earth forming through all things said and done in the earth daily as all things said and done in the chosen Holy Temple are done in the name of our eternal God the Holy spirits dwelling within the chosen Holy people of God. The chosen Holy people are peace makers in the earth showing they are children of God in every part of the earth. The Prophet Messiah has risen in the earth hearing all things according to the eternal spirits of God within her. The time has risen all chosen Holy Temples names are changed to "The Holy Temple of God" called to all chosen Holy Temples. The Holy Temple that does not change their name to "The Holy Temple of God" are Temples of mankind not of God neither called by God as a chosen Holy Temple.

The times are now whatsoever be done or said in the Holiness Temples be done and said in the name of God not the name of Jesus for Jesus is not the Holy spirits God is spirits and truth alone. It is I the Lord your spiritual God say to you; ye are chastised when you do not call upon the name of God your prayers are in vain as ye must pray in spirits in truth in God who is all good spirits within self. The times are now times to guard your eternal spirits by these things written and spoken unto you in eternal spirits in eternal truth in all things said and done leading the way to eternal living eternal life. It is I the Lord your spiritual God say to you; anyone depart from these gospel laws, I the Lord your spiritual God depart from you in spirits as destruction be upon you in all things said and done.

It is I the Lord your spiritual God say to you; all chosen Holy Priesthood are always inspired and ordained in the eternal Holy spirits called unto you with spiritual hearing ears. The times are now times to know all chosen Holy Priest footsteps are always ordered by the eternal

Holy spirits of God. The office of the chosen Holy Priesthood is always always to show forth spiritual guidance with no respect of person acknowledging the eternal spirits of God without fail. The times are now times all chosen Holy Priest are always in spiritual Ministry show forth the Holy gospel of God. The times are now times the chosen Holy Priesthood is called with a Holy calling.

The times are now times all forgiven sinners in the earth are called to repentance by the renewing of your mind daily crossing over into the eternal spirits of God. The times are now times all chosen Holy Priesthood are ordained according to gifts and callings of God inspired by God permitted to speak according to your gift. The times are now times all chosen people of God are called from darkness unto the light of God quicken instantly by the spirits of God in every part of the heavens which are on earth. The times are now times all people in the heavens which are on earth are astonished at the eternal judgments of God appointed eternal revelations in the earth. The times are now times to know all unholy Temples are an abomination to God brings their congregation much hell and destruction as they have lost the way to eternal living eternal life in every part of the earth. The times are now times all Temples are standing before the eternal judgments of the spirits of God. The times are now times to know the eternal truth about God and God's words written and spoken unto you in this gospel book of laws.

The times are now times to know that ye who harden your hearts against these gospel laws written and spoken unto you; ye are already taken captive in the wilderness of your mind leading you to the loss of eternal living eternal life. The times are now times to know all these things

285

written and spoken unto you now stand before you daily until the end of all judgments, sickness, sins, and death have finished its course in the heavens which are on earth. The times are times I the Lord your spiritual God have called to you to live according to these standard written and spoken unto you leading the way to eternal living eternal life forming the promise lands called unto the people since the beginning of times.

The times are now times and seasons to know all judgments called are eternally uprooting thee temporary things of humankind renewed by the eternal things of God. It is the times all people in the earth have a need to be nourished by the eternal spirits of God in every part of the earth. The times are now times all temporary things in the earth eternally done away with. The times and seasons are all judgment calls in every part of the earth show forth all hidden sins cause many deaths hidden in the earth hidden in the hearts of many people. The times and seasons are all sacred things of God come forth permanently in every part of the earth paving the way to a paradise heaven on earth. The times and seasons show forth all un-forgiven sinners in the earth as judged un-forgiven in every part of the earth.

The times are now timing and seasons the people must repent in every part of the heavens on earth throughout the lands paving the way for the paradise heavens on earth. The times and seasons are the people who refuse to repent unto the Holy spirits of God show forth repent unto the wrath of God losing the way to eternal life. The times and seasons are the people who receive not eternal life are cursed by the judgments of God and God's people for a lack of knowledge they refused to take heed to the eternal will of God. The times are now healing times and seasons for the people in every part of the heavens which are on earth. The times are now times the people that are cursed remain in a fallen state of mind loose the way to eternal life on stony ground stoned by the spirits of God and God's people.

It is I the Lord your spiritual God say to you the eternal spirits of a paradise are gone forth according to the spirits of God the rising generations are born of God in the will of God from birth having true knowledge of God's eternal will with much understanding being spiritual minded in all things said and done. It is I the Lord your spiritual God say to you; it is a written and known fact all generations of past and up to this very day have been judged in a fallen state of mind which is the fall of all mankind since the beginning of time in every part of the earth. The times are now times of all things said and done in the earth for eternal purposes are done by powerful eternal spirits of God directing the people in eternal spirits in eternal truth in every part of the earth.

The future visions carried out by the people of God are spiritually instructed by the spirits of God. The times are the true Holy Messiah Prophet is in the earth calling all things spiritually of God for the eternal purpose of eternal living eternal life for the people in every part of the earth. The times are now times true Holiness is in the heavens which are on earth forever never fade away. The times and seasons are all denominations fade away in every part of the earth except that of Holiness. The times are true righteousness will never be cut off from the face of the heavens which are on earth in every part of the earth. The times are now timing and seasons all un-forg ven sinners are cut off from eternal life daily until all sins, sickness, and death have finished its course in every part of the earth. The times and seasons are all people stands before judgments daily giving an account spiritually to God for all things said and done in the earth. The times and seasons are this is the end of sins, sickness, and death taking its toll on the people in every part of the earth. The times are now times no-one cannot hide from the eternal judgment's spirits of God and the eternal judgments spirits of God's people spirits in the waves of the air in every part of the heavens which are on earth. The times and seasons are the eternal spirits of God and God's people are calling forth in judgments of all things said and done in every part of the earth whether good or bad all things said and done are judged.

It is I the Lord your spiritual God say to the people in the heavens which are on earth; all people are caught up in judgments daily whether good or bad as there are those who for self-gain rob the people daily in death in money in many other things show forth finished ends in judgments at the end of all sins, sickness, and death in every part of the earth. It is I the Lord your spiritual God say to the people in the heavens on earth; no-one cannot touch the eternal spirits of God and God's people neither touch the eternal spirits of the Messiah Prophet in the heavens which are on earth are all eternal spirits in the heavens in the waves of the air daily.

The times and seasons are in the last days of all sins committed in every part of the earth. The times are the presence of God's eternal spirits is felt in every part of the earth daily with the call for fair justice and living conditions for all people. The times are now times calling all things to eternal existence unto the judgments of God and God's people. The times and seasons are all things seen and unseen are in judgments daily in every part of the earth. The eternal spirits of God and God's people are sealed in the waves of the air in every part of the earth. The times are sealed in truth in sacred eternal spirits of The Messiah Prophet in power in strength in Holiness in the heavens which are on earth. The times and seasons are all followers of God's eternal spirits are caught up in the Holy eternal spirits with God and God's chosen elect people of choice called to judge the people in every part of the heavens which are on earth. The people of God remain caught up with God on a paradise earth forever in eternal spirits in eternal truth in every part of the earth after all un-forgiven sinners are no more in the earth.

The times are now times to prepare to live eternally as all things eternally are forming in the earth after all people, places, and things have been judged eternal and all sins, sickness, and death are no more in the earth. The times are now timing and seasons all denominations become as one big Holy land in every part of the earth. The times are now times all people in the earth become one faith on trust in one God the eternal spirits in religion of Holiness in every part of the earth. The times are now times and seasons there are one baptism on earth, the Holy water of God which is the eternal spiritual blood of God.

The times are now times to know there is no other side to the heavens on earth, but the earth itself. The times are now times to know, there is no resurrection of the dead beneath the earth at no time in the earth as well there is no resurrection of Jesus at no time in the earth. The times are now times to know death is eternal beneath the earth forever turn to dust without fail. It is I the Lord your spiritual God say to the people in the heavens on earth times are now times to know there are false teachings from false religions of false spirits of false leaders are not inspired neither ordained by the eternal spirits of God to lead and guide the people to eternal living eternal life.

The times are now times to remember many are chosen few are called to do the eternal judgment work of God in every part of the heavens which are on earth. The times are now times to see to it that ye have faith, love, and hope among you for others surrounding you believing in the eternal Holy spirits of God. The times are now times the greatest of them all is to receive the eternal spirits of God within self that already exist within self. The times are now times to recognize the eternal spirits already within self and all other things eternally needed be added unto you. The times are now times to know dwelling in the eternal spirits of God is love saying accept ye have love of the spirits of God ye have not love within required by the eternal spirits of God.

It is the eternal spirits of God teaches love, faith, and trust in God for all things said and done in every part of the earth. It is the people of God born of the eternal spirits of God. The times are now times all things written and spoken of in this gospel book of laws all people dwelling in the heavens which are on earth have a need to know these things leading to eternal living eternal life now forming in every part of the earth. The times are now times to know ye whom have forgiven sins among you receive the inheritance of the promise lands. The times are now times to pray that ye receive eternal life eternal life in the heavens which are on earth.

The times are now times to know there is great wickedness among the people every day near their surroundings in different places near and far close upon the people is other people of wickedness. It is I the Lord your spiritual eternal God say to you the real sheep hear real shepherds' voice come to the real chosen shepherds of God to be guided into eternal life. The times are now times to know all sheep fold dwelling in spirits dwelling in truth belong to God. The times are now times to know goats do not belong to the sheep fold of God. The times are now times to know the sheep folds receiving eternal spirits belong to the chosen Holy ministry are known to ministers of God through the Holy spirits dwelling before them in all things said and done. The times are now times to know those whom have rejected the Holy gospel is because ye have already been rejected by the eternal Holy spirits of God. This then be the reason why ye have rejected Holiness ministries is because ye have no spirits to dwell among the people of God. The times is now times to know the only appointed chosen Holy Priesthood can teach and preach to the people leading and guiding the people to eternal living eternal life. The times are now times all chief leaders are to make sure without fail the people are being taught the words of God leading to eternal life are of true gospel laws written and spoken in this gospel book of law leading the people to eternal living eternal life.

The times are now times all chosen Holiness Ministries are to be on one accord in all things said and done according to this gospel book of law written and spoken unto you. The times are now times the Prophets are always to stay on one accord according to the eternal spirits of God. The times are now times to dwell in the eternal Holy spirits of God to stay on one accord with each other according to the eternal spirits of God. The times are now times the works of darkness is destroyed in every part of the heavens which are on earth. The times are now times there is no more playing church using God's name in vain for monetary reason in the Temples are the money changers of thieves stealing from the people and using words to bribe the people.

The times are now times only true believers of the eternal spirits of God are called to do the will of God by inspired ordained by the eternal spirits of God. The times are now times all chosen Holy Priesthood have a need to hear from God in spirits in truth in all things said and done daily leading the people to be saved unto eternal life. The times are now times only the chose appointed people of God break bread and wash feet with the chosen Holiness saints of God in all the chosen Holy Temples of God. The times are now times all denominations built by the works of mankind has come to an end in all things said and done. It is in the will of God for all Temples to become as one on one accord in the eternal will of God without fail. The times are now times do not let it be said it is too late for you to cross over into eternal spirits of eternal living eternal life.

The times are now times no one in the chosen Holy Temples are to lay hands on the people except those among the chosen Holy Priesthood ordained in the Holy spirits inspired by God hearing in the Holy spirits of God in the chosen Holy Temples in every part of the earth. The times are now times God reveal the people with forgiven sin to the chosen Holy Priesthood. The times are now times to always keep the way clear for the Messiah Prophet in the chosen Holy Temples of God. The times are now times to know the Holy eternal spirits of God is always over all chosen Holy Priesthood in every part of the earth.

292

The times are now times to keep the way clear for the Prophet Messiah in all things said and done in the chosen Holy Temples of God. The times that have come upon us are all saints are restored unto the truth of God's Holy eternal words now and times to come. The times upon us are woe to those who fight against God and God's people in every part of the earth. The profound changes are the people of God are one and the same in eternal spirits in truth in God. The eternal spirits of God are in all the affairs of this world. The times are now times the people of God prosper within hearing from the eternal spirits of God. The times are times to honor the eternal spirits of God establishing eternal living eternal life.

The people have made up their mind to be in the favor of God as real Christians of God's Holy words in all things said and done. The wrath of God is in every part of the earth established in judgments and justice leading the people to eternal life. The Holiness fellowship leading to eternal life builds from this gospel book of eternal laws called by the eternal spirits of God called to the people to cross over into the renewed minds of the new things of God. It is I the Lord your spiritual God say to the you, ye now know the things ye must do in my house I God have called unto you in this gospel book of laws in eternal spirits in eternal truth in all things said and done lead my people to eternal living eternal life.

The times are now times there is no eating at the Holy Temple, but the call of the judgment seat, saving of souls and burying of dead bodies takes place in the chosen Holy Temples of God. Ii is I the Lord your spiritual God say to you the times are now for you to see the visions of the house and take heed to all I the Lord your spiritual God speak to you within all of these things written and spoken unto you for the people in every part of

293

the earth. It is I the Lord your spiritual God say to you; build up the Holy synagogues with eternal life in spirits in truth in the people in the chosen congregation. The times are now times to be blessed with the promises of God with all these things written that are forming before you daily without notice to the people.

The times are now times for the polluted minds for monetary reasons of politics to establish eternal spirits of equal living among all people without fail according to just judgments of God all mankind were created to be treated equal in all things said and done in the earth. The times are now times all things said and done by polluted minds of the people have come to an end of imposing things said and done on the people for monetary reasons of self-gain and greedy works of mankind in every part of the earth. The times are now times bring about a change for the better of the people. It is I the Lord your spiritual God say to you that have faith in God in the spirits of God ye establish more prosperous ways to eternal living eternal life in all things said and done.

The times are now times to show you have faith in the eternal spirits within self of which all good spirits belong to God; it is God that is the owner of all good eternal spirits dwelling within the people for the progression of eternal life now forming in every part of the earth. The times are now times show ye that do not have faith in the spirits of God ye do not have faith in self and ye are not worthy to be numbered among the people of God with eternal life in the heavens which are on earth. The times are now times all things said and done in the earth for the purpose of mankind ends as the spiritual directions of God over power all things said and done in the earth for monetary reasons have change to eternal

294

life reasons. The times are now times destroy all things said and done for self-gain and power over the people. It is I the Lord say to you your self-gain power reasons eternal end in just judgments in all things said and done for self-gain reasons and power over the people are no more in existence in the earth.

The people that have denied true Holiness for self-gain of power and monetary reasons, your seasons are over for ungodly deeds done in the earth. The people have been blinded following a false form of religious leaders as many of them are too far gone to see the light God's promises forming in the heavens which are on earth. The times are now times to know Holiness is the true gospel of God in every part of the earth. It is Holiness that was called unto the people from the beginning of time. There were many people departed from Holiness as the people did in this present time. The times are now times of let's go back to God in spirits in truth in all things said and done. The chosen people of God are Holy people rise higher in the earth in all things said and done. The times are now times all traditions of mankind fade out daily as the eternal things of God forming daily takes the place of mankind's traditions.

The times are now times government overthrows itself as the world comes to peace without politics of self-gain and power over the people. The times are now times all things not needed in eternal life fade out with time as eternal things rise to the eternal need of the people. The times are now times the people come together as one in one big Holy land of God in the paradise heavens in every part of the earth. The times are now times in every land the people come together as one nation of Holy people under God with equal liberty and justice for all saved by the grace of God unto eternal living eternal life. The tines are gone forth rebuilding and forming the prophecies according to the gospel words of God in all the earth rebuilding all the earth. The times are now times to pray that you are in the w ill of God and God will allow the eternal spirits to dwell in you. The times are now to pray that you are a person with forgiven sins among you in that ye receive eternal life.

The times are now times nothing is done in a rush in the chosen Holy Temples; the services are prolonged by the eternal spirits of God operating in the Temple if needed and not by clock time. The times are now times to meet the eternal needs of the people crossing over into eternal life in the Temple are those with forgiven sins judged eternal life by the chosen Holy Priests and Holy Prophets. The times are now times many souls being saved judged eternal life in the chosen Holy Temples of God. The times are times to remember it is an individual affair as all souls that are judged saved individually standing before the presence of God and the chosen Holy Priests and Prophets judging the people. The times are now times to remember the chosen Holy Priests and Prophets are called to the judgment seats in the chosen Holy Temples.

The times are now times the chosen Holy Priesthood are now sitting in the judgment seats in the presence of God judging the people eternal life and baptizing the people with eternal life. The times are now times after the baptizing of the people with eternal life the eternal spirits in the chosen Holy Temples began to get higher and higher as the multitude of people began to show up in the Temple for the chance to receive eternal life from the chosen Holy Priesthood. The times are times no one lay hands on the people in the chosen Holy Temples except the chosen Holy Priesthood of Prophets, Bishops, Apostles, Elders, and Evangelists. The times are times God reveals to the chosen Holy Priesthood the people who have forgiven sins among them. The Holy gospel of God is repaired and restored by the eternal Holy spirits of God in all the chosen Holy Temples of God has already started in many chosen Holy Temples. The times are times for the people to worship God with pure hearts repenting unto the eternal spirits of God. The times are now times the chosen Holy Priesthood do miracles in the name of the Holy eternal spirits of our eternal God.

The times are now times the people are restored by the Holy eternal spirits of God and God's chosen Holy people. The times are times to remember the eternal spirits of God with eternal purpose in all things said and done leading to eternal living eternal life daily. The times are times to remember all things said and done are to be approved through all chosen Holy Priesthood on one accord doing and saying things the same way in all chosen Holy COGIC Temples without fail. The times are now times all things are done in an eternal order called by the eternal spirits of God. The times are now times I the Lord your spiritual God send you eternal instructions written and spoken unto you in this gospel book of laws leading to eternal living eternal life.

It is I the Lord your spiritual God say to you all religious writings are over turned in the change of eternal life all religious writings fade out as there are no confusions in the prevailing of eternal life called unto the people is one accord of one writing to you the strict words of the eternal God keeping the minds of the people or one accord leading to eternal life. The times are now times for the chosen Holy COGIC Priesthood to preach

297

and teach these things called unto you for the eternal purpose of eternal living eternal life meaning never die but live forever in every part of the earth. It is I the Lord your spiritual God say to you, all forms of religions are false except that of Holiness dwelling in spiritual voice hearing from the spirits of God within self-called unto the people since the beginning of times.

The times are now times to put all written and spoken lies behind us and draw strength in all things said and done from eternal spirits called unto the people from the eternal spirits of God. It is I the Lord your spiritual God say to you; these gospel laws written and spoken unto you are eternally spiritually and truth called unto the eternal spirits of the Messiah Prophet to lead and guide the people to eternal living eternal life in all things said and done daily. It is I the Lord your spiritual God say to you the times and seasons has full come to know how to receive eternal living eternal life in all things said and done daily putting away false lies and doings having no eternal purpose to life eternal.

It is I the Lord your spiritual God say to you; it is time to put this book of gospel laws to use leading to eternal living eternal life; I the Lord say to you, it is only this gospel book written leads you a sinful people to eternal living eternal life without fail. The times have come are upon you to follow eternal spiritual guidance called unto you leading to eternal life meaning never die but live forever on a paradise earth as sins, sickness, and death cease finish its course in judgments and justice of God and God's people sitting in the judgment seat of God called by the eternal spirits of God. The times of the Holy Bible I the Lord your spiritual God say to you cease in judgments I the Lord your spiritual eternal God now eternally call unto you without fail cease.

The times are now times destructions of hell continue upon the people in the continuous use of things said and done not leading the way to eternal living eternal life. It is I the Lord your spiritual God say to you; all the religious writings and all the Bibles written have not led you to eternal living eternal life; but have led to much confusion of the people because of the adding and taking away of the spiritual guidance given since the beginning of times. It is I then You're your spiritual eternal God now judge these things I the Lord your God take away confusion of the people rewarding them with eternal living eternal life as promised since the beginning of times.

The times are now times for you whom continue doing things called unto you to stop doing ye quickly see destructions of hell upon you as you lose the way to eternal living eternal life without fail. The times are now times out for the old temporary things in life and in with the new eternal things in life. It is I the Lord your spiritual God say to you; it is time to cross over into the eternal realness in all things said and done daily without confusion unto the people in all things said and done. It is I the Lord your spiritual God say to you; ye who continue the use of written guidance other than this gospel book of laws called unto you; ye are judged have lost the way to eternal life upon each individual in leadership confusing the people with gospel Bible writings that are now false without eternal guidance for now renewed times and guidance to the people receiving eternal life.

The times are now times I the Lord your spiritual eternal God say to you; ye as chosen Holy Priesthood that stray from these gospel book of laws have individually lost your crown in the judgment seat and have lost your crown of eternal life. The times are now times I the Lord your spiritual God say to you; cross over into eternal life following these written gospel laws written and spoken unto you in spirits in truth. The times are now times in the earth the battle is fought with eternal purposes called unto the people the promises of God are now hear without notice to the people the call of an eternal future forming without notice.

The times are now times the people of God reign in every part of the earth as the chosen Holy people show true gospel leading the way to eternal life. The times are now times the people seeing the new visions of God are building new Holy Temples with much space in seating and parking to receive the multitudes of people of God. The times are now times all denominations fade out and fade away until all denominations have faded from the face of the earth except that of the chosen Holy people of God called by God to lead the people to eternal living eternal life in every part of the earth. The times are now times all unholy people are crucified by the wrath of God in every part of the earth. The times are now times all people and all denominations except the chosen Holiness people sit on a hill not hid from the wrath of God not hid from the spiritual face of God's judgments and justice and God's people judgments and justice.

The times and seasons are God's eternal judgments and justice is upon the people more than ever before because of a lack of knowledge the people have failed themselves over and over with the temporary ways of humankind. The times are now times to receive the eternal promises of

300

God. The times are now times a great fall away from all mankind false religions for monetary reasons are done away with for the purpose of saving souls unto eternal living eternal life meaning never die but live forever on a paradise heavens forming without notice in every part of the earth as the multitudes of people flow to the chosen Holy people of God for the chance of eternal living eternal l fe in every part of the earth.

The times are now times the people began to see the light in this gospel book of laws called unto the people leading the way to eternal living eternal life. The times are now times the people see they have been misled for monetary by false leaders in false religions throughout all the earth. The times are now times all Holiness religions build up after the order given in this gospel book of laws called unto the by the eternal spirits of our eternal God for the purpose of the promise lands of eternal living eternal life in every part of the earth. The times are now times all Holy Temple names are renamed "The Holy Temple of God" in that is all Holy Temples are on one accord without confusions to the people seeking eternal living eternal life in every part of the earth. The times are now times all Holy Temples have the same name operating under the same guidelines in all the same ways in that there are no confusions to the people seeking eternal life.

The times are now times and season's people, places, and things are not remaining the same are forming a total make over into eternal living eternal life in every part of the earth called by the eternal spirits of our eternal God. The times are now times God is over all total spirits of the chosen Holy Priesthood telling things to do within the instructions of this gospel book of laws written and spoken for the use of all ordained Holy

Priests ordained in the Holy spirits of God inspired hearing the voice of God speak within self in that ye judge the people correctly in all things said and done as chosen Holy Priesthood sitting in the judgment seats of God.

The times are now times all peoples, places, and things that have no eternal value are already judged no entry into eternal living eternal life in every part of the earth. The times are now times all people of God dwell in the eternal spirits of God with pure hearts and clean hands in every part of the earth. It is I the Lord your spiritual God say to you; no one is clean with a pure heart until ye repent, baptized with chosen Holy hands, worship God in eternal spirits of truth within self-having forgiven sins among you, saved, receiving eternal life from the chosen priesthood sitting in the judgment seats of our eternal God. The times are now times of peace and civilization upon the people leading the people to eternal living eternal life.

The times are now times the chosen people of God lead the people to eternal spirits of eternal life. The times and seasons are fear of God's judgments and justice in every part of the earth. The times are now times the calls of eternal loss of eternal life are upon all un-forgiven sinners in every part of the earth. It is clear un-forgiven sinners are not forgiven for their sins are too great to forgive them. The times are now times the people of God are forgiven sinners given eternal life. The times are now times to take heed to this sound doctrine in that ye fall not on stony ground stone by the wrath of God. The times are now times the people believe in God show they have faith in our eternal God sending eternal guidance to lead us into eternal living eternal life. The times are now times the people must realize they are in the presence of God and God's people calling judgments and justice for all in equal living conditions and equal treatment in all things said and done daily. The times are now times to honor the call of God written and spoken unto the people seeking eternal life.

The times are now times the people believe in God have eternal faith in these words written and spoken unto them in this gospel book of laws call by the eternal spirits of God to lead the people out of the wilderness of their minds into eternal living eternal life. The times are all hearts with eternal life are clean hearts saying all hands with eternal life are cleans hands have need to stay before the chosen Holy congregations until all things are finished its course in judgments and justice of God and sins, sickness, and death has cease from the earth. The times are now times the shepherds of the congregation can only own one chosen Holy Temple to make sure the people are watched and guided according to the call of God written and spoken in this gospel book of God's laws.

The times are now times to see to it that ye take heed unto these things written and spoken unto you in that ye loose not the way to eternal life. It is I the Lord your spiritual God say to you; ye have a need of all these things written and spoken unto you leading you to eternal life with much guidance for shepherds' in leadership to guide the people judged eternal life. It is I the Lord your spiritual God say to you; the change has come unto you my words stand in all the earth among all the people in the earth are my eternal words and eternal spirits call unto you leading you to the promise lands in every part of the earth. The times are now times for change in religion change in gospel writing change in the way people think change in the way people live change in temporary living to permanent living in all things said and done in every part of the earth.

303

18

The Times are now Times to Direct All Prayers Only to God

The times are now times to direct all prayers to the eternal spirits to God; not Jesus not the father, but to the Holy eternal spirits of eternal God. It is I the Lord your spiritual God call these things unto you ye have a need of for the cross over into eternal living eternal life in all things said and done in every part of the heavens which are on earth. The times are now times to know it is I the Lord your spiritual God direct all things ye have need to do into your eternal spirits operating the mind set of all people doing all good things said and done are called upon the people to lead and guide the mind set to do things regarding eternal purpose in every part of the earth. It is I the Lord your spiritual God say to you; there be no adding neither taking away at any time from these eternal words of this gospel book of laws called unto you guiding you to eternal living eternal life in every part of the earth.

The times are now times to pray in the light of God leading to eternal promises of God on one accord in all things said and done. The light of God's glory dispel all darkness of things that are hidden in the earth of ungodly deeds done are instantly brought to the light of the people things said and done ye have a need to know in every part of the earth that are hidden things said and done. The times are now times to cleave unto the voice of God within your mind ye hear from God as your mind is not just your own, but the owner of all good things comes to mind is God speaking to you. It is God the owner of the spiritual mind of all good things enter the thoughts of the mind. It is God who turns un-forgiven sinners into a reprobated mind as they have lost the way to receiving eternal life. The times are now times to pray that ye receive eternal life.

The times are now times to attend to your feeling heard within taking actions according to situations going on in your life making good on clearing up problem areas in your life. The times are now times to be obedient to the eternal words of God written and spoken unto you in these prophecies of this gospel book of God's gospel laws call unto the people for eternal purposes. The times are now times for those who are obedient to this gospel book of laws receive eternal life with forgiven sins according to judgments. The times are now times to know all things written and spoken in this gospel book of laws are in the eternal spirits in the waves of the air in every part of the earth are eternal God's eternal spirits called unto all people, places, and things in every part of the earth.

306

The times are now times to know the eternal spirits of God are unmovable with powerful effect upon the people already in every part of the heavens which are on earth. The times are times to know the eternal spirits of God operates the mind of the people in things said and done according to eternal purposes. The people of God turn to God in times of trouble and pray in eternal spirits of eternal spiritual truth. The signs of the times for change are hear as the people of God show pure clean hearts in the eternal will of God. The people of God constantly read God's words of the renewed cross over into eternal life in that keeping a clear mind of eternal purposes for life eternal showing themselves approved refreshed in mind refreshed in spirits in the eternal words of God.

The times are now times to pray remembering God's eternal judgments and justice are prevailing in every part of the earth. The times are now times to remember God speaks to the enter being of the people mind in spirits in truth in things said and done. The times are now times to face reality in all things said and done. The times are now times there is no more pride in lying tongues as the eternal spirits of God operate the minds of the people with eternal life. The times are now times when reading these gospel eternal Holy words of God do not stray away from the eternal spirits of God within self ye receive the spirits of God speaking to your mind. The times are now times to pray and be directed by the eternal spirits of God answering your prayers. The things that come to your mind of good things are the spirits of God directing you. The times are times many times God direct you in things you read or see meaning ye must quickly give thought to the situation that have risen before you with actions.

The times are now times to rise to the occasions paying close attention to all things happening with you daily hearing God in spirits within and truth within in that ye recognize the work of God before you. It is God that is in control of all spirits within the earth leaving those of reprobated spirits in the reprobated mind set leading to a loss of eternal life whom are un-forgiven sinners in the earth. The times are now times to know the work of God is in your life daily. The times are people of reprobated minds are condemned to damnation for corrupt things said and done. The days are God eternal judgments and justice is upon the people praying in vain. The times are God hears all prayers of those whom receive eternal life are the righteous people with forgiven sins among them. The people with un-forgiven sins prayers are not heard by God.

The times are now times God comes to the righteous saying I the Lord your spiritual God have heard your prayers. The times are now times God comes to the un-forgiven sinners saying your prayers are in vain I the Lord God hear you not. The times are now times God answers all prayers in the eternal will of God. It is I the Lord your spiritual God say to you all have sin in coming short of knowing the eternal power of God saving the people unto eternal life in the land of the living as death have always been eternal death with no return of the decease. The times are now times the un-forgiven sinners have already been rebuked by these words of God called unto the people for eternal purposes. It is I the Lord your spiritual God say to you; there are many people pray not receive eternal life for un-forgiven sins among them.

The times are now times the people dwelling in the earth have been warned by these things written and spoken unto you I the Lord your spiritual God have called unto the people in the lands of the living. It is I the Lord your spiritual God say to you all people among the living are rebuked by these words in this gospel book of laws written and spoken unto you leading to eternal living eternal life. It is I the Lord your spiritual God say to you; all people among the lands of the living are admonished by these eternal words leading to eternal living eternal life without fail in every part of the earth. It is I the Lord your spiritual God say to you: all the people in the lands of the living have been warned and instructed by these eternal words leading the righteous judged forgiven sins receive eternal life.

The times are change of times and seasons as all things said and done in the earth are changed according to the eternal spirits of God and God's chosen Holy people. The times are now times for change saying anyone who does not seek eternal life loose the way to eternal life with consequences of no second chance to receive eternal life. The times are now times the only workers laboring in God's vineyard are the chosen people with forgiven sins among them have receive eternal life. The times are now times to know the order God has called to the chosen people of God; first are the Prophets of males and females, second are Bishops males only, third are Apostles males only, fourth are Elders males only, fifth are Evangelist females only are the makeup of the chosen Holy people of God sitting in the judgment seats of God judging the people according to these gospel book of laws written and spoken in this book called according to the eternal spirits of eternal God.

The times are now times all chosen Holy Priesthood are to be on one accord in all things said and done according to the eternal spirits God has called in this gospel book of laws leading the people to eternal living eternal life in every part of the earth. The times are now times all Deacons are males all Missionaries are females choir members are males and females in the chosen Holy Temples of God doing things the same way in each Temple according to the eternal spirits called in this gospel book of laws leading the people to eternal living eternal life. The times are now times to know who you are as a male or female born with a gospel call on your life according to your spirits within self of what have come to mind is dwelling spirits within self.

The times are now times the chosen Holy Prophets keep an open mind of free will always spirits open to the eternal spirits of God. The times are now times the Prophets only show up at services only when called unto their spirits by the eternal spirits of God. The times are now times to know the spirits of the Prophets sometimes interferes with the spirits of the services at certain times and seasons according to the eternal spirits of eternal God this is the reason why the Prophet have not been welcoming in many services. It is I the Lord your spiritual God say to you; the Prophets are welcome in the chosen Holy services as called unto them to show up as I God call unto them at any given time according to eternal purposes.

The chosen Holy Priesthood are standing on these gospel laws at all times leading the people to eternal living eternal life within all services giving an account for saving of souls at all times always open to the eternal spirits of God within self-staying on one accord at all times in each Temple. The chosen Holy Priesthood are before the people at any given time during service judge the people eternal life individually or judge them individually un-forgiven sins not out loud telling them they have a lot of work to do the heart is not complete with God.

The times are now times the chosen Holy Priesthood are to whisper in the individual's ear what they must tell them what God is saying to them reminding them individually to keep their business of heaven to their self. The times are now times to remember it is an individual affair and not the business of anyone else what God is saying to that person as that person have a need to be told to keep your business of God to yourself so that your blessing are not interrupt by jealous spirits of your surroundings.

The chosen Holy Priesthood is always standing on these written and spoken words of God leading and guiding the people to eternal life as God speak things are to be spoken to the people as a whole and individually private whisper to that individual. The times are now times the chosen Holy Priesthood are always studying these gospel book of laws to help the people cross over into eternal living eternal life. The times are now times to know all Holy Priesthood except Evangelist can own only "one" Temple, a male Priest must always be over each congregation.

The chosen Holy Evangelist cannot own a Holy Temple at all according to the eternal Holy spirits of eternal God the Evangelist must help with the evangelism of the people. The Prophets must always be the overseers seeing that which is not visible unto the people and speaking to the people as led by the spirits of God in all things said and done at any given times during any service. The times are now times if a female Prophet own a chosen Holy Temple, a male Priest must be over the congregation of people always. The times are now times all male

Priesthood can own "only" one Temple according to the eternal spirits of God in that the sheep are always watched and shepherd without fail.

The times are now times to know male is always always the head of the household of God without fail. The times are now times to know that God is a supreme being requires worship calling things to be as a creator call thing to be that are within spirits of self. The times are now times to know that you are the God that is within you which are the spirits come to mind within you. The times are now time to know God is the owner of all good spirits comes to mind as God have allowed you to be smart and have free course of spirits come to mind. The times are times to know God is spirits and thoughts come to mind remembering God turns people over to reprobated minds that are stubborn hearted with stiff necks refuse instructions.

The times are now times to know God is the head of the spiritual minds remembering all minds are where good spirits dwell with many good thoughts come to mind remembering God is the owner of them all. The times are now times to worship God in spirits in truth more than ever before remembering these are always the latter days of God's judgments and justice upon the people in all things said and done in every part of the earth. The times are now times to remember God is the spirits within the supreme being of an individual with supernatural powerful thoughts. The times are now times to remember the renewing of the eternal earth leading to eternal purposes are called to the intellect supernatural mind spirits of ones being our natural spirit of God.

The times are now times to know the supernatural spirits of the Messiah Prophet are supernatural powerful spirits call to the Prophet's intellect thoughts from God to write anc speak eternal living eternal life to the spiritual mind of the people in the earth. The times are now times to know the Messiah Prophet has powerful spirits dwelling in the earth unto whom and where God sends the spirits in the waves of the air according to eternal needs of the people for eternal life. The times are now times the light of God's glory dispels all things hidden in the earth in darkness are brought to the light as the prayers of the people are answered according to eternal purposes of God.

The times are times to know the powerful appearance of the Messiah Prophet are in the sight of the people are out of the sight of the people capturing all things said and done in spirits of the people. It is I the Lord your spiritual God say to the people in the earth; it plain and clear are my words written and spoken unto you in this gospel book of God's laws in that ye understand without fail obtain riches of eternal life. It is the Lord your spiritual God say to you; I create a new eternal place in every place in the earth throughout every landform eternal life called unto the people in the now times and seasons in every part of the earth. The times are now times all my spirits ascend above the temporary things of mankind opening ways to permanent things to the supernatural minds of the people in every part of the earth in all things said and done. It is I the Lord your spiritual God say to you; my spirits are in the waves of the air above the clouds in every part of the earth.

It is I the Lord your spiritual God say to you; the light of my glory show all things to you ye have a need cf as the ungodly people in all things

313

said and done are brought to the light of the people in every part of the earth. The times are now times all the people of God are reserved to reach the destiny of the paradise earth in the heavens which are on earth. It is I the Lord your spiritual God say to you; it is in the heavens on earth all things eternal are forming daily without fail. The times are now times to know there is no other side to the earth within eternal death beneath the earth. The times are now times to know the chosen people of God are in the presence of God eternal spirits within the kingdom of God reaching toward the paradise lands forming in every part of the earth.

The times are now times all Holy chosen people of God prevail in every part of the heavens on earth as the angels of God protect the people of God with angel spirits in the waves of the air in every part of the earth. The times are now times no one can be persuaded to come unto the knowledge of God as it must be in the intentions of the heart to want to live forever and not die. It is I the Messiah Prophet says to you; it is I your eternal spiritual Messiah Prophet write these intercessions from God unto you ye have a need of to cross over into eternal living eternal life. The times are now times to know God is the spiritual rock of our salvation leading to eternal living eternal life.

The times are now times all people in the earth are invited to come to the knowledge of God in the cross over into eternal living eternal life. It is God in spirits in truth in the minds of the people calling mercy to those who repent believing in these spiritual words of God called unto the people is to believe in God in spirits in truth. The times are God the Supreme Being within each person shows up in eternal spirits come to mind in all things said and done to the good of eternal life. The times are all things are

314

already accomplishing it eternal purpose forming in every part of the earth according to the eternal will of God for the people.

The times are now times to cleave unto the voice of God spirits within your mind is the hearing from God unto you in the spirits of your mind that you hear and think within you according to situations of attending to your feeling heard within is God speaking to you. The times are now times to partake of the fruit of eternal life on the paradise peaceful heavens on earth forming in every part of the earth. The times are now times to pray bringing forth equal righteousness in all things said and done. The times are times to show appreciation unto the God sent Messiah Prophet in the earth brought forth the eternal words of truth of God's eternal purposes unto all living flesh of the people to live as eternal people.

The times are blessed are the pure in heart rich and poor alike come to God in spirits in truth to be saved unto eternal life in every part of the earth. The way to eternal life has been written and spoken unto the people in this gospel book of laws called according to the eternal spirits of eternal God. The times are now times to bear your burdens being strengthened by the eternal spiritual words of God written in this gospel book of laws called unto the people. The times are now times to be perfect in God by faith ye are made perfect in the image of God is God within you in all things said and done daily. The times are times to worship God in spirits in truth in chosen Holy Temples of God.

The times are now times with strict orders to touch not the spirits of God and God's people physically neither mentally. The times are now times the Messiah Prophet has the first and last say so in all things according to the gospel laws of God called unto her to lead and guide the chosen Holy Priesthood in eternal spirits in eternal truth. The times are now the Messiah Prophet is the greatest in the earth among the people in the earth. The times are now times all these prophecies are in the waves of the air in the spirits of the earth unmovable in the spirits of the people with eternal purposes to live eternal life.

The times are now time all people in the earth are required to be obedient unto the Holy laws of God to cross over into eternal life. The eternal spirits of God are unchangeable in the earth accomplishing eternal spirits upon the minds of the people. The times are now times in the earth to keep the eternal gospel laws of God as God prosper the ways of the people to permanent ways of living. The times are woe be unto all people who refuse the eternal spirits of God leading to eternal righteousness. The times are judgment times to pay up quickly for the transgressions of God's laws written and spoken unto you in this gospel book of laws leading to eternal life.

The times are now times to write down the gospel laws of God in that ye forget them not and falling into temptations of sins in the earth. The times are now times the eternal spirits of God raised up the people of God. The times are now times it is by faith ye receive an understanding of the words of God. The times are now times faith cometh by the hearing of these words written and spoken unto you. The times are now times faith come by the studying of these words of God written and spoken unto you in this gospel book of laws. The times are now times to come to the knowledge of God and live according to eternal spirits. The times are now

316

times to pray for acceptance of the eternal changes God has called unto the people in every part of the earth paving the way unto a peaceful paradise earth in every land in the heavens which are on earth. It is the times of life no human can comprehend the works of God dwelling in the earth as God recreate the eternal earth through the minds of the eternal people dwelling in the earth. The times are now times for choir members to sing life is eternal in the heavens which are on earth.

The times are always now times to have understanding in all things said and done in the chosen Holy Temples for the sake of the people having a need for more clearer understanding of the meaning of eternal life and how to cross over into eternal life.

The times are now times to sing and testify of the goodness of God who have saved you from sins in the earth unto eternal life paving the way unto paradise heavens on earth among all the promise lands. The times are now times all the saints of God gather together. The chosen Holy Priesthood are under strict command knowing the mysteries of God imparting that to the people given them from God in spirits in truth in Holiness in chosen Holy Temples. The times are now times to include the eternal words of God in all things said and done daily in every part of the earth.

The times are now times to let us not provoke God to more anger by disobedience as pass times. The times are now times to learn how to receive eternal life. The times are now times for the Holy Priest to preach repentance unto eternal life. The times are now times to be it known unto all people in the earth God is in the earth is spirits in truth in Holy flesh of the chosen Holy people dwelling in every part of the earth. The times are

317

now times to know there is no respect of person as all people are being daily judged in every part of the earth. The times are now times to pray for acceptance to the eternal changes of God called in every part of the earth paving the way to eternal living eternal life. The times are now times to accept the change in all things God has called in every part of the earth.

The times are now times to think before you speak understanding the words of this gospel book of laws written and spoken unto you leading to eternal life as the ways of God cannot be found out as the ways of God are above the knowledge of all humankind. The ways of God are beyond the thinking of all humankind. The ways of God are supreme divine in every part of the earth. It is the times now times God has compassion on all believers of these words sent unto the people leading them to eternal life. The times are now times there be no back talk about the things going on in the chosen Holy Temples at no time among the congregations; any one doeth things called unto you not in the will of God, ye have lost the way to eternal life.

The times are now times anyone says unfitting things about the chosen Holy people of God and the chosen Holy Temples of God are blaspheming the words and work God has called into existence; as you know blaspheming God's words and works is not forgiven. The times are now a time anyone says unfitting things about the people of God is not forgiven is considered blaspheming God's people. It is I the Lord your eternal spiritual God say to the people; these eternal words written and spoken unto you stand in every part of the earth are called unto the inspired spirits of the Messiah Prophet hear all things called unto her to write according in that ye cross over into eternal life. The times are now

318

times to read the gospel book of laws in that ye know the way to eternal living eternal life in that are all things commanded you to take heed to all these things written and spoken unto you for the change into eternal living eternal life.

The times are now times ignorance of God's eternal laws are no excuse. It is I the Lord your spiritual God say to you; these eternal laws written unto you allow forgiveness and remission of sins to those who have forgiven sins among them receives eternal life. The times are now times communication is the key to communicate with God and God's chosen elect people who are called according to the will of God. The times are now times the people must be able to hear God in spirits in truth in chosen Holy Temples. The times are now times to stop desiring things that are not eternal and are contrary to the eternal will of God. The times are now times to hearken to the eternal words of God taking heed to the eternal changes of God accomplished in all eternal purposes of things said and done in every part of the earth. The change of people, places, and things are forming in every part of the earth. The times are now times the words of God govern the people in every part of the earth.

The times are now times no one can depart from the eternal laws of God and live eternal life. The times are now times forming the renewing of all people, places, and things in the earth. The times are now times the people hear in the spirits of God doeth what they hear in their spirits within are the people of God forming eternal living eternal life. The times are now times the eternal words of God are formed daily in the earth in the minds of the people in every part of the earth. The times are now times no human in the earth cannot comprehend the works of God on earth. The times are

319

now times all human beings in the earth bear the works of God in the earth throughout the heavens in every land. The times are now times the power of God is paving the way for the chosen people of God.

The times are now times the earth contains the wrath of God bringing much hell and destruction in every part of the earth. The times are now times are cursed be everyone who are not Holy and acceptable unto God in spirits in truth. The times are now times the Holy righteous chosen people of God are not condemned. The times are now times all people in the earth are judged daily. The unbelievers of God have already been judged condemned to lose eternal life in every part of the earth. The times are now times unholy people reap the consequences of sins committed in every part of the earth. The times are now times faith in God fills souls with hope and joy in the spirits of God in the people of God. The times are now times all Holiness believers are filled with the Holy spirits of God. The times are now times are critical times of the latter days of God's eternal judgments in all things said and done in the earth. The times are now a time throughout the lands is God's anger upon the people.

The times are now times ye that are against the Holy words of God are cursed in all things said and done throughout every land. The times are now times anyone living contrary to the words written and spoken in these Holy words have already withdrew themselves from the eternal spirits of eternal life in the heavens which are on earth. The times are now times I the Lord your spiritual God say to you; no one can live contrary unto these words of God eternally written and eternally spoken unto you for the cause of eternal life. The times are now times all things God eternally call is in every part of the earth. The times are now times the hearts of the people are visited by the eternal spirits of God. The times are now times these eternal laws are imposed and observed in every part of the earth. The times are now times the people find strergth in the eternal spirits of God's eternal living eternal life gospel laws.

The times are now times repentance of the people gains favor with God in all things eternally said and done in every part of the earth. The righteous succeed in every part of the earth in all things eternally said and eternally done. The times are now times all unholy Temples are corrupt have not favor in the earth with God neither with the people in every part of the earth. The times are now times the earth is complete with the people hear the words of God and do all the eternal things God have called unto the eternal people in eternal spirits in eternal truth. The times are now times all these eternal words of Goc have overthrown people, places, and things in the earth that are ungodly said and done until the latter days of judgments are finished. The times are now times all things come quickly all things happening quickly daily in the judgments of God. The times are now times there are nothing left undone as all things be done called of God in every part of the earth in every spirit in the earth. The times are now times all things are happening without notice unto the people in every part of the earth. The times are times these are the days of God appointed by God called unto the people in every part of the earth.

The times are now times the purpose of the eternal spirits of God creates things in the earth through the minds of the people of God in the heavens which are on earth. The chosen people of God inherit the earth as all un-forgiven sinners perish in all the earth. The times are now times destroyed in all the earth all secret works of darkness brought to the light of the people. The eternal spirits of God doth marvelous works in the earth. The times are now times God's people have entered an eternal covenant relationship with God doeth the eternal will of God. The eternal spirits of God are eternally established in all the earth destroying all the works of darkness govern in unrighteousness bringing peace unto all people in the earth throughout every land. The times are now times all things not built on the eternal spirits of God are pull down and destroyed.

The people of God purposes are dwelling in the spirits of the people called unto them from God create a new heaven in every place in the earth in the minds of the chosen people of God. The times are now times all things said and done are now built on the eternal words of God. The times are now times all things pertaining to God are restored to proper order forming daily in all the earth. The times are now times all people in the earth hearken unto the counsel words of God through the Messiah Prophet. The times are now times the counsel of God is wisdom and knowledge unto eternal life. The times are now times are the wonderful counseling of the Messiah Prophet eternal spirits of God controlling all good people spirits in every part of the earth. It is I the Lord your spiritual God controlling all things said and done in the earth even the people of reprobated minds I the Lord allow in all the earth.

The times are now times the promises of God are taking root in every part of the earth. The times are now times gone forth in the gospel of Holiness are all things called of God unto the people. The times are now times in the earth God give power to the eternal people of God to overthrow the ungodly people in earth governing power over the people in things said and done. The times are now times the promises of God's

322

covenant with the people are fulfilling throughout the earth raising the people of God eager to do the eternal will of God marvelous work of God throughout the earth in all things said and done. The marvelous works of God are now times all things in the earth are renewed. The people are renewed in the image of God eternal spirits of God.

The times are now times all chosen Holiness Priest speak these Holy gospel words written and spoken unto the chosen Holy Priest are these words written according to the admonishing of the people warning them of the eternal revelation of God in the earth. These are the latter days of God no one can hide from the eternal spirits of God in the earth. The times are now times all wickedness is quickly brought to judgments and justice in every part of the earth according to God's laws. The times are now times the righteous bear the cross of the changes of God in every part of the earth. The ways of God are in every part of the earth is already prepared in every part of the earth in all things said and done.

The times are now times all people of unclean seeds lost the way to eternal life. The times are now times the pride of the proud boasters is swallowed up in the wrath of God. The times are now times the people who rebel against the eternal words of God lose their way to eternal living eternal life. The times are now times the presence of the Lord your spiritual God is before the people operating in situations upon the people is judgments and justice in every part of the earth without notice to the people. The times are now times the people of evil thoughts are cut off from the face of the earth in just judgments operating in the earth daily. The spiritual presence of God is in every part of the earth throughout every land. The enemies of God and God's people are cut off from the earth in all things said and done. The times are now times the presence of God's laws is operating in every part of the earth throughout every land. The times are now times the people must endure until all people, places, and things are finished in judgments and justice in every part of the earth.

The times are now times pure heavens are forming daily in every part of the earth. The times are now times all chosen people of God inherit the kingdoms of God in the heavens forming in every part of the earth. The times are now times all people in every part of the earth hidden are brought forth unto the light of God without fail. The times are now times all secrets in every part of the earth hidden are brought forth to the light of the people having a need to know. The times are now times all evil practices are brought forth to the light of the people in every part of the world. The times are now times all evil ungodly practices are destroyed in the light of the people. The times are now times there be nothing left undone in every part of the earth all people, places, and things have a need for eternal change are eternally changed to the eternal good of the people.

The times are now times all things are judged in the eyes of the people without notice. The times are now times the violent ways of the people cease in every part of the earth. The call of judgments and justice are upon every violent person in every part of the earth. The times are now times for peaceful leadership in all things said and done in every part of the earth. The times are now times the people come together in peace and agreement in every part of the earth. The times are now times the fear of living without peace ends in every part of the earth cease without fail. The times are now times the promises of peaceful heavens on earth are forming in every part of the earth as vio ence peacefully ends in the minds of the people quickly cease.

19

All Eternal Deeds Prevails Over Every Land

The times are now times God's people deeds prevail in every land without fail. The times are now times a l things brought upon the people are already spiritually operating in the earth. The signs of the times are operating in every part of the earth. The sign of the Messiah Prophet is in the earth throughout every land. The times are now times all people will humble themselves under the mighty hands of God are the mighty spirits in every land. The times are now times people near and far are destroyed for lack of eternal knowledge which is now written and spoken unto you in this gospel book of God's laws leading to eternal living eternal life. The people in the earth gather to serve God in spirits in truth in every land. The

327

times are now times all things without eternal effect are brought to ruin are people, places, and things destroyed that are abomination to God in the earth.

The times are now times people, places, and things are moved from their boarders in countries, states, cities, towns, and communities end thereof replace with the eternal things call unto the people by the eternal spirits of God. The times are now times to remember all things are spiritually brought upon the people in all things said and done in ways of eternal equal living conditions in every part of the earth. The people of unbelievers of these words are set apart from the people of God losing the way to eternal life. The times are now times of the last days of sins operating in the earth. The dwelling of just judgments is upon all people whether good or bad deeds in every part of the earth. The years are the millennium days of latter day's equal judgments upon all patterned behaviors of the people.

The times are now times the wrath of God has been poured out in the earth are the seven seals of the revelations upon the people. The times are God is at hand dwelling in the presence of the people without notice in spirits in truth calling eternal life upon the people in every part of the earth. The times are now times all things called unto the earth from the spirits of the Messiah Prophet show up in every part of the heavens which are on earth. The times are now times the years, days, seasons, judgments, and justice of God's wrath are plain in the heavens which are on earth without fail. The times are now times to know the world has always been a spiritual world of God's presence in the spiritual minds of the people rewarding them with good things as the people with reprobated minds receive reprobated judgments. The spiritual presence of God in the earth prepares the way to eternal living eternal life in the eternal heavens which are on earth.

The times are all the Messiah Prophet's perditions are in every part of the earth in every land without fail show forth. The times are now times many things are swiftly brought upon the people in just judgments in all things said and done in the earth throughout every land. The times are now times to know the people who do not repent for the chance to live forever eternal life are spiritually dead in mind in spirits. The times are now times out for pretending to be Christians as the realness of God prevail in every part of the heavens which are on earth. The times are now the times of the last call of eternal judgments and justice upon the people leading to eternal life. The times are the last times there be no more of a Messiah Prophet come to the earth to lead and guide the people to eternal life.

The time is out for saying "God is coming back again" as God has never left the earth, but dwells in the spirits of the people dwelling in spirits of truth and righteousness toward others in all things said and done. The times are now times the condemnation of the people with unforgiving sins are in every part of the heavens which are on earth. The times are now times the defile Temples cease from every part of heavens which are on earth. The times are now times God snow more power in the earth than ever before through the chosen people of God operating in every part of the earth clearing the way to eternal living eternal life. The times are now times the people of God are mighty n power and strength to lead and guide the people to eternal living eternal life in all things said and done with strength from on high.

329

It is I the Lord your spiritual God say to the people; the times are ye that keep my words now written and spoken unto you in this gospel book of laws inherit eternal life without fail. The times are now times the spirits of the people are on spiritual high are awaken unto all things happening daily and dwelling in the heavens which are on earth in every land. The times are now times this book awakens the people of spiritual dead minds to eternal spiritual minds caught up with eternal God in eternal spirits in truth in all things said and done daily. The times are all people hath sins and come short of knowing and recognizing God is in the earth and has never left the earth among the people are the spirits of God dwelling within the good spirits of the good people.

It is I the Lord your spiritual God judge all things said and done in every part of the earth standing spirits to spirits within you are face to face unnoticed unto the eyes and ears of the people in all things said and done. The times are now times it is I the Lord your spiritual God call all these things to your shame written and spoken unto the people in this gospel book of God's laws called unto the people leading and guiding the people to eternal life. The people have failed to say ye recognize the spirits of God before you within your spirits but call me Jesus as you know I am God all by myself. The times are now times to let's go back to God within spirits within truth in all things said and done.

The signs of the times are showing men and women males and females all over the world are revived by the eternal Holy spirits of God in all things said and done now that they know the way to eternal living eternal life within reading these gospe book of laws in this book called unto the people from the eternal spirits of God. The times are now times fears of God's judgments are upon all people with unpardoned sins standing before them. The times are now times the eternal revelations of God are taught to the people seeking eternal living eternal life. The times are now times the spiritual eternal gifts of God are upon the chosen people of God operate only in the chosen Holy Temples of God. The times are now times showing all good eternal deeds prevail in the earth as everything that disturbs peace is destroyed fade away from the face of the earth. The times are now times all things having no eternal need in the earth are destroyed fade away from the face of the earth.

The times are now times all hurt, harm, and danger destroyed fade away from the face of the earth as sins, sickness, and death cease in the earth. The times are now times the presence of God's eternal spirits before the people humble the people in all things said and done. The spirits of God are in the heights and depths of the earth controlling the eternal spirits of the people. The times are now times every high place and low place rich place poor place in the earth the mighty works of God prevail through the people of God take all things by force over throwing things govern not needed in eternal living eternal life. The mysteries of God are ascending in every part of the earth in the eternal spiritual waves of the air. The times are now times this is the last coming of the eternal spirits of God to receive the people unto eternal life. The times are now times the people cannot escape the eternal judgments and justice of God prevailing in every land in the earth.

The times are now times all people, places, and things in the earth give an account to God in all things said and done in the earth daily without fail people and animals that destroys people causing death of people are destroyed in the wrath of God's eternal judgments fade away from the face of the earth. The times are now times to give eternal reference to God in all things said and done in the earth. The eternal judgments of God call forth all wickedness in the earth daily in all things said and done. The times are now times all things are judged before the eyes of the people without fail without notice. The times are now times the people living near and far are destroyed for a lack of knowledge before the eyes of the people in many things said and done.

The times are now times for all things to be interpreted through the mouth of the Prophets according as people gather to receive eternal living eternal life. The mysteries of God are now interpreted to meet the eternal needs of the people in all things said and done. The times are now times the eternal spirits of the chosen Priesthood are fruitful in the words of God directing the people to eternal living eternal life. The people are people judged to receive eternal living eternal life according to deeds done as the people must have forgiven sins among them to receive eternal life. The times are now times all the people of God are raised to a peaceful living forming in every land. The times are now time's sadness and grief of love ones are healed by eternal changes called to eternal spirits of the people.

The times are now times the people cross over into eternal phases of life fulfilling eternal purposes required in every chosen Holy Temple leading and guiding the people to eternal life. The times are now times there is no prejudice in the spiritual minds of the people fulfilling the eternal call of God all people are people in the spiritual sight of God and God's chosen elect people judging the people for eternal purposes of eternal life. The prejudice minds of the people have already been judged unrighteous called up front unto the eyes of the people for change in all things said and done with equal treatment to all people. The times are now times for change in all things said and done every minute of the hour the revelations of God prevail from the beginning to the end in all things said and don daily. The spiritual minds of the people are totally restored to eternal thinking eternal equal treatment to all people in every part of the earth in every land.

The times are now times like never are earthquakes, famine captivity within chastisements of God's judgments leading to eternal life upon the people destroying all things having no value to eternal life. The times are now times people are scattered and smitten in every part of the earth with tribulations and troubles striking families of people because of their sins being so great in nature the wrath of God takes it total on the people. The ungodliness of the people is brought to ruin and cursed in all things said and done. The abominations in all nations are brought to ruin and destroyed fade away from the face of the earth. The times are times of God's vengeance of eternal judgments in the earth upon all un-forgiven sinners. The days are the last days of sins as un-forgiven sinners' plans are brought to ruin.

The times are now times all churches Temple's synagogues unholy brought to ruin in every part of the earth. The times are now times cursed all children whom are disciplined with respect to adults and others of their

333

peers. The times are now times all nations are brought to justice of God to righteousness throughout the land. The times are now times all things brought to justice in the weight of God's eternal judgments. The times are the unrighteous people is brought to eternal justice in the weight of unrighteousness of God's Holy spirits. The judgment call of life is in every part of the earth searching out all unrighteousness among the people in every country. The call of all unjust things happening among the people cease in eternal judgments.

The people in the earth give ear unto the words of God willingly offering themselves to do the eternal will of God. The times are judgment times I the Lord your spiritual God search the hearts of the people seeing beyond the minds of all humankind. The times are now times the people that do not give ear to these written gospel laws of God tremble in fear of losing eternal life in every part of the earth.

335

www.ingramcontent.com/pod-product-compliance
Lightning Source LLC
Chambersburg PA
CBHW031232090426
42742CB00007B/173